The Handbook of
International Trade

The Handbook of
International Trade

A Guide to the Principles and Practice of Export

SECOND EDITION

Consultant Editors:
Jim Sherlock and Jonathan Reuvid

Published in Association with:
The Institute of Export

GMB

GMB Publishing Ltd.
Hereford House
23-24 Smithfield Street
London EC1A 9LF
United Kingdom
www.globalmarketbriefings.com

525 South 4th Street, #241
Philadelphia, PA 19147
United States of America

This edition first published 2008 by GMB Publishing Ltd.

© GMB Publishing Ltd and Jim Sherlock and Jonathan Reuvid

ISBN 978-1-84673-034-4   E-book ISBN 978-1-84673-035-1

British Library Cataloguing in Publication Data

A CIP record for this book is available from the British Library

Typeset by David Lewis XML Associates Ltd

Contents

Foreword

The Institute of Export is pleased to present and wholeheartedly recommend this vital source of reference and advice to all international traders. In particular we commend this book to students studying for the Institute's Advanced Certificate in International Trade examinations wherever they may be based.

The Institute of Export's mission is committed to the enhancement of export performance by setting and raising professional standards in international trade management and practice, principally through the provision of education and training programmes. The Institute is recognized by the Qualifications and Curriculum Authority as an Awarding Body for vocational qualifications and is the only professional body in the UK offering recognized formal qualifications in International Trade.

Dedicated to professionalism and recognizing the challenging and, often, complex trading conditions in international markets, the Institute believes that real competitive advantage lies in competence underpinned by a sound basis of knowledge.

Globalization is an accepted phenomenon of the 21st century. As goods and services increasingly move across international borders ever greater expertise is required to make such activity as smooth as possible. Failure of World Trade Organization talks means that barriers and challenges to that free and smooth flow of trade remain. One sure way of overcoming obstacles is to be in possession of the right knowledge. That is why this Handbook is so important.

The authors of this Handbook are recognized experts in international trade education and business support.

Jim Sherlock, a Fellow of The Institute, and Director – Educational Projects is also a trainer and consultant in International Trade with extensive experience in the UK and other manufacturing sectors. He has extensive experience in the educational sector and is the author of "Principles of International Physical Distribution" together with regular contributions to a number of international trade publications.

Jonathan Reuvid is a well known and respected Sinologist, internationalist, strategy consultant and educationalist. Engaged in the design and delivery of academically accredited educational business and management programmes, as an editor and publisher he has involved himself in a variety of international trade and business books of the highest quality.

Andy Nemes FIEx.
National Chairman, The Institute of Export

Part 1

The Global Economy

1.1

The rationale for foreign trade and its organization

Why countries trade

There are two basic types of trade between countries:

- the first in which the receiving country itself cannot produce the goods or provide the services in question, or where they do not have enough.
- the second, in which they have the capability of producing the goods or supplying the services, but still import them.

The rationale for the first kind of trade is very clear. So long as the importing country can afford to buy the products or services they are able to acquire things which, otherwise they would have to do without. Examples of differing significance are the import of bananas into the UK, in response to consumer demand, or copper to China, an essential for Chinese manufacturing industry.

The second kind of trade is of greater interest because it accounts for a majority of world trade today and the rationale is more complex. The UK imports motor cars, coal, oil, TV sets, domestic appliances and white goods, IT equipment, clothing and many more products which it was well able to produce domestically until it either transferred production abroad or ceased production as local industries became uncompetitive. At first sight, it would seem a waste of resources to import goods from all over the world in which a country could perfectly well be self-sufficient.

However, the reasons for importing this category of product generally fall into three classifications:

- the imported goods may be cheaper than those produced domestically;
- a greater variety of goods may be made available through imports;
- the imported goods may offer advantages other than lower prices over domestic production – better quality or design, higher status (eg prestige labelling), technical features, etc.

Comparative advantage

The law of comparative advantage was first articulated by the 19th century economist David Ricardo who concluded that there is an economic benefit for a nation to specialize in producing those goods for which it had a relative advantage, and exchanging them for the products of the nations which had advantages in other kinds of product. An obvious example is coal which can be mined in open-cast Australian mines or in China with low cost labour and shipped more than 10,000 miles to the UK where a dwindling supply of coal can be extracted only from high cost deep mines. In coal, Australia and China have comparative advantages.

The theory of comparative advantage can be extended on a macro-economic scale. Not only will trade take place to satisfy conditions of comparative advantage; in principle, the overall wealth of the world will increase if each country specializes in what it does best.

Stated at its most simplistic, of course the theory ignores many factors, of which the most important is that there may be limited international demand for some nations' specialized output. Nevertheless, the question arises why specialization has not occurred on a greater scale in the real world. The main reasons, all of them complex, may be summarized in order of significance, as follows:

- strategic defence and economic reasons (the need to produce goods for which there would be heavy demand in times of war);
- transport costs which preclude the application of comparative advantage;
- artificial barriers to trade imposed to protect local industry, such as tariffs and quotas.

The evolution of world trade

In Chapter 1.3, the pattern of world trade over more than a century from 1870 to 2001 is discussed in detail. Overall, merchandise trade grew by an average of 3.4% per annum from 1870 to 1913 in the period up to World War I. Two World Wars interspersed by the Depression and a world slump effectively reduced the annual rate of growth in international trade to less than 1% in the period 1914 to 1950.

Then, as the international institutions which were established in the immediate post-1945 period began to introduce some financial stability and impact, world trade there followed a 23 year period of more buoyant growth averaging 7.9% up to 1973. In the next 25 years to 1998, the average growth rate in merchandise trade fell back to 5.1%. More recently, a less stable period of global economic slowdown saw merchandise exports fall by 4% in 2001, after rising by an exceptional 13% in 2000. Current trends which have surfaced in the early years of the 21st century are identified in Chapter 9.3. Apart from the period between the two World Wars and up to 2001, trade has continuously outstripped growth in the world economy as a whole.

Protectionism

To analyze what happened in the inter-war years of the 1920s and 1930s, it is necessary to understand that the reaction of many governments to economic slump was to protect jobs at home by raising the protection against imports. The most common method of protection is the introduction or increase of tariffs on imported goods. In the 1920s and 1930s, the widespread use of tariffs caused job losses, in turn, in other countries – a reiterative process. In the second half of the 1930s, the prolonged world slump was alleviated, particularly in Europe, by the heavy public spending on defence equipment and munitions in the lead-up to the World War II.

After 1945, there were concerted international efforts to put in place organizations which would reduce the effects of trade protection and any future reductions in world economic activity. The first of these were the International Monetary Fund (IMF) and the International Bank for Reconstruction and Development (IBRD), now known as the World Bank which were established by the Bretton Woods Agreement in 1947. These institutions which have become the cornerstones of international macro-economic management were largely the brainchild of British economist John Maynard Keynes, who was among the first to recognize that reductions in government spending and increases in protection had been major causes of the pre-war depression.

Methods of protection

The tools of protection may be categorized as either tariff or non-tariff barriers.

Tariffs

A tariff is a 'tax' or import duty levied on goods or services entering a country. Tariffs can be fixed or percentage levies and serve the twin purposes of generating revenue for governments and making it more difficult for companies from other countries to do business in the protected market.

The moves towards 'free trade' of the 19th century were largely offset by the reintroduction of tariffs in the early part of the 20th century at rates sometimes as high as 33 and 50%. Since 1945, tariffs have been lowered significantly as a result of eight successive rounds of multilateral trade negotiations under the General Agreement on Tariffs and Trade (GATT), the third institution established following the Bretton Woods Agreement, and its successor the World Trade Organization (WTO).

Non-tariff barriers

Although progress was made in dismantling tariff barriers under the GATT in the period up to 1995 when the WTO was established, the use of non-tariff protection increased during the 1980s, mostly as a substitute for the tariffs which were outlawed.

The following is a list of non-tariff measures which have been deployed by both developed and developing countries:

- Quotas
  A numerical limit in terms of value or volume imposed on the amount of a product which can be imported. Chinese quotas on imported automobiles or French quotas on Japanese VHS equipment during the 1980s are well-known examples.
- Voluntary export restraints
  Agreed arrangements whereby an exporter agrees not to export more than a specific amount of a good to the importing country (usually to pre-empt the imposition of more stringent measures). Such agreements are common for automobiles and electronics, but are also applied to steel and chemicals.
- Domestic subsidies
  The provision of financial aid or preferential tax status to domestic manufacturers which gives them an advantage over external suppliers. The most obvious examples are agricultur,e where both the EU and US have consistently employed subsidies to help domestic producers.
- Import deposits
  The device of requiring the importer to make a deposit (usually a proportion of the value of the goods) with the Government for a fixed period. The effect on cash flow is intended to discourage imports.
- Safety and health standards / technical specifications
  This more subtle form of deterrent requires importers to meet stringent standards or to complete complicated and lengthy formalities. The French bans on lamb and then beef imported from the UK during the 1990s will be long remembered by the British farming industry.

Regions in world trade

Although the multilateral trading system promoted by the GATT and now the WTO has been broadly successful in overcoming protectionist regimes – at least up to the current Doha round – it has failed to prevent the concomitant proliferation of regional pacts and regional trade agreements (RTAs). More than 60% of world trade is regional and almost all major countries belong to at least one RTA. In 2001, 61% of the EU's trade was between member states and 55% of North American trade was between the three NAFTA countries. The jury is still out on whether RTAs can be viewed as stepping stones toward multilateral integration or as discriminatory arrangements that fracture the multilateral trading system. The failure of the WTO summit meeting in Cancun, Mexico in September 2003, subsequent Conference Meetings of Ministers and the further summit in Hong Kong in

December 2005 to reach agreement, have not been encouraging. More recently, there has been an ominous rash of new protectionist measures and RTA negotiations.

There are four basic models of trading block:

Free trade area

Members agree to reduce or abolish trade barriers such as tariffs and quotas between themselves but retain their own individual tariffs and quotas against non-members.

Customs union

Countries which belong to customs unions agree to reduce or abolish trade barriers between themselves and agree to establish common tariffs and quotas against outsiders.

Common market

Essentially, a common market is a customs union in which the members also agree to reduce restrictions on the movement of factors of production – such as people and finance – as well as reducing barriers on the sale of goods.

Economic union

A common market which is taken further by agreeing to establish common economic policies in areas such as taxation and interest rates. Even a common currency is described as an economic union.

The original European Economic Community (EEC) in the mid-1950s, comprising six members, was the forerunner of a number of such agreements. Now with 27 member states, the European Union is still the most advanced economic grouping. However, some of the more recent groupings, notably ASEAN and NAFTA, having created regional trading agreements, account for increasingly significant proportions of world trade.

Table 1.1.1 lists the principal trading blocks in date order of their formation together with details of their membership.

Regional arrangements are an important factor in the organization of world trade. They are beneficial in allowing countries inside the arrangement to acquire some goods at lower prices through tariff reductions than they could from the rest of the world. However, they may also cause trade to be 'diverted' away from efficient producers outside the arrangement towards less efficient sources within. A case can be made that the proliferation of

Table 1.1.1 - The principal regional trading blocks

Trading bloc	Year	Description
European Union (EU)	1957	Austria, Belgium, Denmark, Finland, France, Germany, Greece, Ireland, Italy, Luxembourg, Netherlands, Portugal, Spain, Sweden, United Kingdom. *Since 1 May, 2004*: Czech Republic, Cyprus, Estonia, Hungary, Latvia, Lithuania, Malta, Poland, Slovenia, Slovak Republic *Since 1 January 2007*: Bulgaria, Romania *Pending*: Croatia
European Free Trade Agreement (EFTA)	1959	Norway, Switzerland
Latin American Free Trade Area (LAFTA)	1960	Now known as LAIA (Latin American Integration Association) and superseded by MERCOSUR
Central American Common Market (CACM)	1961	Agreement between a number of central South American States which has agreed a free trade area with Mexico (part of NAFTA)
Association of South-East Asian Nations (ASEAN)	1967	Brunei, Darussalem, Cambodia, Indonesia, Lao, PDR, Malaysia, Myanmar, Philippines, Singapore, Thailand, Viet Nam
Andean Pact	1969	Bolivia, Colombia, Ecuador, Peru and Venezuela. Established a four-tier common external tariff in 1994.
Economic Community of West African States (ECOWAS)	1975	A free trade agreement which has aspects of a common market but which has suffered from regional instability
Australia-New Zealand Closer Economic Relations Trade Agreement (ANZCERTA)	1983	Now signed up to APEC.
North American Free Trade Association (NAFTA)	1989	Canada and the USA with Mexico since 1993.
Mercado Commun Del Sur (MERCOSUR)	1995	Argentina, Brazil, Paraguay and Uruguay
ASEAN Free Trade Area (AFTA)	1991	Planned successor to ASEAN from 2003
South Asian Association for Regional Cooperation (SAARC) Preferential Trading Agreement (SAPTA)	1993	Bangladesh, Bhutan, India, Maldives, Nepal, Pakistan, Sri Lanka

self-protecting trade blocks reduces the levels of potential benefits to be gained from world trade.

The UK's changed status in world trade

The EU is now the most important market for most UK exporters, accounting for around two-thirds of the UK's trade. The ratio represents the most dramatic difference between Britain in 1970 and Britain today.

In 1970, most of the UK's trade was with markets beyond Europe, mainly Commonwealth countries including Australia, New Zealand, Canada, the Caribbean, West and East Africa. Within the 20 years following, as a result of the UK joining the then EEC, the situation was reversed with UK trade focused on Europe, and the Commonwealth countries becoming relatively minor trading partners.

The consequences for both UK manufacturing industry and the Commonwealth have been far-reaching:

- the countries of the Commonwealth had to make trading arrangements of their own, having lost previously captive UK markets.
- much of the agricultural product previously imported by the UK from the Commonwealth is now sourced from within Europe.
- the UK has lost many of its markets for low-tech, low cost goods.
- UK exporters have tended to become higher-tech and more expensive.
- UK exporters have had to learn to do business in foreign languages and, with the advent of the EU monetary union, in euros rather than sterling.

In fact, the UK has always experienced difficulties with trade in manufactured goods. Even during the halcyon British Empire days of the late 19th and early 20th centuries, the UK was heavily dependent on the import of cheap raw materials from the colonies and Commonwealth in larger volume than the goods exported. However, throughout that period the UK continued to run substantial surpluses on its trade in services which largely offset the deficits on merchandise trade. During the period 1816 to 1995, the UK registered surpluses on goods account in only 6 years and only 3 deficits on services and investments.

During the past 50 years the UK has drifted into deeper deficits in merchandise trade, alleviated to some extent by the production of North Sea oil and gas. At the same time, the City of London no longer dominates world financial markets and the 'invisible' earnings which it generates are no longer sufficient to offset the deficits in trade of goods. The advent of the eurozone and the installation of the European Central Bank (ECB) in Frankfurt threatened a shift in Europe's financial centre of gravity but, so far, London has maintained its dominant position in securities and money markets. However, it is significant that the traditional UK investment banks and brokerage houses are now mostly in foreign ownership and the current bid by NASDAQ, the US securities market, for the London Stock Exchange at the end of 2006 poses a fresh threat .

Of course, commercial services comprise much more than banking, insurance and other financial services. They also include:

- the tourist trade. UK expenditure by foreign visitors less spending abroad;
- shipping and aviation freight services;
- communication services (telecommunications, postal and courier);
- computer and information services;
- royalties and licence fees;
- personal, cultural and recreational services;
- other business services.

In arriving at the net effect of 'invisible' transactions on the balance of payments, government disbursements, interest and profits earned abroad and emigrants' remittances are also taken into account. Their role is referred to again in Chapter 1.2.

The interplay of the deficits on merchandise trade and surpluses on commercial services since 1990 is detailed in the various figures of Chapter 1.3.

Organizations in world trade

Earlier in this chapter, the significance of three international organizations of key importance formed in the immediate post-World War II period was discussed in the context of the campaign against protectionism. The aim of all three organizations was to attempt to establish international approaches to trade and to economic development which would enhance world wealth while helping countries to adjust to economic fluctuations.

The IMF (International Monetary Fund)

The IMF's prime task is to try to regulate the way in which countries adjust to fluctuations in exchange rates. The IMF was set up to provide a way in which countries experiencing trade deficits could borrow funds to pay their debts from a central source. Member countries subscribe amounts of their own currencies and gold which are used, in theory, to assist deficit nations. For that purpose, the IMF also established a regime of currency rates and a form of 'world money' called 'Special Drawing Rights'.

Over the last 60 years, the IMF has undoubtedly contributed significantly to the way in which world trade has been able to expand. It has also played a crucial role in helping to rescue the economies of countries from bankruptcy through external debt.

Indeed, it is difficult to imagine how Argentina or Brazil could have survived their post-millennium financial crises without continuing IMF intervention.

The World Bank

The World Bank was established – as its original title implies – to help with post-war reconstruction. It was initially known as the 'International Bank for Reconstruction and Development'. Since 1945, the World Bank has taken on the role of providing loans at preferential rates mostly to developing countries for projects which will assist and accelerate their economic development. Typical projects are irrigation and hydro-electricity schemes, roads and power supply.

From the 1980s onwards, the World Bank has taken on a new role supporting the IMF in 'debt relief'. Between 1960 and 1980, many countries, particularly in South America and Africa, had accumulated substantial external debt on which the annual interest alone created real hardship. The scale of the debt was also creating the risk that a country would simply 'renege'on its debt which would create a domino effect as others followed suit.

By 1992, the 33 most indebted low-income countries faced debts with a present value that had doubled over 10 years to over six times their annual exports. The Paris Club and other bilateral creditors began to re-schedule and forgive debts from the late 1980s. However, a new debt relief initiative was required by the mid-1990s, and in 1996 the IMF and the International Development Association (IDA, the World Bank's concessional lending arm for poor countries) launched the Heavily Indebted Poor Countries (HIPC) Initiative which was enhanced in 1999 to a wider group of countries and to increase the Initiative's link to poverty reduction. To date, 29 countries are benefiting from HIPC debt relief.

Following the 2005 Gleneagles Summit of the G8 group of nations, the World Bank together with the IMF and the African Development Bank have been implementing The Multilateral Debt Relief Initiative (MDRI). The MDRI forgives 100% of eligible outstanding debt owed to the three institutions by all countries reaching the completion point of having satisfied the conditions of the HIPC Initiative. By the end of 2006, 19 countries had reached the completion point.

The General Agreement on Tariffs and Trade (GATT)

The GATT, which was superseded by the World Trade Organization (WTO) on 1 January 1995, was set up to try to avoid the competitive tariff wars of the 1930s.

The GATT was signed at Geneva in 1947, and came into operation in 1948.

Over a series of protracted negotiations, known as 'rounds', from 1945 onwards GATT established binding agreements on its members to reduce tariffs.

Each round reduced general tariffs further, thereby creating the conditions for steady increases in world trade. Under the GATT arrangements any proposal to impose a new tariff had to be submitted to GATT and any disputes between members were, in theory, to be settled by reference to GATT.

GATT rules for preventing infringements of tariff concessions and keeping the channels of trade open are based on two principles :

- most-favoured nation treatment for members; and
- non-discrimination.

However, many captions are allowed. Controls in conflict with the rules are permitted if they were in operation when the General Agreement was concluded, or, in the case of new members, when they first enter into negotiations. New restrictive measures of a discriminatory nature are allowed under certain conditions, the most important being safeguarding the balance of payments.

Since the conclusion of the Uruguay Round in December 1993, progress has been slower although WTO membership has continued to grow, notably with the addition of China in December 2001, and more effective dispute resolution procedures have been adopted. The more recent problems of the WTO which have been exposed during the current stalemate of the Doha round, not least those related to subsidies for EU agricultural products and tariff protection for US farmers, are discussed in Chapter 9.3.

1.2

Balance of payments – measurement and management

Measuring trade

In Chapter 1.1 we distinguished between international merchandise trade and trade in commercial services. The interplay between the two is the key element in national trade and balance of payments accounting of which the main elements are illustrated in Table 1.2.1.

In the past it was common UK practice to distinguish between 'visible' and 'invisible' trade, meaning effectively the tangible items and the intangible items. The formal published trade figures now have the two headings: 'balance on goods' and 'balance on services' as in Table 1.2.1.

Other items of what used to be part of the invisibles account are now treated under the new heading of 'UK Assets and Liabilities'.

International balance of payments ratios

There are three yardsticks of international trade which are quoted commonly by economists and others seeking to compare trade performance between countries relative to their economies:

- *ratio of trade at market prices to gross domestic product (GDP)*. For example, China now has a surprisingly open economy with a ratio of 44% in 2001, while Japan's ratio of trade to GDP was only 18%.
- *ratio of current account balance to GDP*. The ratios of the UK's and USA's deficits to GDP are 1.7% and 5.1% currently while those of some of the EU accession states exceed 40%.
- *terms of trade*. This more sophisticated measurement is the ratio of a country's prices of exports to those of its imports and is an indicator of competitiveness.

Imbalances in trading accounts

The surplus or deficit resulting from the sum of the balance on goods and the balance on services is known as the 'Balance of Trade'.

Table 1.2.1 - Balance of payments accounting

Balance on goods	The account for trade in manufactured goods and raw materials.
Balance on services	The account showing balances on trade in services.
Current account	The account which includes virtually everything which would be recognised as trade as well as some other things such as net investment income. Included are: Balance on goods Balance on services Balance on investment income Balance on Government transfers
UK assets & liabilities Account	A new account introduced in the mid-1990s to show the UK's net earnings or net payments in respect of what it owns in the rest of the world.
Balance of payments	The overall 'accounts' for the UK's trade with the rest of the world.

The ultimate result of the collection of UK trade figures is a net total known as 'Balance of Payments'. This figure represents formally the final surplus or debt resulting from all UK transactions with the rest of the world in any given year.

It is customary to apply the term 'current account balance' to the reported net surplus or deficit for a given period or the current year to date.

The objective for trade balances objective is to achieve 'equilibrium' or sufficient surpluses to pay off a country's debts but not over such a period as to damage trade by affecting the exchange rate. A country whose balance of payments shows consistent deficits is said to be in 'disequilibrium'. Technically, the term 'disequilibrium' applies equally where consistent surpluses are experienced but this is a more desirable result and is rarely referred to under the heading of disequilibrium.

Managing disequilibrium

A country with a surplus in its balance of payments is said to be a 'creditor nation'. It can add this surplus to its reserves or lend it to other nations to enable them to improve their economies.

Conversely, if a country incurs a deficit in its balance of payments, it is said to be a 'debtor nation' because it has spent more than it has earned. It must finance this deficit either by drawing upon its reserves or borrowing externally.

Clearly, a country's reserves of gold and foreign currencies are not inexhaustible and, sooner or later, it would have to negotiate loans and eventually repay them. We have already mentioned the role of the IMF as a provider of loans for this purpose. IMF loans are generally granted with stringent conditions attached as to the management of the borrowing country's economy. In the 1970s the UK negotiated significant loans from the IMF in order to cover accumulated deficits. Changes in domestic economic policy, in agreement wit the IMF, enabled the loans to be repaid quite soon.

A country with a persistent balance of payments deficit must take appropriate measures to rectify the situation which would depend upon the causes of the deficit. If it is due to its imports, measures must be taken to restrict imports while stimulating exports. If it has been caused by an excessive outflow of capital, then measures must be taken to control overseas investment.

As we shall discuss in Chapter 9.3 at the end of this book, both the UK and the USA are in deficit at the end of 2003 and remedial action is likely to become necessary.

Some of the measures which a country may take are summarized as follows:

Import controls

In theory, there are two methods of controlling imports, the protection tools described in Chapter 1.1:

- import quotas and
- import duties (tariffs)

Import quotas provide restrictions to the total number or value of goods which may be imported into the country during a specified period.

The imposition of import duties is intended to reduce demand for the commodities in question by increasing the price to the ultimate user.

As signatories to the GATT and its successor the WTO, the boundaries within which the UK or the USA can impose import controls or tariffs, even to address disequilibrium, are severely restricted. As a full member of the EU the UK can depart from the common external tariff only in the most exceptional circumstances.

Export incentives

A government might grant its exporters generally, or in specific industries, subsidies or taxation reductions to enable them to reduce their prices and undercut foreign competitors. Such incentives are also outlawed by the WTO ad would certainly contravene EU agreements if applied to trade within Europe.

Monetary measures

Since the use of import controls and export incentives is constrained, the UK usually resorts to monetary measures when there is a balance of payments deficit.

Recognising that the fundamental cause of current account deficits is usually excessive home demand for imported goods and the absorption of home-produced goods which may otherwise have been exported, the government may adopt one or more of the following measures:

- *increase interest rates* - thereby discouraging borrowing and consequently tightening and reducing spending power. Higher interest rates also attract foreign short-term capital.
- *open market operations* - by selling securities in the open market the government reduces the amount of money in circulation which diminishes purchasing power.
- *special deposits* - in the form of directive to the banks to deposit a certain proportion of their funds with the Bank of England where they are frozen.

This reduces the liquidity of the banks, which in turn restricts bank lending and diminishes purchasing power.

Fiscal measures

A government can also reduce spending power more directly by means of higher taxation, hire-purchase controls, etc.

Devaluation

The purpose of devaluing a currency is to make a country's exports cheaper to overseas buyers and, at the same time, its imports dearer. This method is applicable when a system of fixed exchange rates is in place, but is usually the measure of last resort.

Under a system of floating exchange rates, the exchange value of a currency will gradually depreciate if it is overvalued, which will have the same effect as a devaluation. The currencies of developing countries which are 'pegged' by a fixed rate (or within a narrow fixed band) to a more stable 'hard' currency, such as the US dollar, are effectively insulated from the market forces related to its own country's economy.

Managing exchange rates

The history of exchange rates is complex. In the early days of trade exporters would accept payment only in commodities which were considered to have intrinsic value, such as gold, silver or jewels.

This approach continued until well into the nineteenth century when certain currencies came into use for trade, notably the pound sterling, the Dutch guilder and the French franc reflecting the growth of Empires during that century.

The British Empire's wealth enabled the British Government to back every single pound note with an equivalent amount of gold. The level of trust in paper currency became so great that large areas of the world traded and maintained reserves in sterling.

These territories became known collectively as 'the Sterling Area', a vast expanse of British Government-backed paper which became a major embarrassment to successive governments of the 1950s and 1960s when countries began to convert their reserves to gold or US dollars.

In about 1873, the need to know the value of a trading currency led to the establishment of the 'Gold Standard' with currencies pegged in terms of their values in a specific weight of gold and each other. The Gold Standard created the first system of fixed exchange rates and provided the confidence required for a significant expansion in world trade. The standard began to break down after 1918 and disappeared during the 1930s. The lack of formal exchange rate mechanisms contributed to the collapse in world trade during that inter-war period.

After World War II the IMF established a new system of fixed exchange rates which was also fixed against gold but more remotely. Each country assigned a value to its currency in terms of an ounce of gold (which was valued then at $35). Nations were only allowed to adjust their exchange significantly in extreme circumstances but could make minor adjustments (up to 10%) in circumstances which were described as 'fundamental disequilibrium'.

Few countries used this facility (only 6 between 1947 and 1971) and, by the 1960s, the system had become highly unstable. By 1971 continuing US difficulties caused the Americans to announce that the dollar would no longer be convertible into gold. Soon afterwards the British and French Governments also came off the gold standard.

Since that date the main system of exchange rate 'management' has been to allow currencies to float within reasonable limits against other currencies. In its European Community phase the EU operated several fixed and semi-fixed systems during the 1970s and 1980s, the last of which deteriorated into a smaller 'Deutsche Mark' area. However, the establishment of the European Monetary Union with the formation of the European Central Bank (ECB) and the launch of the euro-currency from 1 January 1999 has put in place a single currency throughout the Euro-zone which currently includes all members of the EU15 except for Denmark, Sweden and the UK.

The UK retains the pound sterling which the British Government allows to float whilst monitoring its position closely. The 10 members of the Euro-zone have foregone the ability to devalue or revalue a national currency individually.

1.3

Patterns of world trade

International trade in the twentieth century

The endeavours of participating nations in the GATT and its successor, the WTO, to expand the Free Trade environment in the past sixty years may be appreciated best in the historical context of the growth in trade throughout the 20th century.

In Table 1.3.1 the rate of growth in the volume of merchandise exports for 11 countries and the world is summarized for the period from 1870 to 1998. In global terms, the annual average compound growth rate between 1913 and 1950 was less than 1%, compared to pre-1913 growth of 3.4%. The following 23-year period was one of strong international trade expansion with annual compound growth averaging 7.9%, which then eased off to 5.1% over the 25-year period 1973--98.

Comparing the two most recent periods, among developed economies annual average growth fell back with the exception of the UK where the growth rate increased from 3.9 to 4.4%. In Europe, most striking was the fall in the growth rate of merchandise exports from Germany from 12.4 to 4.4% as the post-war reconstruction period of German industry came to a close, while the annual growth in exports from the USA remained at the 6.0% level. However, the fall in merchandise export growth has been most marked in the case of Japan, where the annual rate fell by almost two-thirds from 15.4% over 1950--73 to almost European levels (5.3%) during the 1973--98 period.

By contrast, the volume of merchandise exports from developing countries in Asia and Latin America soared. China's annual growth rate more than quadrupled from 2.7 to 11.8%, while Mexican export growth rose from 4.3% to 10.9%.

The growing significance of merchandise exports to the economies of individual countries is illustrated in Figure 1.4 which charts over six selected years in the same span of the past 130 years how exports as a percentage of GDP at 1990 prices fluctuated. Globally, exports fell back from 9.0% of GDP in 1929 to 5.5% in 1950 before recovering to 10.5% in 1973 and moving forward to 17.2% in 1998.

Broadly, the developed countries conformed to this pattern with much higher rates of export ratios in Europe and lower rates in the USA and Japan. By 1998 the exports/GDP ratio had reached 25.0% in the UK and 38.9% in Germany. For the USA and Japan the ratios were 10.1 and 13.4%

Table 1.3.1 - Rate of growth (%) in volume of merchandise exports, 11 countries and world, 1890–1988 (annual average compound growth rates)

	1870–1913	1913–50	1950–73	1973–98
France	2.8	1.1	8.2	4.7
Germany	4.1	-2.8	12.4	4.4
Netherlands	2.3	1.5	10.4	4.1
United Kingdom	2.8	0.0	3.9	4.4
Spain	3.5	-1.6	9.2	9.0
United States	4.9	2.2	6.3	6.0
Mexico	5.4	-0.5	4.3	10.9
Brazil	1.9	1.7	4.7	6.6
China	2.6	1.1	2.7	11.8
India	2.4	-1.5	2.5	5.9
Japan	8.5	2.0	15.4	5.3
World	3.4	0.9	7.9	5.1

Table 1.3.2 - Merchandise exports as a percentage of GDP in 1990 prices, 11 countries and world, 1870—1998

	1870	1913	1929	1950	1973	1998
France	4.9	7.8	8.6	7.6	15.2	28.7
Germany	9.5	16.1	12.8	6.2	23.8	38.9
Netherlands	17.4	17.3	17.2	12.2	40.7	61.2
United Kingdom	12.2	17.5	13.3	11.3	14.0	25.0
Spain	3.8	8.1	5.0	3.0	5.0	23.5
United States	2.5	3.7	3.6	3.0	4.9	10.1
Mexico	3.9	9.1	12.5	3.0	1.9	10.7
Brazil	12.2	9.8	6.9	3.9	2.5	5.4
China	0.7	1.7	1.8	2.6	1.5	4.9
India	2.6	4.6	3.7	2.9	2.0	2.4
Japan	0.2	2.4	3.5	2.2	7.7	13.4
World	4.6	7.9	9.0	5.5	10.5	17.2

Source: Appendix 1.6.1, sources for Fig. 1.6.1, Maddison (1997), Table 13

respectively. The highest export/GDP ratio for 1998 among developed countries was recorded in the Netherlands at 61.2%.

Among developing countries, in spite of their superior rates of export growth since 1973, export/GDP ratios are comparatively modest. In 1998 Mexico's merchandise exports represented 10.7% of GDP, while China's export/GDP ratio was only 4.9%, giving a foretaste of the likely impact of Chinese exports on world trade as its per capita industrial output approaches more developed economy levels.

More detail on the evolution of exports round the world is given in Table 1.3.3, where the value of merchandise exports at constant 1990 prices for 35 countries is tracked for the same six years over the 1870-1998 period.

Trends in merchandise trade and commercial services by region

The growth by region in the value of world merchandise trade and world trade in commercial services between 1990 and 2001 in terms of annual percentage change are charted in Tables 1.3.4 and 1.3.5.

Merchandise trade

After increased exports of merchandise in all regions in 2000, of which the EU's increase of 3% was lowest, all the groupings in Figure 1.3.4 except for Central and Eastern Europe, the Baltic States and the CIS (5%) and China (7%) suffered export declines in 2001.

The EU

In terms of merchandise trade, the EU (within Western Europe) was the world's biggest grouping in 2001 in both exports ($2,291 billion) and imports ($2,334 billion) with imports marginally exceeding exports. The rate of growth of imports fell from 6% in 2000 to just 1% in 2001, while exports actually declined in 2001 by 1% against 4% growth the previous year.

Including the new members who joined in May 2004, the merchandise trade of the enlarged EU25 has shown healthy growth over the most recent five-year period to 2004 for which statistics are available. Exports rose 11% to $3,714 billion and imports by 10% to $3,792 billion. Figure 1.3.5 shows exceptional growth of 19% for both imports and exports in 2004, the year in which the 10 new members joined and a similar surge is shown for the whole of Western Europe. The value of both exports and imports climbed above $4,000 billion that year.

Table. 1.3.3 - Evolution of world exports from 1870 to 1998 at constant 1990 prices

	1870	1913	1929	1950	1973	1998
Austria	467	2,024	1,746	1,348	13,899	69,519
Belgium	1,237	7,318	7,845	8,182	61,764	175,503
Denmark	314	1,494	2,705	3,579	16,568	49,121
Finland	310	1,597	2,578	3,186	15,641	48,697
France	3,512	11,292	16,600	16,848	104,161	329,597
Germany	6,761	38,200	35,068	13,179	194,171	567,372
Italy	1,788	4,621	5,670	5,846	72,749	267,378
Netherlands	1,727	4,329	7,411	7,411	71,522	194,430
Norway	223	854	1,427	2,301	11,687	58,141
Sweden	713	2,670	4,167	7,366	34,431	103,341
Switzerland	1,107	5,735	5,776	6,493	38,972	78,863
United Kingdom	12,237	39,348	31,990	39,348	94,670	277,243
Total	30,396	119,482	122,983	115,087	730,235	2,219,205
Australia	455	3,392	3,636	5,383	18,869	69,324
Canada	724	4,044	7,812	12,576	60,214	243,015
United States	2,495	19,196	30,368	43,114	174,548	745,330
Total	3,674	26,632	41,816	61,073	253,631	1,057,669
Spain	850	3,697	3,394	2,018	15,295	131,621
USSR	n.a.	6,666	3,420	6,472	58,015	119,978
Argentina	222	1,963	3,096	2,079	4,181	23,439
Brazil	854	1,888	2,592	3,489	9,998	49,874
Chile	166	702	1,352	1,166	2,030	18,228
Colombia	114	267	811	1,112	2,629	11,117
Mexico	242	2,363	3,714	1,999	5,238	70,261
Peru	202	409	1,142	1,172	4,323	6,205
Venezuela	n.a.	1,374	2,593	9,722	23,779	29,411
Total	2,126	8,966	15,300	20,739	52,178	208,535
Bangladesh	–	–	–	284	445	4,146

Table. *1.3.3 (continued)*

	1870	1913	1929	1950	1973	1998
Burma	–	–	–	269	235	1,075
China	1,398	4,197	6,262	6,339	11,679	190,177
India	3,466	9,480	8,209	5,489	9,679	40,972
Indonesia	172	989	2,609	2,254	9,605	56,232
Japan	51	1,684	4,343	3,538	95,105	346,007
Pakistan	–	–	–	720	1,626	9,868
Phillippines	55	180	678	697	2,608	22,712
South Korea	0	171	1,292	112	7,894	204,542
Taiwan	–	70	261	180	5,761	100,639
Thailand	88	495	640	1,148	3,081	48,752
Total	5,230	17,266	24,294	21,030	147,733	1,025,122

Source: Volume movement in Western Europe, Western Offshoots and Japan from A. Maddison, *Dynamic Forces in Capitalist Development*, OUP, 1991, Appendix F, updated from OECD, *Economic Outlook*, December 1999. Spain 1826–1980 from A. Carreras, ed., *Estadísticas Históricas de España: Siglos XIX–XX*, Fundación Banco Exterior, Madrid, 1989, pp. 346–7. USSR, Latin America and Asia from sources cited in A. Maddison, *The World Economy in the Twentieth Century*, OECD Development Centre, 1989, p. 140, updated with volume movements derivable from IMF, *International Financial Statistics*, various issues. Brazil 1870–1913 from R.W. Goldsmith, *Brasil 1850–1984: Desenvolvimento Financeiro Sob um Século de Inflacão*, Harper and Row, Sao Paulo, 1986, pp. 54–5 and 110–111; Peru 1870–1950 from S.J. Hunt, "Price and Quantum Estimates of Peruvian Exports, 1830–1962", Discussion Paper 33, Research Program in Economic Development, Princeton University, January 1973, (1929 weights for 1900–50, 1900 weights for 1870–1900): Venezuela 1913–29 from A. Bapista, *Bases Cuantitativas de la Economica Venezolana 1830–1989*, C. Corporativas, Caracas, 1991, and 1929–92 from ECLAC sources. 1990–8 movements from ADB, OECD, ECLAC, IMF.

Table 1.3.4 - Growth in the value of world merchandise trade by region (1990-2001)

	Exports				Imports			
	Value	Annual percentage change			Value	Annual percentage change		
	2001	1990–01	2000	2001	2001	1990–01	2000	2001
World	5984	5	13	–4	6270	5	13	–4
North America[a]	991	6	14	–6	1408	7	18	–6
Latin America	347	8	20	–3	380	11	16	–2
Western Europe	2485	4	4	–1	2524	4	6	–3
European Union (15)	2291	4	3	–1	2334	4	6	–3
C./E. Europe/Baltic States/CIS	286	7	26	5	267	6	14	11
Central and Eastern Europe	129	8	14	12	159	10	12	9
Russian Federation	103	–	39	–2	54	–	13	20
Africa	141.2	3	27	–5	136	3	4	2
Middle East	237	5	42	–9	180	5	13	4
Asia	1497	7	18	–9	1375	6	23	–7
Japan	403	3	14	–16	349	4	22	–8
China	266	14	28	7	244	15	36	8
Six EastAsian traders	568	7	19	–12	532	6	26	–13

[a]Excluding Mexico throughout this report.

Note: It should be mentioned at the outset that there are breaks in the continuity of the figures at the country and regional levels.

Source: WTO (www.wto.org). More recent changes in the pattern of world merchandise trade over the five years ended 2004 are highlighted in Table 1.3.6. The period was one of more prosperous activity for World trade with both exports and imports rising 9% to $8,907 and $9,250 respectively. Growth in 2004 was particularly strong with foreign merchandise trade rising 21%.

Table 1.3.5 – The pattern of world merchandise trade

	Export			Imports		
	Value 2004	Annual Growth %		Value 2004	Annual Growth %	
	US$ billion	Five Yrs.	2004	US$ billion	Five Yrs.	2004
World	8,907	9	21	9,250	9	21
North America	1,324	2	14	2,013	5	17
South & Central America	276	9	30	237	4	27
Europe	4,031	11	19	4,140	11	20
- EU25	3,714	11	19	3,791	10	19
CIS	266	16	37	172	21	30
- Russian Federation	183	15	35	96	21	27
Africa	232	12	32	212	13	27
Middle East	390	10	29	252	12	27
Asia	2,388	10	25	2,224	10	27
- China	593	24	35	561	26	36
- Japan	566	4	20	455	5	19
- Six Asian traders	880	7	24	785	6	27

Source: World Trade Organization statistics

Table 1.3.6 – Top 10 exporters and importers in merchandise and commercial services

US$ billion and percentages

	Exports		Imports	
	Value	Share of World Trade		Value	Share of World Trade
United States	1,129	10.1	United States	1,733	15.7
Germany	1,044	9.4	Germany	911	8.2
China	655	5.9	China	606	5.5
Japan	634	5.7	United Kingdom	591	5.3
France	531	4.8	Japan	541	4.9
United Kingdom	521	4.7	France	525	4.7
Italy	428	3.8	Italy	417	3.8
Canada	378	3.4	Netherlands	344	3.1
Netherlands	374	3.4	Canada	335	3.0
South Korea	298	2.7	Spain	302	2.7
Total	5,992	53.9		6,305	56.9

Source: World Trade Organisation Statistics
Note: Hong Kong, China is omitted from top 10 exporters (US$314 bn) because its trade in goods includes significant re-exports or imports for re-exports.

Asia

Asia was the second largest exporting region ($1,497 billion) with exports exceeding imports by $122 billion in 2001 and has comfortably maintained its ranking since. Following the 1997/8 Asian financial crisis, the annual growth in exports recovered from 6% negative to 18% positive in 2000 before falling back 9% in 2001. The decline in 2001 was attributable to a reduction in Japanese exports of 16%. Likewise, imports revived from 1998's decline of 18% and peaked at 23% growth in 2000.

Over the five-year period to 2004, Asia maintained a 10% rate of growth in both exports and imports similar to Europe reaching $2,388 billion in exports and $2,224 billion in imports. The biggest contributor to Asia's growth was China with exports rising 24% to $593 billion and imports 26% to $561 billion.

North America

In 2001 North America (excluding Mexico) was the world's second largest importing region ($1,408 billion), although only third in exports ($991 billion). However, export growth recovered by 4% in 1999 (1998 -- 1% negative) and peaked at 14% growth in 2000 before declining 6% in 2001. Imports achieved 14% growth in 2000 against 5% in 1998.

More recently North American exports (including Mexico) grew more slowly over the period to 2004 reaching $1,324 billion; however they did register superior growth of 14% in 2004. Import growth averaged its lower 1998 rate of 5% but in 2004 rose by 17% to $2,013 billion as the US trade gap widened further. However, its world ranking in imports fell to third place against the fast expanding Asia region.

Central and Eastern Europe

Although exports from Central and Eastern Europe increased only marginally in 1999 by 1% against a 10-year average growth rate of 7%, growth was more robust in 2000 and 2001 (11%) to a total of $129 billion. Imports declined by 1% in 1999 against 10% average for the decade, but grew strongly in 2000 and 2001 to a total $159 billion. Thus, the annual trade deficit for the region was maintained at the level of $30 billion from 1999.

The Baltic States and CIS countries together achieved an export surplus of $31 billion in 1999 with exports slowing by 2% and imports by 24% but in 2001 the trade surplus narrowed to $19 billion.

Since then foreign trade of the Russian Federation has advanced strongly with exports rising for the five years ended 2004 by an average 15% to $183 billion, peaking at 35% in 2004. Over the same period annual import growth averaged 21% rising to 27% in 2004 when the value of imports reached $96 billion. The healthy current account balance is maintained by the ever-growing revenues earned from Russian oil and gas exports.

Trade statistics for the eight leading CEE member states that joined the EU in 2004 are folded into those for the EU25 in Table 1.3.6.

Middle East

The Middle East trade surplus in 2001 was $57 billion with OPEC oil exports accounting for most of the export total of $237 billion. Although exports grew by 42% in 2000, significantly higher than in other region except the oil-producing Russian Federation (39%), they fell away by 9% in 2001.

Figure 1.3.6 shows that over the five years to 2004 the growth in Middle East exports rose by 10% average to $390 billion while import growth averaged 12% to $252 billion. As in the case of China and Russia, 2004 was a peak year for exports (+29%) and imports grew also at a similar rate of 27%.

Africa

African imports were at a similar level ($128 billion) to the CEE in 1999 but grew more modestly in 2000 and 2001 to $136 billion. Exports from Africa grew more rapidly from $117 billion (1999) to $141 billion (2001) thereby achieving a small trade surplus.

Africa's exports reached $232 billion in 2004 having grown at an average rate of 12% over five years (2004: +32%) maintaining the small trade surplus over imports of $212 billion although they grew at an annual average of 13% (2004: +27%).

Latin America

Latin America's exports grew strongly by 20% in 2000 but fell back by 3% in 2001 to $347 billion, resulting in a regional trade deficit of $3 billion.

Excluding Mexico, South and Central American exports grew by 9% average from 1999 to 2004 ($276 billion) while import growth averaged 4% to 2004 ($237 billion). As in other regions outside North America and Europe, growth of both exports (30%) and imports (27%) accelerated in 2004.

Commercial services

The pattern of 2001 world trade in commercial services was rather different from that of merchandise trade, as Table 1.3.5 demonstrates. Although the world average annual growth rate in the value of exports over the 10-year period to 2000 at 6.5% was the same as for merchandise trade, the decline in the export of commercial services in 2001 was only 0.5% compared to 4.5% in the case of merchandise. Both Western Europe and North America (again, excluding Mexico), the first and third exporting regions, were net exporters of commercial services to the values of $31 billion and $10 billion respectively.

By contrast in 2001, Asia, now the second-ranking region in commercial services, was a net importer to the value of $54 billion. Neither Central and Eastern Europe nor the Baltic States and the CIS registered as significant in commercial services world trade.

Foreign trade between trading blocs and their members

Regional merchandise trade may also be analysed in terms of intra- and extra-exports and imports between the principal trading groups1 and their members: APEC, EU, NAFTA, ASEAN, CEFTA, MERCOSUR and AN-DEAN. The data for 1990, 1995 and 2001 is displayed in Figure 1.8 in respect of percentage share of exports/imports and annual percentage change, and in value for 2001.

In the case of APEC, the most diverse of the groupings, exports between the 21 country membership in 2001 exceeded exports to other regions in the ratio 71.8 to 28.2. Similarly, the ratio of intra-imports to extra-imports was 69.9 to 30.1.

Exports between the 15 members of the EU in 1999 exceeded exports to other regions in the ratio 61.85 to 38.15 while intra- and extra-imports followed a closely similar pattern.

Given the comparatively recent formation of the NAFTA, it is encouraging to find that in 2001 intra-exports and intra-imports represented 55.5% and 39.5% respectively of total exports and imports.

Among the four other trade groups the incidence of intra-exports and imports is less dominant. The proportion of intra-exports between the 10 ASEAN and 4 MERCOSUR members was 23.5% and 17.3% and, similarly, 22.8% and 18.9% respectively for intra-imports.

Intra-trade between the 7 members of CEFTA (exports: 12.4; imports: 9.9%) and 5 members of the ANDEAN group (exports: 11.2%; imports: 13.3%) were less significant but have been growing quite strongly in the case of the ANDEAN 5. Clearly, there are potential foreign trade benefits for all trading blocs from enhanced free trade between them if the Doha round of WTO negotiations can be revived and pursued to a positive conclusion. The alternative scenario is discussed in Chapter 9.3.

Extra- and inter-regional merchandise trade

North America

North America's biggest regional export markets are Asia and Western Europe, accounting respectively for 19.0% and 20.9% of total exports in

Table 1.3.7 - Growth in the value of world trade in commercial services by region (1990-2001) The pattern of world merchandise trade

	Exports			Imports		
	Value 2004 US$ billion	Annual Growth % Five Yrs.	2004	Value 2004 US$ billion	Annual Growth % Five Yrs.	2004
World	8,907	9	21	9,250	9	21
North America	1,324	2	14	2,013	5	17
South & Central America	276	9	30	237	4	27
Europe	4,031	11	19	4,140	11	20
- EU25	3,714	11	19	3,791	10	19
CIS	266	16	37	172	21	30
- Russian Federation	183	15	35	96	21	27
Africa	232	12	32	212	13	27
Middle East	390	10	29	252	12	27
Asia	2,388	10	25	2,224	10	27
- China	593	24	35	561	26	36
- Japan	566	4	20	455	5	19
- Six Asian traders	880	7	24	785	6	27

Source: World Trade Organization statistics

Table 1.3.8 - Merchandise trade of selected regional integration arrangements, 2001 ($billion dollars and percentages)

	Value	Share in total exports/imports			Annual percentage change		
	2001	1990	1995	2001	1990–01	2000	2001
APEC (21)							
Total exports	2700	100.0	100.00	100.00	7	17	–8
Intra-exports	1938	67.5	73.06	71.78	7	20	–9
Extra-exports	762	32.5	26.94	28.22	5	11	–4
Total imports[a]	2969	100.0	100.00	100.00	7	21	–7
Intra-imports	2076	65.4	71.74	69.92	8	20	–8
Extra-imports	893	34.6	28.26	30.08	6	24	–2
EU (15)							
Total exports	2291	100.0	100.00	100.00	4	3	–1
Intra-exports	1417	64.9	64.01	61.85	3	1	–2
Extra-exports	874	35.1	35.99	38.15	5	7	0
Total imports	2334	100.0	100.00	100.00	4	6	–3
Intra-imports	1421	63.0	65.23	60.89	3	1	–2
Extra-imports	913	37.0	34.77	39.11	4	15	–4
NAFTA (3)							
Total exports	1149	100.0	100.00	100.00	7	15	–6
Intra-exports	637	42.6	46.06	55.46	9	18	–6
Extra-exports	512	57.4	53.94	44.54	4	11	–6
Total imports[b]	1578	100.0	100.00	100.00	8	18	–6

Intra-imports	624	34.4	37.72	39.55	9	17	−7
Extra-imports	954	65.6	62.28	60.45	7	19	−6
ASEAN (10)							
Total exports	385	100.0	100.00	100.00	9	19	−10
Intra-exports	90	20.1	25.52	23.46	11	28	−12
Extra-exports	295	79.9	74.48	76.54	9	16	−9
Total imports	336	100.0	100.00	100.00	7	22	−8
Intra-imports	77	16.2	18.89	22.77	10	28	−12
Extra-imports	260	83.8	81.11	77.23	6	21	−7
Total exports	138	—	100.00	100.00	—	13	11
Intra-exports	17	—	14.54	12.37	—	14	14
Extra-exports	121	—	85.46	87.63	—	13	11
Total imports	168	—	100.00	100.00	—	12	8
Intra-imports	17	—	11.28	9.91	—	13	12
Extra-imports	151	—	88.72	90.09	—	11	8
MERCOSUR (4)							
Total exports	88	100.0	100.00	100.00	6	14	4
Intra-exports	15	8.9	20.51	17.26	13	17	−14
Extra-exports	73	91.1	79.49	82.74	5	13	9
Total imports	84	100.0	100.00	100.00	10	8	−6
Intra-imports	16	14.5	18.07	18.88	13	12	−11
Extra-imports	68	85.5	81.93	81.12	9	8	−5

Table 1.3.8 (continued)

	Value	Share in total exports/imports			Annual percentage change		
	2001	1990	1995	2001	1990–01	2000	2001
ANDEAN (5)							
Total exports	53	100.0	100.00	100.00	5	34	–9
Intra-exports	6	4.2	12.16	11.19	15	30	14
Extra-exports	47	95.8	87.84	88.81	4	34	–12
Total imports[c]	44	100.0	100.00	100.00	9	9	12
Intra-imports	6	7.7	12.88	13.32	14	29	8
Extra-imports	38	92.3	87.12	86.68	8	7	12

[a] Imports of Canada, Mexico (1990–99), Peru, and Australia are valued f.o.b.
[b] Imports of Canada and Mexico (1990–99) are valued f.o.b.
[c] Imports of Peru and Venezuela are valued f.o.b.
Note: The figures are not fully adjusted for differences in the way members of the arrangements in this table record their merchandise trade.
Source: WTO (www.wto.org)

2001. Asia accounted for 32.7% of total US imports of which 9.9% were sourced from China. A further 19.5% originated from Western Europe.

Western Europe

For Western Europe, extra-trade accounted for about one-third. The 32.5% of exports shipped in 2001 from Western European countries to external markets were diffused relatively evenly between North America (10.2%) and Asia (7.9%) with the remainder distributed between Latin America, Africa and the Middle East in almost equal proportions.

Of the 33.6% of imports sourced outside Western Europe, 11.3% were imported from Asia, 8.0% from North America, 6.7% from Central and Eastern Europe and CIS countries and 3.0% from Africa.

Central and Eastern Europe, the Baltic and CIS states

The exports of Central and Eastern European countries, the Baltic and CIS states outside the region are sold primarily into Western European markets. The two other significant regional markets are Asia and North America.

Latin America

By contrast, more than 60% of Latin America's exports are sold to North American markets, with Western Europe and Asia its more important secondary regional markets.

Asia

North America is also the primary extra-export market for Asian goods with Western Europe the dominant secondary market. Asia is the primary export region for Middle Eastern merchandise with Western Europe and North America its major secondary markets.

Africa

Finally, Africa follows a similar pattern to Central and Eastern Europe, the Baltic and CIS states with more than half of export goods shipped to Western Europe and the bulk of remaining extra-exports to North America and Asia.

The world's leading exporters and importers

Merchandise trade

The top 10 exporting and importing countries in world merchandise trade and commercial services, excluding intra-EU trade, are identified in Table 1.3.9.

Table 1.3.9 – Top 10 exporters and importers in merchandise and commercial services

	Exports		US$ billion and percentages	Imports	
	Value	Share of World Trade		Value	Share of World Trade
United States	1,129	10.1	United States	1,733	15.7
Germany	1,044	9.4	Germany	911	8.2
China	655	5.9	China	606	5.5
Japan	634	5.7	United Kingdom	591	5.3
France	531	4.8	Japan	541	4.9
United Kingdom	521	4.7	France	525	4.7
Italy	428	3.8	Italy	417	3.8
Canada	378	3.4	Netherlands	344	3.1
Netherlands	374	3.4	Canada	335	3.0
South Korea	298	2.7	Spain	302	2.7
Total	5,992	53.9		6,305	56.9

Source: World Trade Organisation Statistics
Note: Hong Kong, China is omitted from top 10 exporters (US$314 bn) because its trade in goods includes significant re-exports or imports for re-exports.

The total value of merchandise and commercial services exports from the Top 10 exporters in 2004 was $5,992 billion against $6,325 billion in imports by the Top 10 importers.

In individual country terms, the US ranks first ahead of Germany in second place, both for exports and imports. China now holds third place in both exports and imports. Both Germany and China are net exporters whereas the US, as already noted, is a net importer.

Japan ranks fourth as an exporter but fifth in imports, showing a strong trade surplus, whereas the UK is a net importer, in spite of its strong performance in commercial services, lying fifth in the Top 10 as an exporter but fourth as an importer.

The remaining countries that appear in the league table as both exporters and importers enjoy trade surpluses.

Part 2

International Marketing - principles and practice

2.1

Principles

The marketing concept

There is no argument about the concept of marketing but there are constant arguments about the best way to define it. The consequence of this is that there are literally hundreds of definitions of marketing, all of which can claim to be correct. This does not mean that opinions differ about the essence of marketing but that we can have different attitudes towards a single concept.

Whilst we have the old clichés such as 'Marketing is selling goods which don't come back to customers who do', it is in fact possible to classify definitions into three basic attitudes:

Group one

This consists of definitions with the strong implication in them that a producer is doing something that involves consumers as nothing more significant than pawns in a game, with profit as the end goal.

– The income-producing side of the business. Mcnair, Brown, Leighton & Englent

– The process of determining consumer demand for a product or service, motivating its sale, and distributing it into ultimate consumption at a profit. *L. Brech*

– The planning, executing and evaluating of the external factors related to a company's profit objectives. *G. M. E. Ule In D. W. Ewing (Ed)*

– The primary management function which organises and directs the aggregate of business activities involved in converting customer purchasing power into effective demand for a specific product or service and in moving the product or service to the final customer or user so as to achieve company-set profit or other objectives. *L. W. Rodger*

– Deciding what the customer wants; arranging to make it; distributing and selling it at the maximum profit. *Durham University Careers Advisory Service*

Group two

Consists of a number of definitions with the implications that the producer is doing something FOR consumers rather than TO them, but still doing it to suit their own purpose.These definitions are, like those in Group One, very much concerned with a means to a profitable end. They are completely company-centred.

– Getting the right goods to the right people in the right places at the right time and the right price. *Anon.*

– Marketing development is systematic forward planning so as to ensure matching of resources to fit market trends and to ensure continued growth for the enterprise. *R. Glasser*

– The total system of interacting business activities designed to plan, price, promote and distribute want-satisfying products and services to present and potential customers. *W. J. Stanton*

– The activity that can keep in constant touch with an organisation's consumers, read their needs and build a programme of communications to express the organisation's purpose. *Kotler & Levy*

Group three

These definitions move us significantly forward by introducing the idea that there is an element of willingness on the part of consumers as well as producers to join in the process. The vital words 'transfer', 'society' and 'needs of consumers' appear in these definitions, although they remain company-centred. Marketing is seen by these authors as a **transaction** of some kind.

– The economic process by means of which goods and services are exchanged and their values determined in terms of money prices. *Duddy & Revzan*

– Selling is preoccupied with the seller's need to convert his product into cash; marketing with the idea of satisfying the needs of the customer by means of the product and the whole cluster of things associated with creating, delivering and finally consuming it. *T. Levitt*

– The business activities involved in the transfer of goods or the acquisition of services. *R. Webster*– The organisation and performance of those business activities that facilitate the exchange of goods and services between maker and user. *L. W. Rodger*– All activities intended to stimulate or serve demand *G. A. Fisk*

To go just one stage further there are definitions which consolidate the tendency of Group Three to think in terms of transactions. They say that marketing can in fact be thought of as a social exchange process.

– The medium through which the material goods and culture of a society are transmitted to its members. *E. J. Kelley*

– The establishment of contact. *P. T Cherrington*

The latter is included because it is probably the shortest definition you could find. However these last two, while being interesting in their own right, have little practical value to the exporter.

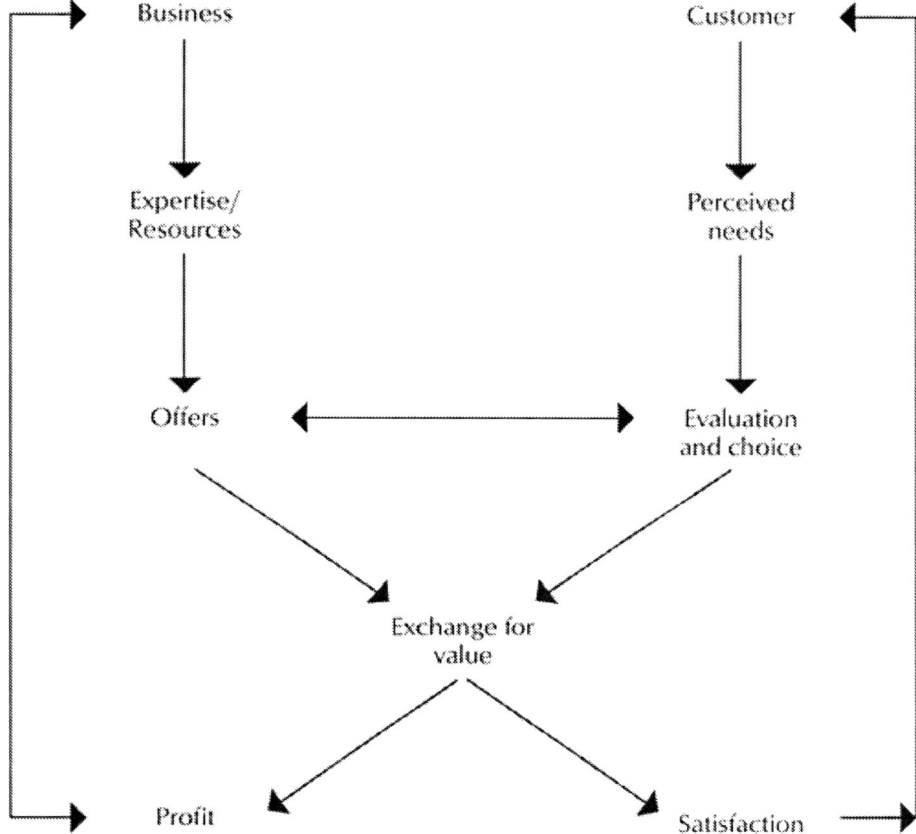

Fig. 2.1.1 - The exchange process

The group that contains definitions that are most appropriate for international marketing is undoubtedly group 3, in that they not only contain a need for consumer satisfaction but also the need for the establishment of some sort of relationship or partnership with overseas buyers. This will have some resonance with most practising exporters.

The exchange process

The idea that international marketing can be seen as an exchange process can be broken down into its constituent elements in the diagrammatic form shown in Fig. 2.1.1.

This demonstrates the two sides of the exchange; the business on one side using its expertise and resources to offer products and services on to a market made up of potential customers who have their own ideas about what they need and do not need. The business that most closely matches its products and services to the buyer's perceptions of their needs will be more likely to achieve its goal of profits and will be more likely to produce satisfied customers.

The other point about this diagram is that it is not a process that has a start and a finish. Businesses should be constantly questioning what they do with their expertise and resources in terms of offers on to the market simply because the perceived needs of the customers are dynamic, that is, subject to change, and, in international trade, may be very volatile.

The marketing process

In fact we could take this a stage further. Perhaps the most important question any business should be continually asking itself is:

'What business am I in?'

You may think that this is a pointless question and that every business knows its business. But you could be wrong.

The fact is that many businesses can get so focused on their products and services that they can be very short sighted regarding the actual expertise and resources which they possess. There are a number of case studies illustrating this, one of the more obvious ones being Bic who, when asked by consultants what business they were in, replied, of course, that they were in the 'pen business', more specifically the low price pen business.

The consultants conducted a marketing audit, an in depth investigation of the strengths and weaknesses of the marketing function of a business, and came back with their perception of Bic's business. They said that Bic's expertise and resources were in 'disposable plastic'. Not a very revolutionary statement but one which revolutionised Bic's attitude towards it business. It was not a pen manufacturer but a 'disposable plastic' manufacturer, more specifically extruded plastic containing metal inserts. What came next, the very first disposable razors, to be followed by disposable lighters, disposable toothbrushes, disposable perfume dispensers etc. etc.

Fundamental questions can sometimes produce answers which fundamentally change the nature of a business.

Back to our marketing definitions. While there may be innumerable definitions of marketing it is possible to pick out a couple of elements which are common to all of them, in fact the elements of a concept of marketing:

- Customer Orientation
- Profit
- (or other objective)

That is to say that all of a marketing company's activities are centred around the needs of the consumer and the whole process starts by finding out what the customer wants. This is the opposite of a product orientated

PRODUCTION → SELLING → PROFIT THROUGH SALES VOLUME

Figure 2.1.2 - The selling process

company which attempts to produce what it chooses to produce and then sell it into the market.

Another cliché: 'marketing is about making what we can sell, not selling what we can make.'

All of this is not because we like to please our customers, which of course we do, but primarily based on the fact that a satisfied customer is a more profitable customer.

However, it has to be said that definitions of words can help understanding but the more practical question concerns the **HOW?** of marketing rather than the **WHAT?**.

That is, if a company were to accept the need to be responsive to market demand, to be 'customer orientated', as a means of becoming more successful in competitive markets, then how would it go about doing it? Firstly, the difference between selling and marketing is important.

The following tables illustrate the basic difference in the processes, the major point being that selling starts with production, followed by the need to sell enough to make a profit, whilst marketing starts with market research in order to identify current market needs and profits from a satisfied customer.

The other important distinction is the fact that selling is totally a one way process whilst marketing is based on continuous feedback from the customer and adaptation by the company to changes in consumer demand.

Figure 2.1.4 is perhaps more instructive as an overview of the marketing process and helps us introduce physical distribution as a vital element of that process.

The beginning of this process is research carried out as a continuous activity in the market place, often underpinned by the internal research and development which improves a company's capability to produce. Once research has identified **WHERE** demand exists, and the company is capable of producing goods or services to meet that demand, then decisions need to be made as to **HOW** that demand might be serviced successfully.

The so called '4 Ps' approach is a simplistic, but nevertheless useful, interpretation of the basic decision making areas of the marketing plan.

All important strategic decisions which successful companies make can be categorised into the four elements of:

• PRODUCT
• PLACE (or DISTRIBUTION – the '3 Ps and a D' doesn't really have the same ring to it!).
• PRICE
• PROMOTION

MARKETING → INTEGRATED MARKETING → PROFIT THROUGH
RESEARCH   PLAN   CONSUMER
                                             SATISFACTION

Figure 2.1.3 - The marketing process

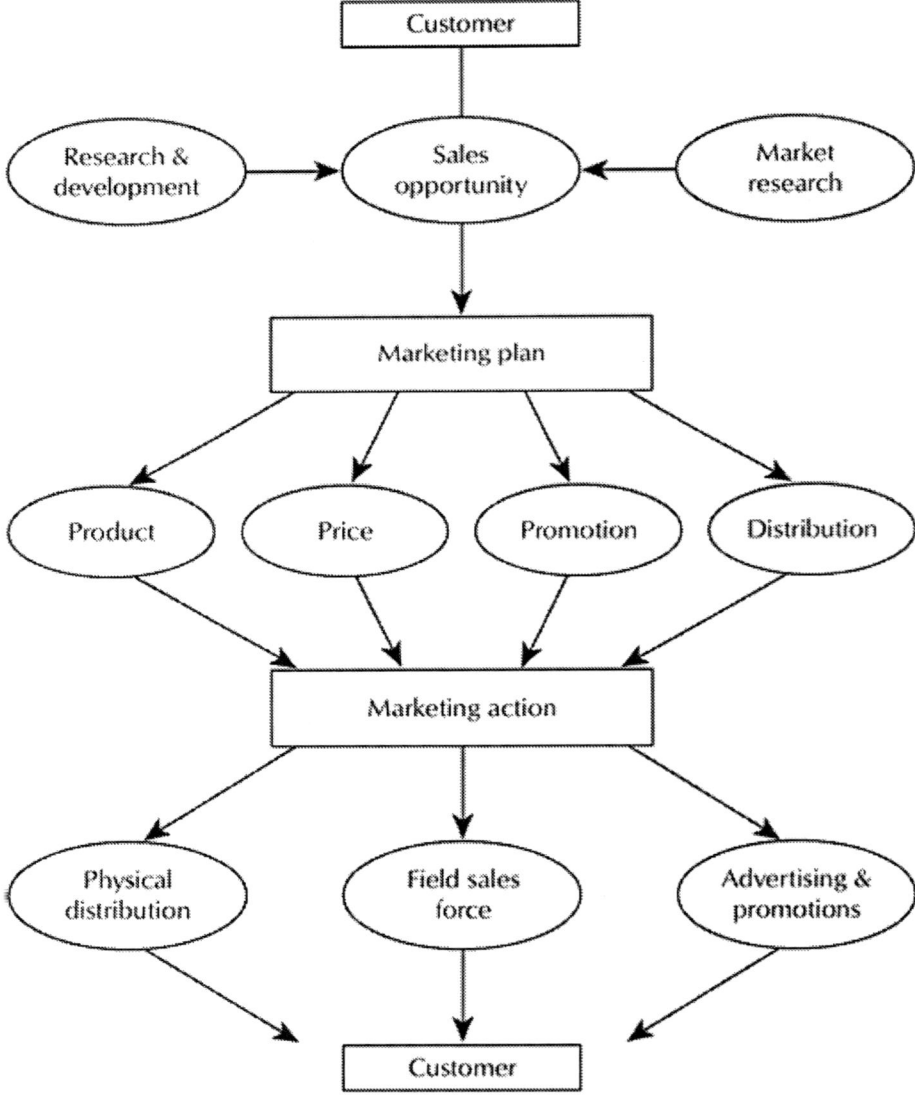

Fig. 2.1.4 - The marketing process

Often referred to as the 'Marketing Mix' - that is a cluster of elements which all have to interact together in a cohesive plan. The right mix is the recipe for success!

There are other structures for the elements of the mix, notably the concept of the '7Ps' which adds to the above:

- PEOPLE - considerations of the personnel involved and their responsibilities and needs
- PROCESS – administrative processes necessary for implementation
- PHYSICAL – actual evidence of implementation, change and outcomes

And a list of twelve elements produced by Professor Neil Borden of the Harvard Business School:

- Product planning
- Pricing
- Branding
- Channels of distribution
- Personal selling
- Advertising
- Promotion
- Packaging
- Display
- Servicing
- Physical handling
- Marketing research

All of which are contained within the more simplistic 4 Ps approach.

No amount of planning is beneficial without real implementation of the plan in practice and Table 2.1.2 illustrates the more obvious and visible activities of a company. Planning is not a process that can be seen but it does result in the high profile activities of selling, promotion and physical distribution which are clearly visible as the practical results of the planning.

Later in this chapter we will look a little more closely at the elements of the plan with specific reference to overseas markets, but first the point should be made that the process is the same whether we consider home or overseas trade. It is not the marketing process which changes from home to export markets, or even from one export market to another, but the application of that process which will differ from one market to another.

The concept of market orientation, by definition, means that companies will attempt to discover the differences exhibited from one market to another and adapt to them in order to maximise profitable business. The differences encountered between the UK home market and overseas markets form a formidable list, and it is an ignorance of these differences which very often explains the failures of UK companies overseas.

The internationalisation process

All trading organisations exist in a market environment which is always dynamic, that is, subject to change, and often volatile. In many cases these market movements are very unpredictable and adapting to them is a difficult task for even the most flexible of companies.

The market environment is made up of a whole range of **UNCONTROLL-ABLES**, and the elements of the marketing plan, the **CONTROLLABLES**, represent the company's attempt to operate with maximum success in the face of the uncontrollable elements of the market.

A comprehensive list of the factors which may differ between the UK and overseas markets, and in fact between one overseas market and another, would occupy a disproportionate section of this book, but a brief list of the most obvious points is provided through a useful acronym – PEST.

Political / Legal -	leading to a wide variety of regulations and legislation. May also effect the stability, or otherwise, of the commercial environment.
Economic -	type of economy - mixed private and public, state planned, etc. level of economic development – primary, secondary, tertiary competition - the number, size and quality will vary.
Socio-economic -	cultural / religious - in many markets these two factors may be one and the same thing. They can lead to many problems in product design, packaging and promotion in particular.
	commercial practices - what is perceived as sharp, or even illegal, practice is not the same in all markets.
	taste - very few products are sold in exactly the same form all over the world.
	language - totally innocent words in one language can be quite offensive in another.
	climate - there are obviously extreme differences from one part of the world to another.
Technological -	what is obsolete in one market may be 'state of the art' in another.
	the ways in which products are used may be not quite as intended.
	levels of maintenance will differ enormously.

Another version of the acronym is PESTLE which lists 'Legal' as a distinct category and adds 'Environment' which address things like green issues, health and safety, levels of re-cycling, etc.

Whilst it could be argued that many of these distinctions could also apply to the regions of a domestic market, like the UK for example, there is little doubt that the extent of the differentials is invariably far greater when operating in overseas markets.

This is by no means a full list but does serve to illustrate the point that the international trader is attempting to operate in a potentially infinite number of differing commercial environments, each market segment requiring individual approaches, which means that what is successful in one market is by no means sure to work in others.

It is the company's ability to make the right decisions in those areas within its control, in order to accommodate the differences in the range of markets with which it deals, which makes the difference between success and failure. One of the first things the exporter has to accept is the need to **DIFFERENTIATE** from one market to another if profitable sales are to be maximised.

It is the decisions made in the areas actually under the control of the exporter which illustrate this differentiation in practice, that is, within the areas identified as the 4 Ps earlier in this chapter. Of course, All of these decisions should be based on a firm foundation of accurate and topical market information.

Market research

Quality research underpins all successful export marketing and, if carried out professionally, will always be cost-effective in that any research costs will be recouped by the benefits derived from the proper identification of market potential, the maximum exploitation of that potential and the avoidance of mistakes.

This, and other basic questions regarding marketing research could be illustrated in diagrammatic format in Fig. 2.1.5.

What is the purpose of Market Research? The simple answer is that it helps decide **WHERE** the company will operate, in terms of a logical market selection strategy, and then **HOW** those markets will be exploited for maximum returns.

Market selection

It is clearly important for exporters to develop a market selection strategy which means they choose the markets rather than the markets choose them. But first we should ask the important question as to whether we should in fact be exporting in the first place. It might seem a little illogical in a text book focused on international trade but there are situations in which many companies would do better if they did not export. One of the reasons for this is that many companies are actually exporting for the wrong reasons.

Bad reasons for exporting include:

- *Disposing of excess production*
  Not only does this devalue the potential of overseas markets but also evidences no permanent commitment to export, in that if and when the home market takes up the excess then the export markets are ignored. It is no surprise that such an attitude does nothing to develop overseas

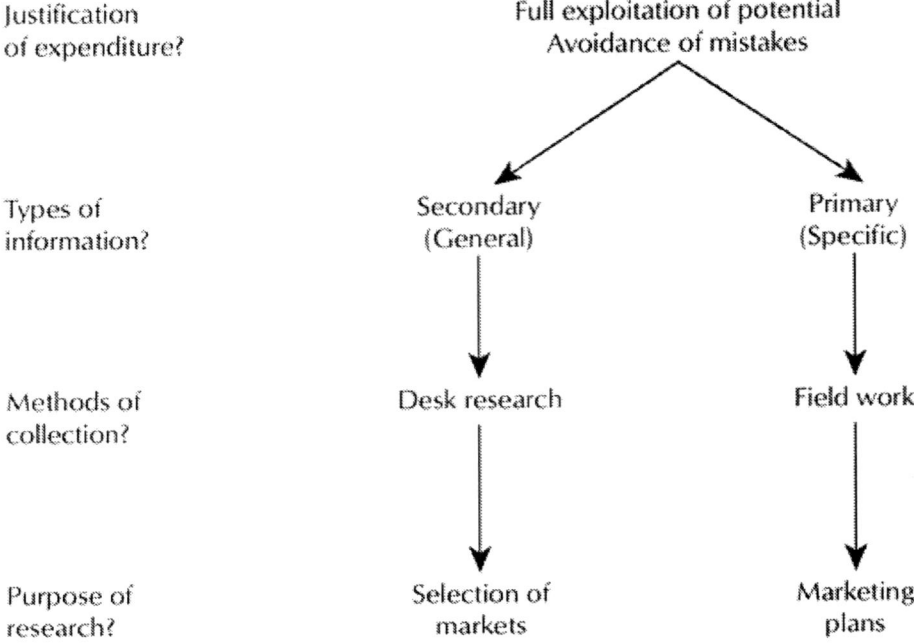

Fig. 2.1.5 - The basics of market research

sales. A company with a permanent excess of production capacity should also be considering the efficiency of their capital investment. A permanent excess points to an underlying structural problem.

• *Marginal cost pricing*

Sometimes linked with the above and based on the, often incorrect, assumption that sales in export markets have to be made at low prices. This process of pricing goods based on a recovery of direct costs only, and making no contribution to indirect costs, is one which can be legitimate as a short term policy in markets quite separate from those paying the full price. In this respect, export markets are prime targets but too many companies simply adopt marginal pricing as a permanent policy, without considering the great potential for profitable sales overseas if they were only to approach the markets more professionally.

• *Prestige*

Some companies operate under the, misguided, opinion that there is somehow great merit in dealing with a very large number of overseas markets. They appear to think that such a global image is evidence of their success. The truth is that in many cases they are trading badly in a large number of markets because the span of control is so wide. Such companies would often do much better if they were to be more selective about the markets with which they deal rather than adding new markets just because they are there.

Good reasons for exporting include:

Good reasons for exporting include:	
Increased profits	either by an increase in volume sales based on the expansion of the size of a company's market network. or, and it is often possible, by obtaining better profit margins in export markets compared with home market levels.
Spread of risk	a selective and controlled market expansion policy will decrease the company's dependence on, for example, its home market. Given the instability of most markets it is clearly preferable for a company to avoid having ' too many eggs in one basket ', as it were.-
Extension of the product life cycle	as is examined later in this chapter, there is often a situation in which the decline of the home market for a product, perhaps because of technical obsolescence, is not reflected in other markets. Because they are at a different stage of their economic development, they can often offer an expanding, as opposed to a declining market.
Even out seasonal fluctuations	products which have a seasonal demand can benefit from the fact that such a cycle is not the same in every part of the world. In simple terms it is always summer somewhere for the deck chair manufacturer.
National interest	it is the interests of the UK economy, and therefore of all UK companies, that we should maximise our export business. OK, not much of a reason, except that there are a variety of government services and incentives available to the exporter, many of which are free, which are specifically designed to encourage them to export.

So the first decision a company should make is the conscious one to enter overseas markets. This should be based on a long term commitment to export and a logical and informed market selection strategy.

Market selection criteria

Market Research is essential if you are to take control and if YOU are to decide where to do business. Good quality Desk Research will often supply sufficient Secondary Information to allow informed management decisions based on the following criteria:

Potential

The most obvious attraction of new markets is the potential they offer for increased business. This can he measured in a number of ways. The most obvious would be pure sales value, but also volume or profit or even market share could be of as much interest, depending on the company's particular requirements. For example a company with a large production capacity would perhaps be more interested in the volume of units sold than the profit margin on each item A company looking for control in a market may value a large market share, even if that means lower profit margins.

It should also be borne in mind that current market size is not necessarily guaranteed to remain unchanged and trends in the market must also be considered.

Accessibility

Not only must new markets offer current, and future, potential; that potential must also be accessible to the exporter . This is of very great importance in international trade where barriers to trade exist which may make certain markets inaccessible to certain suppliers.

From the purely physical distribution point of view, there is hardly a place on earth to which an exporter could not physically deliver goods. The problem is the cost of such physical distribution which is clearly not the same for every supplier in an overseas market.

The UK exporter has to compete with domestic suppliers in overseas markets and with competitors who are geographically closer, whilst facing greater physical distribution costs. It is no surprise that Canada's biggest single foreign supplier is the United States of America or that the Irish Republic's number one supplier is the UK Even if this problem can be overcome, the exporter is still faced with a bewildering array of barriers to trade in the form of regulations which affect goods imported into a country.

Many of these rules and regulations are based on legislation in the country of destination and are often operated by the Customs & Excise authorities of those countries. They can he broken down into two broad categories :-

1. Tariff barriers
    1. Customs Duties
    2. Taxes
    3. Excise
    4. Levies
    5. Licensing
    6. Quotas
2. Non-tariff barriers
    1. Health, Safety and Technical standards (may be part of tariff controls
    2. Cultural eg taste, religion, language etc.
    3. National buying preferences
    4. Collaboration eg cartels

Many of these can simply debar entry into the market, as they are generally designed to do. It should also be noted that suppliers can also find that export controls in their own market impose significant barriers.

Similarity

Finally, given that the above requirements are met, the exporter would wish that any new markets are as similar to current markets as is possible. There is no great merit in expansion into markets which exhibit totally different characteristics to current ones. The less changes that are necessary to the current marketing plan, the easier will be the market development.

The fact that almost 65% of UK exports are to western Europe, and another 15% or so to the USA, does indicate that whether or not exporters actually apply the above criteria consciously, they do operate in practice. It should be noted that it is a little simplistic to describe an overseas market purely in geographic terms. To identify a market simply by political boundaries, as in France or Germany, very rarely represents the actual nature of the market. What the exporter must endeavour to do is define the segment of the market which contains its potential purchasers. This may be in terms of an end user profile describing the typical consumer or an identification of the industrial sector in which it resides, which will give a very clear concept of the segment of the market which will be targeted in the marketing plan.

Managing the mess

The above is particularly and most obviously useful if you are in the position of a company about to start exporting and, of course, deciding to do it right. However, we have to accept that in many cases the damage has already been done. Historic accident has provided us with a range of overseas markets with which we now have to be deal. Perhaps we can learn something from **PARETO'S LAW.**

More commonly known as the 80 / 20 rule, Pareto's Law states that the typical situation for any company is that 80% of its trade will come from 20% of its customers; illustrated on a graph your sales profile is likely to look something like Fig. 2.1.6.

First it should be said that every company should know exactly what their version of the above graph looks like;

that is, there should be a clear and quantitative measure of where the business is coming from.

Secondly your customers can be categorised in accordance with how important they are to the business.

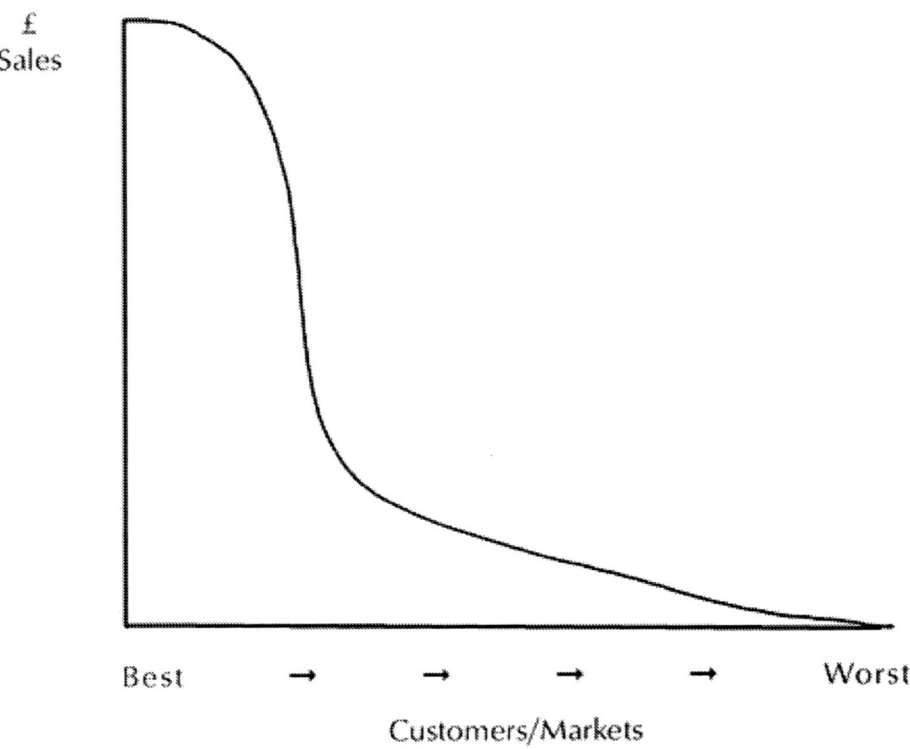

Fig. 2.1.6 - Pareto's Law – the 80/20 rule

Class A	Key markets which take priority over most of the others.
Class B	Two types; some are declining Class A markets in which easy business can be taken without any effort;
	others are potential Class A markets which is where yout focus really should be.
Class C	No priority at all. Trading only at premium prices, or through local distributors, ensuring that a profit can still be taken on small orders. May require realistic minimum order values.

It could be that a form of scoring chart might help to rate potential markets against each other. For example rating a range of criteria from 1 – 10 (10 being the best) would at least start to provide an objective and quantifiable comparison. At the beginning of this process it may be that some boxes have to be left blank and others are just assumptions, but the closer we get to the identification of target markets the more information we should have collected.

But you could customise a version to meet your specific requirements.

2.2

Methods of market research

The two basic reasons for market research, that is market selection and market planning, do actually correlate with the two distinct methods for the collection of information.

Thus the process of market selection can often be achieved through the use of DESK RESEARCH, sometimes referred to as Armchair Research. This involves the company in collecting information without actually venturing into the overseas market.

Such information will invariably be SECONDARY information, in that we are secondary users and it is available to other companies. The sources of such information are very wide ranging in a developed market like the UK

Sources of information

Two main areas:

1. Material available within the company
2. Independent external sources

Within the company

Sales, production, cost, credit andcustomer Information. Sales analysis is particularly important as it indicates:

- market share (% of total consumption/imports)
- rates of consumption
- seasonal variations
- long term trends
- price/volume relationships

This information can be analysed by market, product or customer (or combinations of all three), but must be systematically compiled and continually updated.

However raw data, such as a list of monthly sales figures, needs to be processed into information which actually tells us something. It is also the case that much of the market information we can collect is quantitative. It is this area of marketing where statistical techniques become very useful. But first, there are other secondary sources of information.

External Sources (Secondary)

Business Links comprising DTI/FCO and Chamber of Commerce services integrated as UK Trade & Investment (previously Trade Partners UK) providing international trade advisors to SMEs and a range of web based services including, in their own words:

- *Preparing to Trade – Your local International Trade Adviser can help you to assess your firm's needs and plan for sustainable success in your chosen market. We can also advise you on the linguistic and cultural challenges of operating overseas.*
- *Support to Succeed – Our highly regarded Passport to Export programme combines many of our services in a cost-effective package for new and inexperienced exporters.*
- *Information and opportunities*
  UK Trade & Investment's national and international network can help you gather intelligence on target markets and overseas business opportunities.
- *Opportunities – Sales leads are the lifeblood of any business, which is why our staff overseas are always looking for business opportunities in your chosen markets.*
- *Aid-Funded Business Service – The team liaises on your behalf with all the main international aid-funding agencies.*
- *Market and Sector Research – Our staff in British consulates and embassies around the world can undertake bespoke research into potential markets for your goods and services. You could also conduct research of your own - we show you where to start.*

Making it Happen

- *To be a successful exporter you need to spend time in your markets and build lasting commercial relationships with your clients and partners.*
- *Market Entry – UK Trade & Investment helps groups of UK companies attend major international trade shows and take part in British overseas trade missions.*
- *Marketing Support – We can help to create a buzz about your products in the overseas trade press by producing professionally translated press releases for new and innovative products.*

Specific services worth noting are:

- Sales Leads Database (see 'Business Opportunities' on web site)

- OMIS (Overseas Market Introduction Service) - Basic market information, potential agents and distributors, local contacts, market assessment for products and services etc.
- Export Marketing Research Scheme (50% of cost up to £20,000 operated by British Chambers of Commerce)

Plus other organisations:

- Customs & Excise - Import and export statistics, tariff levels, tariff and non-tariff barriers.
- Trade Associations - Specific product/market information.
- Banks - General economic and financial information.
- Regular market reports.
- Business Information - eg Coface, Dun & Bradstreet, credit organisations, insurance companies etc.
- Market Research - Existing reports or original research
- Consultants
- Bibliographic -Very wide range of published/web & ICT Databases based information.

The general problem for UK exporters is not a lack of secondary information but exactly the opposite. It is necessary to be as specific as possible about the objective of the research in order to pinpoint the relevant data.

Statistics

As mentioned earlier, whatever the source or method of research used, much of the information generated is quantitative hard data and therefore often need to be statistically processed and analysed to provide useful information.
    NB All figures used are fictitious.

Presentation of data

- orderly presentation of the original figures;
- to show some identifiable pattern in the figures;
- to summarise the figures;
- to make public relevant data on which future statistical studies may be based (eg government departments and trade associations).

Diagrammatic presentation of data

Various alternatives may be grouped under this heading. They include:

- pictograms
- statistical maps
- bar charts (simple, component, percentage component and multiple)
- pie charts

Table 2.2.1 - Imports of cars by country of origin and year ($m)

	Japan	Germany	USA
2001	43	77	105
2002	67	82	125
2003	98	80	110
2004	123	85	102
2005	188	88	95

Source: HM Revenue & Customs

Pictograms

This term describes a method of presentation which uses pictures to represent data. There are two basic types:

(a) pictograms where the picture is always the same size, and magnitude is shown by the number of pictures.
(b) pictograms where the *size* of the picture changes to indicate magnitude or value.

The problem with this type of presentation is that the size of the picture may deceive the eye and visual comparison of the figures may become very difficult since the pictures will not show very slight differences in magnitude with any clarity.

Bar charts

In the simplest of these, data is presented by a series of bars, and the magnitude of the particular figure is represented by the height of each bar.

In their method of construction, bar charts are similar to graphs, which will be discussed later. They are preferable to pictograms, largely because of their greater accuracy and because they are easier to construct.

Simple Bar Charts:	May be used where changes only in the totals indicated by the bars are needed.
Component Bar Charts:	Are applicable where it is necessary to indicate not only changes in the totals, but also the size of each part within a specific bar amount
Percentage Component Bar Charts:	Where the most important factor to be indicated is relative size of the component parts.
Multiple Bar Charts:	Where there is a need to express changes in the values of the component figures, and the overall total not important (see Fig. 2.2.1).

Pie charts

These may be defined as circles divided by lines radiating from the centre, much like the spokes of a wheel, or, rather like slices of cake or pie, from which the name derives.

Graphs

In simple terms, a graph may be described as a representation of data by a continuous curve or straight line on squared paper. It is important to note that a line on a graph is always referred to as a *curve*, even though it may be a straight line.

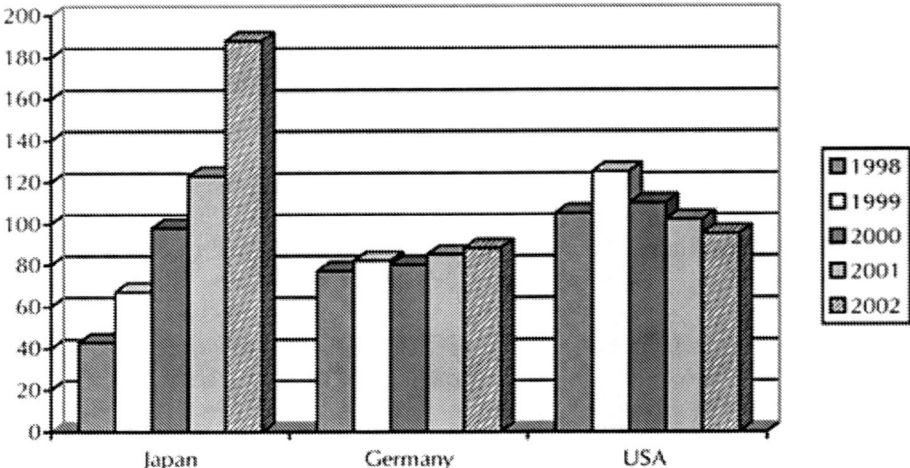

Fig. 2.2.1 -- Multiple Bar Chart

Considerations in constructing graphs:

- construct so as to provide an accurate and useful impression;
- the "independent variable" is that which is unaffected by the other variables (sales volume, consumption, market size, etc) - it is always located on the horizontal axis;
- the starting point for the vertical axis is always zero (0) to avoid giving the wrong impression (even if a "break" is used to cut out unused amounts);
- the axes should be clearly labelled with both the nature of the variable (sales, distance, volume) and the units in which it is expressed (£'s, kilometres, miles, tonnes, etc.);
- curves drawn on the graph must be distinctive since the objective of the graph is to present the data and give an immediate visual impression of pattern, direction or trend in the figures (different colours, etc for different variables);
- it is important to indicate the source clearly.

Frequency distribution, measures of location and dispersion

In some instances, the data collected will be difficult to handle and comprehend in its original form. Consider the example below in Table 2.2.2 and try to draw some conclusions from it.

Most of the figures are in the 300s with one or two 400s to be seen, but can you detect any pattern? In many instances it will be important to identify points of concentration since these may be of special significance.

Car Imports by Country 1998-2000 ($m)

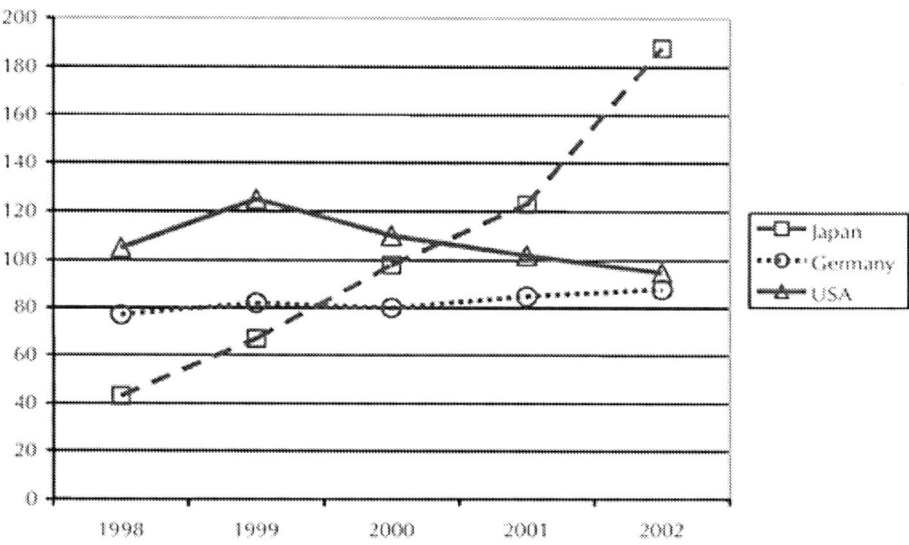

Fig. 2.2.2 - Mathematical graph

It is possible to simplify this table one stage further. Since some of the figures repeat (303), it would be simpler to list each figure once, and in a second column to indicate the number of times it is repeated.

For statistical purposes, the number of times a figure occurs is called the' frequency'
. Table 2.2.4 represents an *ungrouped frequency distribution*, ie a list of figures occurring in the raw data, together with the frequency of each figure.

NB:The sum of the frequencies is expressed (Sf) and must equal the number of items making up the raw data.

Grouped Frequency Distributions

It is possible to improve further still on Table 2.2.4 in terms of clarity and simplicity by condensing the information into a form which indicates more directly the significance of the data concerned. By grouping the figures into classes, we can reduce the number of figures considerably.

The information in Table 2.2.4 might alternatively be presented as the *grouped frequency distribution* shown in Table 2.2.5:

It may be seen that, as an effect of grouping, some pattern can be detected in the figures. In Table 2.2.5 the expenditures cluster around 300 to under 320, and at 340 to under 380. The main drawback with such groupings is that although a pattern may emerge, the result is also a loss of information.

Table 2.2.2 - Raw data

Advertising expenditure by European pet food manufacturers in 2005

(£000s)

307	322	361	345	357
319	311	387	335	372
309	312	382	370	351
348	339	364	373	369
340	367	388	378	412
322	401	351	365	355
323	339	354	306	396
316	392	343	390	317
300	301	319	354	303
353	378	326	341	352
333	349	303	386	357

Arrays: The figures in Table 2.2.2 represent a simple random listing as they were collected, and hence they are denoted 'raw data'. A usual first step would be to re-list the figures in order of magnitude to present them more meaningfully, and such an ordered listing is known as an ' array'.

Table 2.2.3 - An array of the raw data in table 2.2.2

(£000s)			
300	341	355	378
301	343	357	378
303	345	357	382
303	348	361	386
306	349	364	387
307	351	365	388
309	351	367	390
311	353	370	396
316	354	372	401
317	354	373	412

Table 2.2.4 – Ungrouped frequency distribution constructed from the array in table 2.2.5

£s	Frequency	£s	Frequency	£s	Frequency	£s	Frequency	£s	Frequency
300	1	319	2	341	1	355	1	378	2
301	1	322	2	343	1	357	2	382	1
303	2	323	1	345	1	361	1	386	1
306	1	326	1	348	1	364	1	387	1
307	1	333	1	349	1	365	1	388	1
309	1	335	1	351	2	367	1	390	1
311	1	339	2	352	1	369	1	392	1
312	1	340	1	353	1	370	1	396	1
316	1	-	-	354	2	372	1	401	1
317	1	-	-	-	-	373	1	412	1

Total Frequency (Sf) = 55

Table 2.2.5 - Grouped frequency distribution

£s Expenditure		Frequency (f)
300	- under 320	13
320	- under 340	8
340	- under 360	15
360	- under 380	10
380	- under 400	7
400	- under 420	2

Total Frequency (Sf) = 55

Means, medians and modes

In the field of statistics, we can identify three main types of *averages*, these are the

- arithmetic mean (usually referred to for simplicity as the 'mean')
- median
- mode

Mean	The typical average- the numbers are added up and divided by the number of items added.
Median	The median can be defined as the middle value of a distribution ie the middle item when the data is arranged from bottom to top ie an array.
Mode	The mode is defined as the most frequently-occurring value in the distribution. As the value which occurs most frequently it is the most representative of the typical item.

Choosing between mean, median and mode

In choosing an average, we might consider the following:

The Mean is most suitable if we wish to know what the consequence of an equal distribution would be. For example, per capita income (the total income of a nation, divided by the total population).

The Mean, however, makes use of every value in the distribution and can, therefore, be distorted by extreme values

The Median will be chosen if we wish to know the half-way value, with as many above as below (the average age of the population, for instance).

The Mode is the appropriate average to use where we want to find out the most typical value of a series.

2.3

The marketing plan

The Marketing Plan is sometimes referred to as the Marketing Mix because it represents a mixture of decisions made in specific areas but which must blend together. 'The correct mix is the recipe for success' (sorry!). The exporter has to make decisions designed to exploit, to the full, the potential identified in overseas markets. As we have seen it is possible to rationalise these areas into the four broad categories of Product, Price, Promotion and Place.

Product

All exporters must accept the fact that most successful products are modified for sale in overseas markets. Very few products are sold in exactly the same form in all markets and the reason for, and nature of, modifications will differ from one market to another Illustrative of this point is the fact that most products which are thought to be the same throughout the world are, in many cases, not the same at all eg Coca Cola.

The reasons for such product modifications are numerous but include:

- Official regulations/trading standards/power supplies
  Enormous differences exist in health, safety and technical standards, voltages, calibrations, fittings, controls, instructions etc. etc. A manufacturer of electric coffee percolators found that they could not export them to Canada, unless they contained a form of electric wire made nowhere but in Canada! With no mains electricity how can we sell washing machines to African villagers or Indian peasants? The answer is to DE-INVENT, by producing special hand-driven machines. (Incidentally OMO washing powder is the number one brand in West Africa).
- Size, weight and volume
  French women tend to have bigger feet than English women, whilst Japanese women have smaller feet. Many Finns sleep in smaller bedrooms than are usual here. The larger retail packages found in the USA are increasingly common in other developed countries.
- Colour
  In some parts of the Far East, dentists often buy brown black teeth for their patients' dentures because chewing betel nuts stains the teeth. Australians live in a country where eucalyptus trees dominate their

rivals. Their colour key for green is in consequence the eucalyptus leaf. Unlike a UK national for whom grass green is standard. Emerald green the colour of the Muslim religion, is a favourite colour in Pakistan, where also saffron yellow, the colour of the robes of the Buddhist monks, is particularly disliked. White is associated with death in Malaysia. Purple with voodoo in parts of Africa (and even parts of the USA).

- Aesthetic features
  Round or oval tables do not sell well in the Czech republic, where nearly everyone prefers rectangular tables. Canadians, New Zealanders and Australians, like the British, prefer to buy bedroom, dining room and lounge suites, and are keen on matching kitchen cabinets. Elsewhere, for example in Holland, people enjoy bringing together a pleasant collection of odd pieces.

- Physical taste
  Coca Cola recipes vary from country to country, and across the world, Nescafe has been offered in forty different flavours. Equally the British have their own distinctive taste in beer.

- Raw materials
  In India, Hindus refused to buy British bone china as soon as they found that the ground bones mixed with the clay were those of their sacred animal, the cow. Pork products and derivatives find similar problems in Muslim countries.

- Method of use
  In Holland, a bicycle is ridden by many to get them to and from work and to make trips to the shops and friends' homes. The Dutch, therefore, want a strong, reliable machine which can stand up to long years of constant use. In America it is mostly bought as a teenager's toy, or a piece of leisure or keep fit equipment. Depilatory creams are used by men in West Africa as an alternative to shaving.

- Climate
  In hot countries, cars need air-conditioning systems. In monsoon conditions, they require exceptionally effective and reliable windscreen wipers. Where winters are rugged, the starters must function in icy conditions and heaters must be powerful.

The above are just a small number of examples of product modifications, and reasons for them, from the many that exist in international trade. There are some products which are sold without modification throughout the world, for example Scotch whisky, and some -but only some - French perfumes, but even then certain brands will be more or less popular from one market to another. Also some products, usually high technology, which are used in the same way in all parts of the world, may not be modified, but even then other aspects of the marketing plan will almost certainly differ.

To be technically correct we should in fact refer to Product/Market strategies, as each product package should relate to a specific market segment. This process is known as *Product Positioning* and links in with the segmentation process mentioned as part of market selection.

Exporters must also realise that buyers are often not buying just the physical entity of the product, but a whole package of things which go with it. This is known as the *Total Product Concept* and includes elements such as reliability, reputation, image and prestige as well as the more tangible parts of a package deal such as the packaging itself, credit terms, guarantees and warranties and pre- and after-sales service.

The role of marketing research

The value of market research is not only in ensuring that the product is suited to market requirements, but also that costly mistakes are avoided - like the UK company that produced a range of ladies' fashion garments for Scandinavian countries. Naturally they produced a winter range because it is often cold in that part of Europe. Unfortunately, they realised too late that the UK concept of a winter and summer range of clothes was of no relevance to Scandinavian countries, where the distinction between 'indoor' and 'outdoor' is far more important. The market is actually for lightweight, indoor, clothes; functionality is more important than fashion for outdoor wear.

The list of expensive mistakes is almost endless. A bone china dinner service specially designed for Italian taste, did not sell at all due to the absence of a pickle bowl. White false teeth produced for the Far East did not match the betel nut stained teeth of the potential recipients, who objected to a mouth which resembled a piano keyboard.

Packaging may be more important than the product as the company selling powdered milk into West Africa discovered. Their traditional metal container was replaced by a more cost-effective container but the customers found it difficult to carry water, and even more difficult to cook, with a cardboard box. The company totally misunderstood the usage of their product. As did the exporter of depilatory creams who discovered, too late, that the majority of their west African market was male, and not female, who used the cream as an alternative to shaving.

Even when the product is right for the market, the name it is given can render it unsaleable. Some years ago the Chevrolet Nova caused quite a stir in Latin American markets; 'no va' is Spanish for 'won't go', and Toyota's competitor to the Mini would not have sold so well if they had persisted with the name 'Toyolet'. It may therefore be necessary to sell the same product with a range of different names.

Basic market research could, and in some cases did, avoid the long term cost of such mistakes.

Finally, exporters have to accept that even if current demand is being satisfied it is unlikely that the situation will never change. All products go through a Life Cycle which begins with an Introduction to the market,

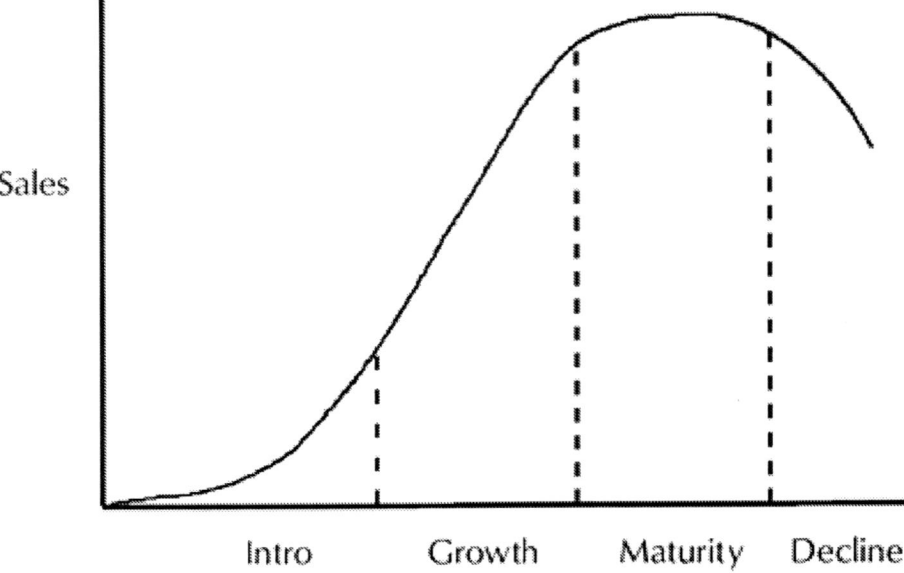

Fig. 2.3.1 – The product/sales cycle

followed by a period of Growth and then a Maturity when the best returns are made, but this is eventually and inevitably followed by Decline.

All products eventually decline; the problem is to determine the time scale (see Fig. 2.3.1).

The profile will differ from product to product and, clearly, the time scale is the most difficult element to predict although generally we would expect:

SLOW	Chemicals, Extractive Industries etc.:
FAST	Clothing, Electrical Goods etc.:

In fact fashion or fad products might have a very short life as in Fig. 2.3.2.

The application of the theory is essential to long term product replacement and development strategies as the development of replacement products must begin, at the latest, during the mature phase of current products.

However it may be that we are not actually replacing a product but looking to extend its life through either modification (Fig. 2.3.3) or a range of marketing activities (Fig. 2.3.4).

Activities designed to extend product life cycles can include:

• Promotion eg advertising campaign, exhibition, special offers etc.
• Re-packaging
• Re-naming/branding and of course
• Expansion into new markets ie exporting

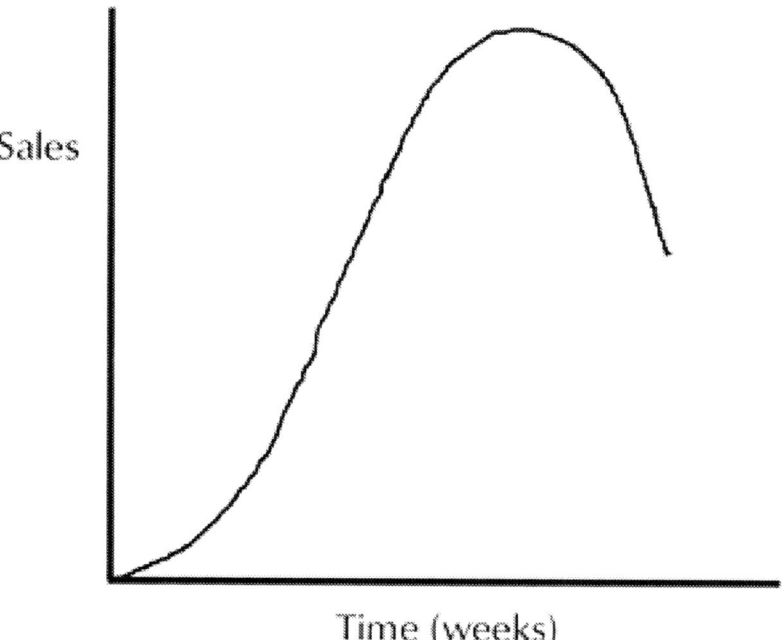

Fig. 2.3.2 - Fashion/fad product life

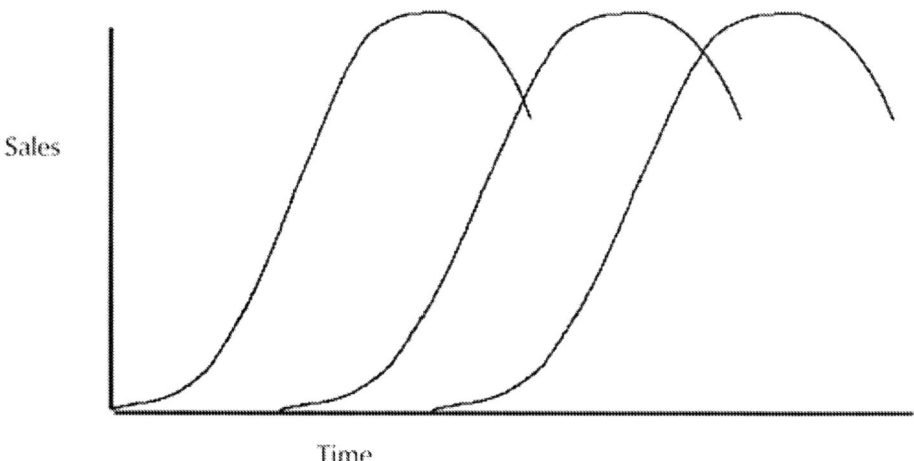

Fig. 2.3.3 - Extended product life through modification

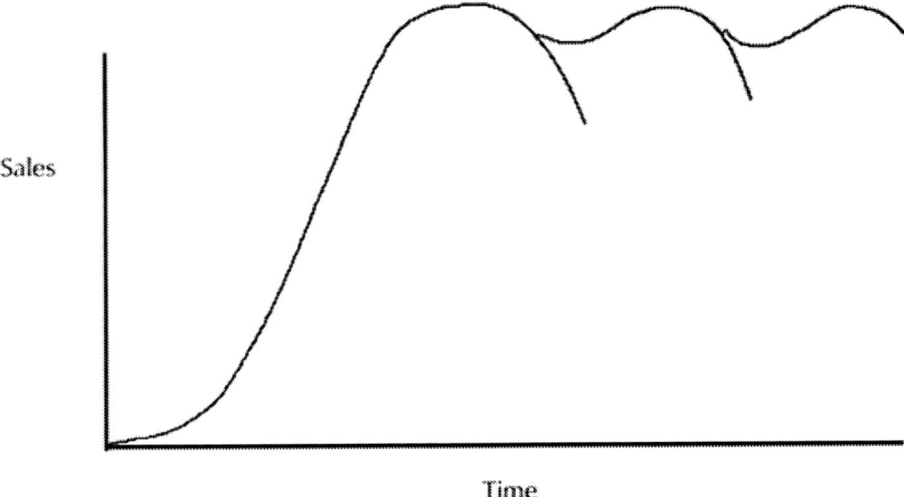

Fig. 2.3.4 - Extended product life through marketing activities

The Boston Matrix

An old concept but one which still has its uses in generating an objective view of, what is sometimes, a messy portfolio of products. Most companies will deal in a number of different products , some with hundreds, and a method of taking an objective view of it is based on the concept that there are only four categories of product, illustrated in Fig. 2.3.5.

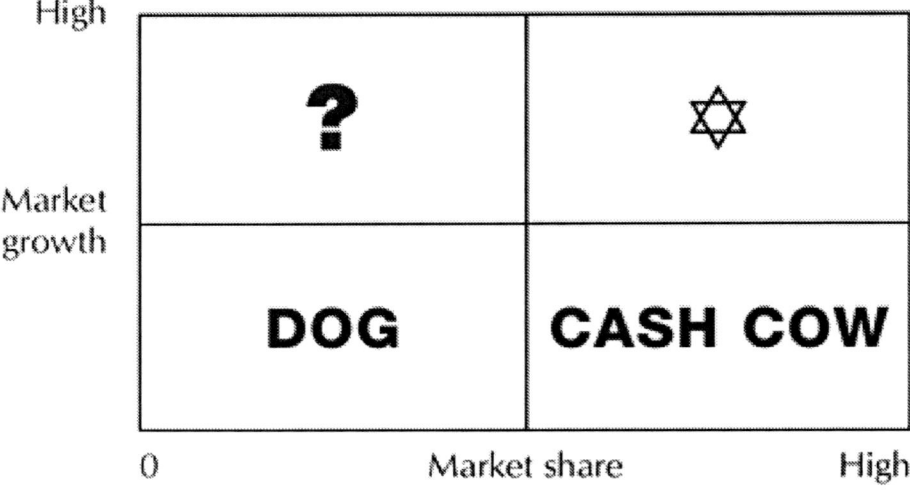

Fig. 2.3.5 - The Boston Matrix

		Stage in the life cycle
?	High growth, low market share	Introduction
Star	High growth, high market share	Growth
CASH COW	Low growth, high market share	Maturity
DOG	Low growth, low market share	Decline

Good management is about maintaining a spread of products at different stages of their life cycles and avoiding the situation in which the portfolio is full of dogs or, almost as bad, full of question marks.

Price

Price, as an element of the marketing mix, may be designed to do more than just maximise profits. It may attempt to create a market share, generate early cash recovery, establish compatibility across a range of products (price lining), or generate a specific rate of return.

Basically the exporter has two choices in arriving at a selling price. The most common, because it is the easiest, is the least effective and that is Cost Plus pricing. The direct, and hopefully indirect, costs are calculated and a percentage profit margin is added. This produces the minimum price the company is prepared to accept, the same price for every customer and every market. The final Delivered price may differ, because the physical distribution costs are different, but the bottom line Ex Works price remains the same.

All companies should have a very clear idea of their minimum price levels but this strategy ignores the possibilities for more profitable sales should the buyer be prepared to pay more.

Sensible companies need to know the price the market will bear to complete the picture. Such information gathered from market research and, it has to be said, trial and error, will lead to an understanding of the maximum price the company can achieve. It will also naturally lead to a system of differentiated pricing in that the price obtainable from one market, and even one customer, will differ from place to place.

Between the two extremes it may be that companies can find compromises based on a variable add-on to a basic cost or in situations where it is simply a case of matching the main competitor's price in the market, as in Fig. 2.3.6.

The truth is often even more complex, as most products exhibit some sort of price-elasticity. There is rarely a price the market will bear, but different prices will generate different sales volume. The typical situation is that the lowest price will generate the highest volume sales, and vice-versa. What

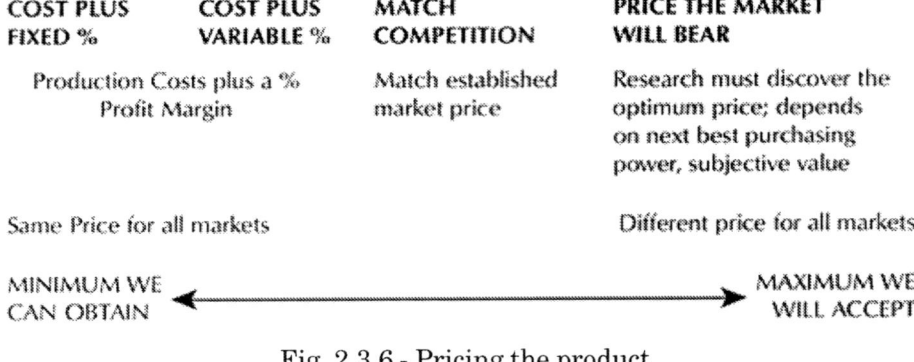

COST PLUS FIXED %	COST PLUS VARIABLE %	MATCH COMPETITION	PRICE THE MARKET WILL BEAR
Production Costs plus a % Profit Margin		Match established market price	Research must discover the optimum price; depends on next best purchasing power, subjective value
Same Price for all markets			Different price for all markets
MINIMUM WE CAN OBTAIN			MAXIMUM WE WILL ACCEPT

Fig. 2.3.6 - Pricing the product

exporters need to establish are the price-volume relationships which exist for their products in overseas markets (see Fig. 2.3.7).

In practice the extremes of this curve are very unreliable and the exporter will attempt to define the range P1 to P2 and its relationship with V1 and V2 as being more predictable, as illustrated in Fig. 2.3.8.

Many companies, knowing the minimum and maximum price parameters in their markets, are able to use price as a marketing tool. They may choose *Skim* pricing strategies to take high profit, low volume, sales, or use

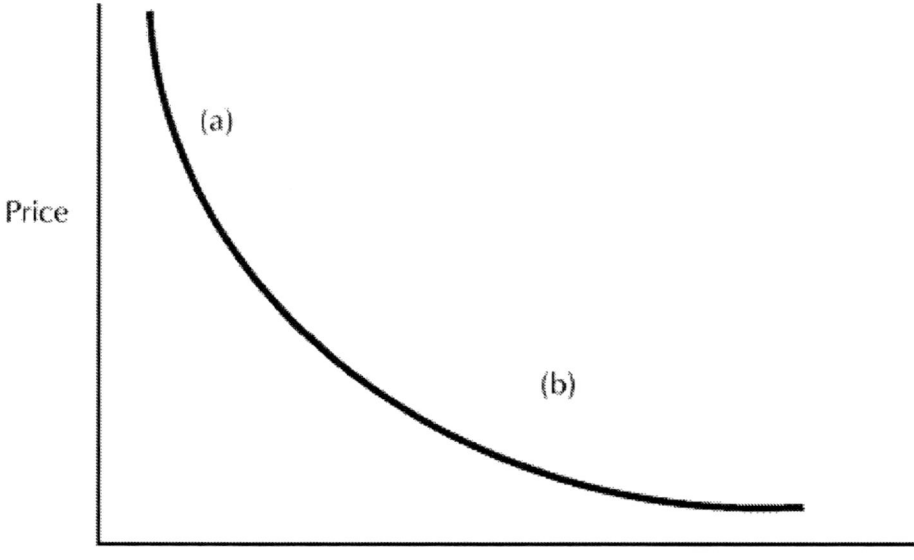

Fig. 2.3.7 - Export price-volume relationship
a) The highest price will generate the lowest volume sales
b) The lowest price generates the highest volume sales

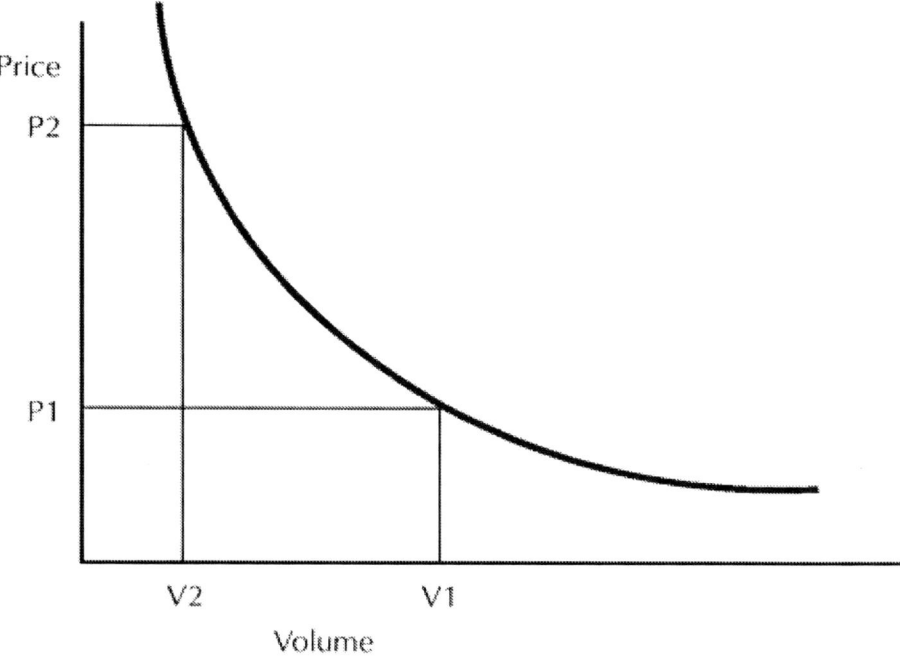

Fig. 2.3.8 - The reliable range of the price-volume curve

Penetration pricing to take high volume , low profit, sales. Or a range of options in between.

In extreme cases a company may even accept loss-making sales in the interest of long-term gains. All of these strategies will be supported by the other elements of the marketing plan.

To operate successfully the exporter must have a very clear understanding of all business costs, the margins necessary to achieve profit targets and the price / volume relationships available in each of their markets.

Differential pricing

A range of different prices for different markets can lead to a number of practical problems in addition to the obvious one of a customer finding out that other buyers are obtaining the same products at lower prices. Specifically these are:

Parallel exports

A situation in which an exporter finds that exported products, sold at prices lower than, for example, their home sales price, actually find their way back into the home market and undercut their own home sales. This is a major problem with consumer products in general and branded products in particular but can affect any goods. The only way to control such movement of goods is to tie up the overseas buyer in contractual obligations which preclude re-exports or sales outside their own country. Appointing them as sole distributors may well be the only way to agree such a restriction. There is also, of course, the final censure: refuse to supply goods.

Anti-dumping legislation

A consequence of the situation described above may also be the accusation that the exporter is dumping products. The definition of dumping is quite specific: it is not to do with excess production or selling below cost but, specifically, if the export price is lower than the home price of a product (the Current Domestic Value) then the exporter is dumping. This means that most exporters are dumping somewhere and some are dumping everywhere. In practice, whilst legislation exists, many countries do not use it extensively or even at all. The exceptions to this are the developed economies such as the EU and the USA. Where an exporter is building a significant market share then an accusation of dumping can certainly slow down growth and may, if the accusation is sustained, lead to an anti-dumping duty which can price the product out of the market.

Promotion

All goods need promotion in order to sell. The type and extent depends on the products themselves, sales outlets, distribution channels and the end user. We must remember that UK sales are to broadly similar users. Overseas markets present a far greater range of situations and require a clear policy of DIFFERENTIATION in all aspects of the Marketing Mix.

Most exporters are able to manage some aspects of promotional mix, such as personal selling or exhibitions, but for more specialised activities it is important to bring in specialist help. The complexity of the promotional mix can be simplified by identifying the four categories of promotional activity.

- Advertising
- Publicity
- Personal selling
- Sales promotions which can be defined as:
  - Advertising -"Any paid form of non-personal presentation and promotion of ideas, goods, or services by an identified sponsor" (media options - press, TV, radio, cinema, outdoor).
  - Publicity - "Non- personal and unpaid publication or broadcast."
  - Personal selling - "Oral presentation in conversation with one or more prospective purchasers for the purpose of making sales. "
  - Sales promotion - "Those marketing activities, other than advertising,

publicity and personal calling, that stimulate consumer purchasing and dealer effectiveness."

Objectives

It is important that some thought is given to the purpose of any promotional activities other than the obvious one of selling more goods or services. These objectives could include the need

- to create awareness and knowledge of our goods.
- to establish a company image or brand name.
- to stimulate an interest and then a preference for our product.

Promotion Budget

Since promotion involves expenditure, it is important to determine how much is to be spent. This can be done in two basic ways

The most common method is to allow a percentage in the selling price to cover promotional costs.

£ per unit: eg		
Cost of raw materials	16	
Direct costs	8	
Indirect costs/overheads	18	
Profit	12	
Selling price	54	
Promotion @ 10% of selling price	6	(ie 11.11.% mark up)
Final selling price	60	

The advantages are that money spent does not affect profits, and the more units sold, the more money is available for promotion.

The disadvantage is that substantial sales have to be made before money is available ideally promotion should generate sales, not vice-versa. This problem can be overcome by investing income at an early stage - based on sales forecasts rather than actual sales. This approach is sometimes referred to as an investment budget approach.

Also, there is an automatic increase in the promotional spend as sales increase when in fact it might be more logical for the spend to reduce as the product becomes established in a market.

	£ per unit
Sales forecast	200,000
Promotion budget @ 5%	10,000
Agent's contribution	5,000
Promotion budget	£ 15,000

It should be noted that it would not be unusual for the local agent or distributor, if applicable, to make some contribution to promotional activities which will support their work in the territory. There is no harm in asking and ideally the company's agency agreement includes a clause formalising such an arrangement.

The alternative 'task method'

The company decides the specific objective ie a percentage increase in sales and then attempts to calculate how much would need to be spent to achieve that objective. This is obviously more difficult to do, at least with any degree of accuracy, but does mean that there is a clear relationship established between the cost of promotion and the specific benefits. It may be that some experience needs to be established in particularly markets before such a process achieves any degree of accuracy.

Only as a very general rule, the percentages spent on promotion would vary:

Industrial / capital goods	$\frac{1}{2}$%	3%
Consumer goods	5%	50%

In the latter case it may be that a large part of the promotion budget is expended on the product packaging which should logically be perceived as part of the promotional costs.

Advertising

Press

Can be categorised into specific types:

• Newspapers (local and national)
• Magazines (general and specialised)
• Trade publications

As in the UK, we often find regional divisions in the circulation of newspapers and a political bias is common but in overseas markets other factors can also distinguish one publication from another. Language, religion and race can often be more important and local specialist advice is essential before choices are made regarding the location of advertisements. Similarly, magazines will often have a specific circulation. All publications should be able to supply quantitative information regarding their size and type of readership.

Trade publications are incredibly numerous, covering what might seem to be some very esoteric specialisms. The advantage is obviously that it is possible to hit the right type of buyer for your goods and it is possible to include technical details.

It is important to select the most appropriate outlet in line with cost, the object being to hit the maximum number of potential buyers at the minimum cost. In order to do this we must have a very clear idea of our end-user in order to properly target all marketing activities, particularly promotion.

Television

Clearly, television represents a massive advance in mass communication media which is now being enhanced by the spread of electricity and increases in world-wide standards of living. It is, of course, expensive, but gives immediate impact and large coverage. However,

it is difficult to be exact about the target market, although figures on audience composition are often available programme by programme. Therefore, this medium tends to favour mass market consumer goods rather than those with a more specialist market. Remember that commercial television is not always allowed overseas and the cost of the advertising slot may be much less than the cost of production.

Apart from the actual content of the ad, which requires professional advice and must consider the cultural mores of the market, we must also consider:

- running time
- regional versus national
- timing
- colour or black and white
- language
- accents

Radio

Television sells - Radio reminds. There is invariably a greater choice of outlets within radio, and coverage of commercial stations has increased enormously over the last 20 years. The medium can be very useful in developing countries particularly where there are high levels of illiteracy and areas of the population are isolated. The same rules as TV apply but particular care should be taken with the voices used and especially the accents.

Remember that whilst commercial television and radio in the UK is based on the hire of a time slot, with advertisers having little influence on programme content, there are many other countries which follow the American model in which the advertisers actually sponsor the whole programme and thus have a far more direct control on content.

Cinema

TV did tend to reduce cinema attendance figures in developed countries but this trend is now reversing. However, in many developing markets, cinema can still be the main form of entertainment or, at least, still attract large audiences: eg Africa . There is still a provision by mobile cinemas of open air shows, which can attract audiences of several thousands, and which incorporate short film lets or slides. An advantage is that the shows can be localised rather than national.

Outdoor

Planning authorities may limit sites but they are usually associated with heavy concentrations of people: eg rail / bus stations. Be aware that hot climates may affect the life of billboard advertisements and it is not uncommon for a hand painted hoarding to be used rather than paper posters. Their main purpose is to act as reminders and they do allow visual images to be used which can be very effective. The organisation of such advertisements will often be controlled by a local agent, in which case it is important to confirm that the posters do actually exist . Photographs can help but independent confirmation is preferable.

What all advertising is attempting to do is to generate **A I D A**
Attention
Interest
Desire
Action

Advertising is distinctive because it is:

- *PUBLIC*, which imparts legitimacy on the product
- *PERVASIVE*, repetitive and widespread
- *EXPRESSIVE*, allows dramatisation
- *IMPERSONAL*, monologue not dialogue

Publicity

Some companies use professional Public Relations consultants or have a staff resource to prepare news stories and features. Without consultants' advice it is still possible to disseminate information overseas through the Central Office of Information and the BBC External Services. It is often necessary to create a newsworthy theme to generate wide spread use. Press releases should be written not from the point of view of the company but from the point of view of the media which we hope will reproduce them. The less editing needed the more likely they are to be used.

Newsworthy items are distinctive because they:

- Have high veracity – accepted as (more) authentic than if sponsored by the seller.
- Are off guard – hits those who otherwise avoid ads and salesmen.
- Have dramatisation – like advertising.

Always be careful with translations. Many mistakes originate from simple errors in the translation of advertising copy from one language to another. The Parker leak-proof fountain pen which prevented the embarrassment of ink stained shirts found a totally new market when embarrassment was translated, in Spanish, as 'emberazer' which actually means 'pregnancy'. Parker had apparently produced a new form of contraceptive!

Almost apocryphal is the case of the company who manufactured depilatory creams. They planned an expensive magazine promotion in the Middle East which involved the use of an advertisement which had been successful in a number of other areas. This involved two colour photographs depicting a pair of shapely legs before and after the application of the cream. The process was fluently described in the advertising copy below the illustrations.

This company was not caught by a problem with the Arabic translation because they had learnt that the only safe way to translate from one language to another is to have one translator handle the English to Arabic, and another then translate the Arabic back into English. In this way, any problems in interpretation are usually revealed. The problem in this case was not the quality of the Arabic but that they had not considered the fact that Arabic reads from right to left, and they had not reversed the photographs. They seemed to be promoting something that made hair grow.

As a final example, even the largest of companies can get caught in the language trap. Coca-Cola's famous global message that 'Coke gives life' was variously translated as ' Coke raises the dead' and ' Coke brings your ancestors back from the grave'.

Personal selling

Successful face to face selling in overseas markets requires a clear perception of the needs of the customer and an adaptation to the wide ranging political, legal, economic, technical and cultural factors which will differ from one market to another,

Face to face selling is distinctive because it involves :

- *Personal confrontation* - immediate, interactive, flexible;
- *Cultivation* - relationships may develop;
- *Response* - buyer may feel under some obligation – greater need to attend and respond.

The sales interview

The bad salesperson sells product	**FEATURES**
The better salesperson sells	**BENEFITS**
The best salesperson satisfies	**NEEDS**

Preparation for a sales interview

Be clear about your objectives eg information gathering, information giving, action generating.

Once you have determined your objectives, you must ascertain the background information that you will require before the meeting can take place. It will include the following:

- The prospect company
  - Possible requirements
  - History of relationships between them and your company
  - Existing company and competitive product usage
- The person
  - Their function and responsibilities
  - Their likely concerns and attitudes
- Your company
  - What are you able to commit to
  - Do you have sufficient product knowledge
  - Do you have sufficient authority

Structure of a sales interview

Be clear in your own mind how you would like the meeting to go.
  What topics do you want to discuss, and in what order?
  When you are selling, remember the old communications maxim:

- *Tell them what you are going to tell them;*
- *Tell them;*
- *Tell them what you have told them.*

(NB: A good maxim for any type of presentation)

Sample structure of a sales interview... first visit

- Opening
  - Social - breaks the ice
  - Business - why you are there, present agenda
  - Check how much time is available
- Create Interest
  - Give them a reason to talk to you
  - Give a quick overview of your role
- Explore Needs
  - Get them talking
  - Qualify their requirement and your capability
  - Put them into their "comfort zone"
- Present your products
  - Total offering
  - Relate to their requirements
  - *BENEFITS* of using your company's products – not its *features*
- Summary
  - Summarise what has been discussed and agreed
  - Highlight major reasons for using your company
  - Confirm next action

As you depart, find a closing, phrase that indicates how much you are looking forward to working with them.

The selling concept

Wrong	The high pressure approach (as in Fig. 2.3.9)
Right	The natural sales approach (as in Fig. 2.3.10)

Sample structure... further visits

For subsequent meetings the structure will vary depending on your objectives. As a guide, you should still follow the above rules for the Opening and Summary sections of the meeting and then remember the following sequence:
   Past
   Present
   Future
This will ensure that any suggestions for the future are clearly related to current and previous ways of working.

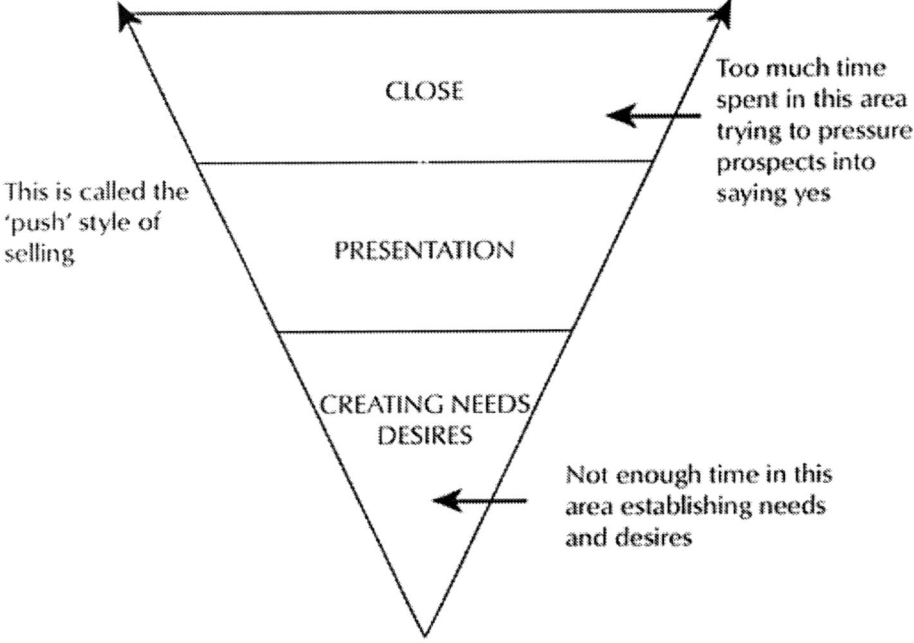

Fig. 2.3.9 - The high pressure approach

During the meeting

Spend more time questioning and listening than you do talking about yourself and your products.

Take notes. It helps you to remember what was said and demonstrates interest in what your prospect is saying.

Use brochures to illustrate the points that you are making and, where appropriate, write comments on the brochure to "personalise it" to your prospect. However, remember to leave a spare copy for your prospect to pass to other people.

Take every opportunity to create or use visual aids.

Follow up

Always document *your* understanding of what has been agreed.

Every meeting should be followed-up in writing.

The objective is to demonstrate your understanding of their present needs, act as a reminder of the agreed actions, assist in shutting out other suppliers and provide your prospect with as much justification as is necessary to assist them in presenting a persuasive argument within their own organisation.

If the sale involves a series of meetings the combined letters will form the basis of the persuasive argument within your offer document.

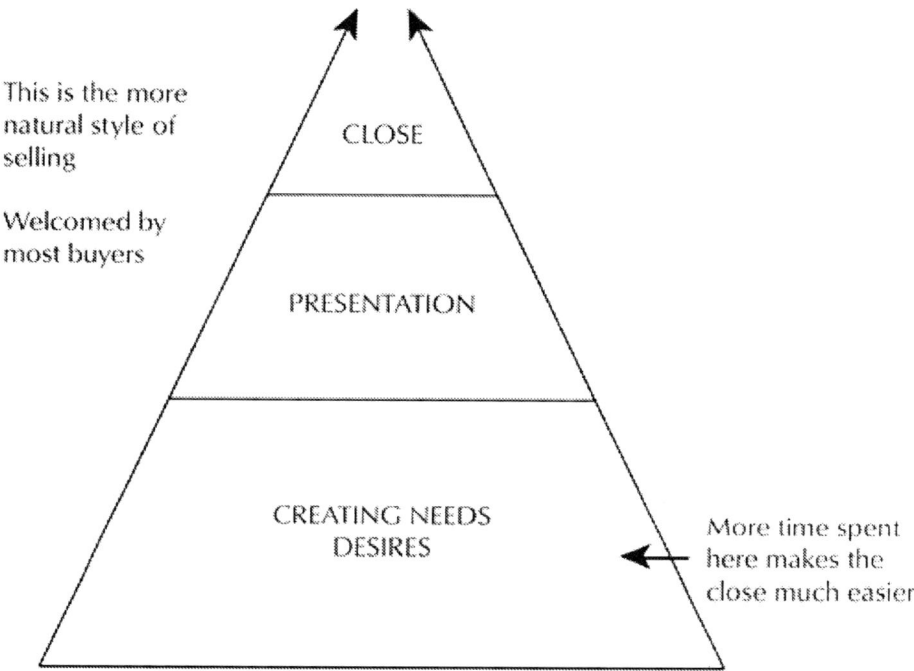

Fig. 2.3.10 - The natural sales approach

Handling objections

Question		to clarify understanding and regain control
Answer	if true	agree
		put into perspective
		outweigh with other benefits
		compensate with alternatives
	if untrue	you must protect your prospect's ego
		explain the true picture
		accept that you may have to offer proof
		apologise for the misunderstanding
	if speculative ...	agree possibility
		diminish probability
Check		to confirm that they are happy with your answer.

Closing the sale

The request for the order should follow naturally - if you do not ask you do not get!

Examples of closing questions:

- *Will you go ahead now ?*
- *Is there a reason for you not going ahead ?*
- *Would you like the agreement to start at the end of the month ?*
- *Suppose we were able to .... would you go ahead then ?*
- *Is it that you don't want ....?*
- *You have agreed that you like ....should we start at the end of the month?*

Nobody ever lost an order because they asked for it . Many people have lost orders because they did not ask for them !
Nobody will buy from you when they :

- do not understand WHAT they are buying; or
- do not understand WHY they are buying it; or
- do not WANT the benefits; or
- do not TRUST you to deliver the benefits.

Literature

It is important not to cut costs in this area as the whole company may often be judged purely on the appearance of its literature. In overseas markets literature is often the first contact and may need to contain a range of relevant information.
Consider:

- Make-up - loose leafed (to allow the replacement of pages), colour or black and white, paper quality, illustrations (often greatest cost) etc.
- Inclusions - type and number of illustrations, company information, technical information, price lists, samples etc.
- Languages - which ones , all in one or separate brochures (other languages may require more copy space).

As they can often be very expensive it is necessary to avoid wastage as much as possible. Ways to do this include making up selective brochures for individual enquirers, maximising accuracy and topicality of the mailing lists used, mail shots with leaflets not full catalogues, ensuring that an agent uses them selectively. and even attempting to have them returned for reuse.
Where direct mail shots are to be used, consider:

- Number of shots - it is often necessary to repeat with modified materials.
- Accuracy of mailing lists - these can be derived from your own research. (see sources of information earlier) or purchased from specialist organisations.
- recording systems - log all responses, follow up all replies with relevant copy.

- catching attention - without an immediate impact the material goes straight into the bin.
- generate an interest - use appropriate language and approach.

We must accept that the maximum direct response we are likely to receive may be as low as 10%.

Choosing advertising media

It is best to concentrate, as it is seldom possible to use all the media.
We must:

- Decide exactly the target audience and concentrate on the media which reaches the greatest number at lowest cost.
- Use the media constantly or not at all; repetition is essential.
- Make sure ads. appear at the proper time.
- Develop close working relationship between the campaign and sales staff:eg compel the distributor to build up stocks before the campaign begins; co-operation between promotion and sales production and despatch is essential.

Sales promotion

Includes a wide variety of activities, other than advertising, publicity and personal selling which have a particular application in overseas markets. These include:

- Exhibition and trade fairs displays
- Demonstrations
- Offers
- Merchandising (point of sale promotion)

How to exhibit

Selection of exhibition –

- Location – demand within the market buyers from other markets;
- Content – specific trade sector general fairs;
- Timing – in line with our marketing plans budget, availability, production capacity;
- Cost – is there a better way to tap into customers budget availability?
- Reputation - record of success, average attendance; our competitors present.

Schedule of events

- Information collecting exercise on market, customers, competition etc;
- Obtain plans of hall (or visit if possible) – deciding siting of stand (if we have a choice) and size;
- Finalise decisions regarding design of stand – consider: availability of electricity, water, lifting equipment, etc. Plans may need sending to organisers, information to our local agent, often beneficial to show products actually working;
- Approximately 8 weeks before – invite all potential customers to the stand;
- Decide staff: – consider language, range of skills required – sales, technical; need a team – or can 2 suffice?
- Ensure stand materials are shipped in good time to arrive – and that no damage is evident on arrival;
- Staff arrive – ideally with enough time to acclimatise – and also to manage: stand re-adjustments; literature and samples available (shipped with stand units); replacement equipment (if possible); Incidentals eg spare bulbs, refreshments, handouts, order forms, etc.
- Day before – final check on working modals, incidentals etc., maybe contacts with customers to ensure attendance, finalise attendance rotas;
- During exhibition – make sure every visitor gets attention; maintain detailed contact records.

Some attempt must be made to collect and measure results of participation to facilitate a subsequent cost/benefit analysis. It may be the case that all other promotional activities are linked to the timing of the exhibition – as this is the only activity over which we have little timing control . Other activities such as mail shots, advertising, merchandising activities, personal visits etc., must all be built around exhibition.

2.4

Practice – distribution

The final, and many would say, most important of the 4 Ps is the decision as to the channels of distribution to be used. The fact is that most exporters feel the need, and often the necessity, to have intermediaries representing their interest and based in their overseas markets. Consider what are the options:

- DIRECT – which means direct to the end user
- COMMISSION AGENT – sometimes referred to as broker
- DISTRIBUTOR – sometimes referred to as wholesalers, stockists, dealers etc.
- RETAILER
- LOCAL COMPANY – in many forms: eg sales office, stockist, assembly, manufacture
- LICENSE / FRANCHISE

Their basic functions are described in the sections that follow:

Agent

- Represents a number of Principals for specific products in a specific territory;
- Responsible for selling, promotion, order getting, debt collection, problem solving etc. but does not normally handle goods.
- Receives a Commission payment on sales in that territory (usually between 5% and 10%).

The commission may be:

- a standard rate for all sales
- different rates for orders received through the agent and those received direct
- different rates for different products
- different rates for different customers
- a sliding scale based on order value or total turnover.

Agent's commission calculation

Common mistakes that many exporters make are to do with:

1. The price basis on which commission is paid.
   We should pay commission only on the Ex Works (EXW) value of the goods. There is no justification for an agent to receive commission on the ancillary or third party costs that may be included in an export price eg freight, insurance, documentation etc. You are making no profit on them (or shouldn't be!) so why should they?
2. The actual calculation of the commission amount.
   Hard as it might be to believe, many exporters do not calculate the commission that they pay to their agents correctly.

Lets look at the wrong way (with simple numbers) ... Assuming an agent is receiving 10% commission on the EXW value of the goods:

	$	
EXW value	100	per unit
add on for the agent's commission at 10%	10	
selling price to the buyer	110	per unit

The buyer pays on time and at the end of the month we pay our agent their commission , ie *10% of the EXW selling price of $110 = $11*

We have added on a cost of $10 per unit but are paying a commission of $11 per unit. Multiply that by dozens of orders and thousands of units and the exporter is losing a significant amount of money.

So how do we do it right? The mistake is to confuse the *Mark up* (added on to the basic EXW value) and the *Margin* (percentage of the gross selling price which is paid to the agent). *Solution ?*

	$	
EXW value	100	per unit
mark up for the agent's commission at 11.11%	11.11	
selling price to the buyer	111.11	per unit

We pay our agent 10% of the EXW selling price of $111.11 = $ 11.11. The fact is that the Mark Up has to be larger than the Margin Round numbers.

- To pay *5%* commission add on *5.26%* (call it 5.5 %)
- To pay *7.5%* commission add on *8.11%* (call it 8.5 %)
- To pay *10%* commission add on *11.11%* (call it 11.5 %)

Distributor

Purchases goods from the manufacturer at a discounted price and resells into the specified territory at a profit.
 Can be:

sole distributor	no other distributors will be appointed in the territory but the manufacturer may also deal direct with buyers.
exclusive distributor	no other distributors appointed and the manufacturer will not deal direct.

In addition to all the duties of the agent, distributors may also hold stock of finished goods, parts, components and repair materials and may provide pre- and after- sales service, maintenance, repair, etc.

Local company

Direct investment in the overseas market, possibly with other organisations (particularly local national) in the form of a joint venture, or as an independent project. May be anything from a simple sales office to a stock holder to an assembly resource to a full scale manufacturing unit.

Licensing/franchise

Sale of 'intellectual property' such as know-how, patents, trade names or marks or copyright, in return for disclosure fees and royalties.

Selection of intermediaries

There is a multitude of factors to be taken into consideration in selecting intermediaries. The following draft checklist is detailed to help you ensure that no important step in the selection process is omitted.

Choosing the method

All strategic decisions made in business, including the selection of the method of distribution, are based on three criteria:

Product	Consumer / Industrial	
	Manufacturing patterns	One or multiple sources of manufacture

	Purchasing patterns	Order values, product quality
	Product needs	Lead time expectations
		pre-sales service (advice, design etc.)
		installation
		after sales service
		customer induction / training
		repair / replacement
		specialised storage
		security
Market	Physical distribution / delivery methods	
	Activities of competition	
	Availability	
	Regulations / custom and practice	
	Consumer practices	
	Special arrangements (cartels ?)	
	Economic / political stability	
Company	Managerial resources and experience	
	Financial resources	
	Strategic organisation ...who makes the decisions ?	
	Company policy ...maintain brand name, licensing etc.	
	Company image	
	Existing arrangements	

and the overall considerations that the channel choice has to :

- fit into the overall marketing plan;
- operate within the desired time scales; and
- allow freedom for future developments.

Job specification

It is essential that a clear picture of the role to be filled is decided and THEN to find the person or organisation which 'fits the bill'. We do not appoint an intermediary and then see what they can do for us.

This is particularly the case if we are using third parties to research the market. Therefore, a pre-search requisite is the drafting of a job specification, as in the following Draft Job Specification.

Draft job specification:

A commission agent/distributor is sought in .... to act as a sole representative for the promotion and sale of the Principal's products.

The intermediary will be required to:

☑

1. Ensure that the method chosen is suitable.	
2. Draw up a clear job specification.	
3. Conduct desk research to produce a long list of possibles.	
4. Selection criteria	
a) Products currently handled	
b) Level of product knowledge	
c) Level of market knowledge	
d) Business acumen	
e) Reputation	
f) Marketing expertise	
g) Sales/promotional expertise	
h) Financial standing	
i) Facilities	
5. Compile shortlist and conduct further research if necessary	
6. Personal visit	
7. Appoint. . . Trial period (12 months?) Written agreement	

Checklist for selection of intermediaries

- Actively promote the Principal's name and products
- Identify and actively pursue prospective customers
- Arrange and conduct personal sales interviews with such customers
- Negotiate sales orders with prospective customers
- Follow up all new and established contacts on a regular basis
- Manage a sales force of sufficient size and capabilities to adequately cover the territory
- Liaise between the Principal and buyers with regard to orders, specifications, deliveries, payments, complaints and any other issues appertaining to the development of the Principal's business in the territory

Optionally:

- Hold agreed levels of stock in the territory
- Provide agreed pre and after sales services
- Install, maintain, repair or replace all products in line with the Principal's warranties
- Train new users where applicable
- Provide adequate show room/demonstration facilities
- Make direct deliveries to buyer's premises

The appropriate candidate would be required to meet the following criteria:

1. Product knowledge
    1. a level of technical knowledge in precision engineering
    2. specific knowledge of aerospace and petro-chemical industries
    3. appropriate qualifications and/or experience
    4. ability to absorb and understand the capabilities of the Principal to produce
    5. ability to negotiate with technical specifiers
2. Current Principals
    1. small number of current Principals
    2. with compatible product ranges
    3. reputable Principals
    4. sufficient length of representation
    5. no representation with directly competitive suppliers
3. Market knowledge
    1. general knowledge of the commercial practices of the market
    2. relevant linguistic abilities., both conversational and technical
    3. general knowledge of industrial infrastructures
4. Sector knowledge
    1. specific knowledge of practices in the targeted sectors
    2. specific knowledge of the main end users
    3. broad knowledge of competitors and their activities
    4. relevant personal contacts

5. Facilities
    1. adequate office premises and administrative systems
    2. appropriate location/s
    3. secretarial support
    4. installation and after-sales service
    5. e-mail capabilities
    6. transport
    7. storage
6. Financial standing
    1. corporate history
    2. adequate funds and capital base
    3. appropriate trading history
7. Management expertise
    1. appropriate management experience
    2. appropriate sales and marketing experience
    3. appropriate sales and marketing qualifications
    4. experience in appropriate exhibitions, presentations and other promotional activities
8. Personal qualities
    1. reputation in the industry
    2. willingness to develop technical knowledge
    3. willingness to provide market information
    4. keenness to develop greater market share
    5. straightforward and honest
    6. flexible and adaptable
9. Sources of information:
    1. Trade partners UK
    2. Databases and bibliographic
    3. Trade Associations
10. Marketing Consultants
    1. Chambers of Commerce (Joint Chambers)
    2. Foreign Embassies
    3. Customer's recommendation
    4. Other exporter's recommendation
    5. Direct approaches from overseas

Selection criteria

- Products currently handled
  Compatible not competitive
  Reputation of current range
  Number of principals
- Level of product knowledge
  Technical knowledge
  Staff qualifications

Training facilities
- Level of market knowledge
Buyers, competition, conditions
Personal contacts
- Business acumen
- Reputation
- Financial standing
Capital
Balance Sheet
Trading history
- Promotional expertise
- Facilities
Warehousing
Showrooms
Transport
Assembly/Manufacture

Produce short list

- Personal interview - to confirm researched information eg facilities, market knowledge, product knowledge to asses personal qualities eg keenness, selling ability, honesty, integrity, business acumen, sense of humour.

It is only at this stage that subjective criteria should apply. In view of the protection that many agents and distributors receive in law (particularly in the European Union) great care must be taken in their appointment. In particular it is advisable to:

- Include measurable indicators of performance eg sale targets.
- Include a fixed duration for the agreement.

Motivation

One of the major problems for many exporters is motivation. You want to ensure that your products receive a fair share of the agent's attention – preferably more. How can this be achieved?

The vital point is to accept that what motivates the agent is different, sometimes drastically, from what motivates you, the Principal, as Table 2.4.1 table illustrates:

Table 2.4.1 Motivations of principal and agent

YOUR NEEDS	AGENT/DISTRIBUTOR NEEDS
Volume/Revenue	Profit
Small number of high market shares	Large number of small market shares
Small number of Principals	Large number of Principals
Brand awareness	Risk spreading
Ability to expand and develop	Security of tenure
Investment in development	Cost control
Commitment to you	Commitment to them

The fact is that the needs of the two parties involved in this arrangement are almost diametrically opposed. The agent/distributor wants to make money by taking easy business for a large number of principals and keeping costs low. The principal wants a committed agent investing time and effort in achieving high market shares. The trick to motivation is to address their needs and not your own. The only real way to do this is by providing them with added value through :

- Staff training
  Not just on your company's products but including general management, administration, marketing, sales techniques, IT, etc.
- Management systems
  Develop their recording systems, accounting, cost controls, stock controls, profit management. etc.
- Resources updates
  Actual provision of hardware and software systems (at no cost to them)
- Personal
  Addressing their need for security, harmony, esteem and acceptance through regular contact, social relations and goodwill – and, of course, conspicuously honouring all your duties under the agreement.

Local company

A local company can be set up in a variety of forms:

- Sales office – anything from one person working from home to a fully staffed department
- Stockist – in effect a wholly owned local distributor (which may still stock and sell compatible products)
- Assembly – import of components and sub-assemblies to be assembled for the local market and possibly for export

- Manufacture – a full manufacturing facility using local or imported materials and labour producing goods for the local market and export (the origins of the multinational company - MNC)

With a variety of ownership:

- Wholly owned subsidiary
- Joint venture - invariably with a local national individual or company (in some countries a non-national can own no more than 49% of the equity in a company)

The regulations governing the establishment of local companies vary from market to market. There are often limitations on the percentage of foreign ownership, the nationality of employees and the transfer (repatriation) of profits. They may be companies set up from 'scratch' or by taking over national companies.

Why an exporter might set up a local company

- Sales volume too great for an agent/distributor to handle
- Tariff barriers in the importer's country
- Lower costs eg labour, raw materials, transport etc.
- Spring board for local and surrounding markets
- Restrictive purchasing policies in overseas market
- Need for quality after-sales service
- Releases production capacity

Some markets actively encourage foreign investment eg Eastern Europe, but exporters must be aware of any restrictions and of the potential danger of appropriation of foreign assets.

Licensing

The licensing of 'intellectual property' includes one or more of:

- Patents (design or process)
- Trade and brand names
- Copyright
- or simply 'Know-how'.

These will allow an overseas company to manufacture goods for sale in the local market. Licensing agreements often involve 'disclosure payments' as lump sums following the provision of information and then regular payments of a share of the licensee's profits (known as 'royalties') during the period of the agreement (typically 10 years plus).

Why licences are granted

When appointing licensees the same reasons apply as for the formation of local companies plus:

- More control of selling operation (prevents cheap copies)
- Standard company policy: eg Coca-Cola
- Royalties are often immune from exchange/transfer control
- Local companies will develop eventually, anyway, possibly by securing a license from another licensor.

Licensing is actively encouraged by many developing countries as their governments will have more control of the licensee than of a foreign owned subsidiary but the investment needed can be a problem. An alternative arrangement may be part-ownership of the licensee, similar to a joint venture, where the exporter also finances the setting up of the licensee.

Conclusion

The selection of the correct Marketing Mix for a particular market is obviously not a simple thing for the average exporter. It requires quality research, an understanding of the options and a little experience would not go amiss. But any planning is better than none and every company, including small ones, will benefit from any research and planning it is able to do, because the more a seller is able to identify and react to market demand the more successful they will be.

Earlier we introduced the concept of Customer Orientation and emphasised its importance in dynamic and competitive markets. This concept is important in home markets but becomes essential when the exporter is faced with the almost infinite variety of situations encountered in overseas markets. The more volatile the market, then the more important it becomes for the seller to adapt and accommodate. The UK exporter that ventures into foreign markets thinking that they are simply extensions of the home market will invariably face a rude awakening.

Part 3

The Legal Environment

3.1

An overview of UK law

The making of law

Law in the UK today is made by Acts of Parliament. These Acts must be passed by the House of Commons, the House of Lords, and finally signed by the Queen. (In practice, the Queen's seal is affixed for her by a committee and assent is never witheld). Lawyers call Acts of Parliament 'Statutes'.

One feature of English law which distinguishes it from the continental system is that, in addition to legislation passed by Parliament, the law is made and developed by the decisions of the courts. Court decisions not only establish the legal position between the parties to a legal dispute before the court, known as 'litigants', but also establish the law for the future by constituting 'precedents' which will be followed by judges in future cases. Nevertheless, as the highest authority in the land, Parliament can pass an Act to overrule a case if it so chooses.

The incidence of European Union Law

European Law now applies in the UK without being adopted by an Act of Parliament following the European Communities Act 1972 5.2(1). The UK courts are bound to give effect to European Law.

Occasionally, due to an oversight of Parliament, a statute is inconsistent with EU law, in which case the UK courts must follow EU law. On occasion, where Parliament has intended to pass a law inconsistent with EU, the courts should uphold the statute.

Hierarchy of precedents

Precedent evolves as a result of the hierarchy of the courts, defined in Table 3.1.1, and efficient and accurate law reporting.

Over the centuries, precedent has allowed a uniform law to be moulded; the developing concept is referred to as *stare decisis* (which means 'let the decision stand'). Binding and persuasive precedent is very important to the English legal system and allows a degree of certainty and fairness. Since a higher court has greater jurisdiction than a lower court within the hierarchy, its decisions will be more authoritative in the interpretation of the law and its application to the facts of a dispute.

Table 3.1.1 - Hierarchy of precedents

EUROPEAN COURT OF JUSTICE	Binds all courts on points of EU Law
HOUSE OF LORDS	Binds courts below but not itself
COURT OF APPEAL CIVIL DIVISION	Binds courts below and itself (unless an error of law is made)
HIGH COURT	Binds courts below but not itself
COUNTY COURT	Does not bind any court

It follows that the decision of a higher court, and the reason or reasons for that decision (*ratio decidendi*), will be binding on a later hearing of a court lower in the hierarchy when it is asked to decide a case on similar facts. The reasons for deciding are the element of the judgement which is most important for the system of binding precedent.

However, decisions of courts lower in the hierarchy can be of only persuasive authority for higher courts. In the course of giving judgement, a judge may make comments not directly relevant to the dispute in question which are described as *obiter dicta*. Such statements can only ever form persuasive precedent, no matter what the place in the hierarchy of the court in which they were made.

The application of higher court precedents is not entirely rigid. Judges will not always follow faithfully all decisions of the courts. They retain some discretion to develop the law, depending upon the individual circumstances of any particular case. In fact, when giving 'interpretations of the law' judges often change the law in very radical ways. A judge may have to decide what Parliament intended the law to be when it used certain words in a statute and that interpretation will bind inferior courts as to the their meaning. Judges also have to apply or extend the law in cases which they adjudicate by deciding what exactly was decided in superior courts in similar past cases.

Sources of law

The main sources of law, as described above, are statutes and decided cases.

Public and private law

Public law

By definition, public law is that law administered by and for the benefit of the general public. The two most important branches are:

• CONSTITUTIONAL LAW
• CRIMINAL LAW

Constitutional Law is the law dealing with Parliament, Government, elections to Parliament and the relationship between the individual and the State, or the country in which the individual lives.

Criminal Law comprises the rules which tell us what we must not do. Breaking these rules entails arrest, prosecution and punishment.

For the purposes of this handbook, the details of constitutional law and criminal law need not detain us. Other branches of public law include

Administrative Law, which stems from the need for government to appoint officials to administer various activities, and Community Law which is imposed by the European Union to achieve its aims. The aspects of community law which are relevant to international trade, notably competition law and the law of agency, are dealt with in the further chapters of Part Three.

Private law

Otherwise called 'Civil Law', Private Law derives its name from the private decision of the individual whether or not to sue another. The outcome of a claim for breach of contract does not concern the nation as a whole, although it may provide a precedent for others in similar contractual circumstances. Civil or private law is a wider area of law than public law and encompasses the following branches:

- The Law of Contract
  Chapter 3.2 discusses the law of contract and contractual disputes in some detail. The actual Law of Contract deals with claims by people for loss they have suffered as a result of breach of contract which is the main area for disputes in international trade. There is a popular misconception that a contract has to be written to have binding force. In practice, most everyday contracts are made verbally e.g when buying a train ticket or ordering a meal in a restaurant.
- The Law of Tort
  Derived from the French word meaning 'wrong', a tort is a wrong for which the wrongdoer can be sued for damages. The following are the main categories of tort:
- Negligence
  Carelessness leading to injury. Motoring accidents caused by negligence are a common example.
- Trespass
  Trespass generally means going on someone else's property without permission. More specifically, trespass to goods means damaging someone else's goods and trespass to the person gives rise to claims for assault.
- Defamation
  Saying things about someone else which are untrue and which lower their reputation constitutes defamation. Defamation in writing is classified as Libel and often results in the award of damages.
- Nuisance
  The tort of nuisance refers to the disturbance of a neighbour's enjoyment of and peace in their home.
- Consumer Credit and Sale of Goods
  Personal transactions in goods or services on credit are covered by the Consumer Credit Act (1974) which gives the individual very considerable

rights. Sale of Goods law deals with the rights of consumers who buy defective goods and many other questions connected with sale of goods.

- Agency Law
  Agents are people appointed by another to make contracts for them. Agency Law applicable to the use of agents in international trade is dealt with in chapter 3.5. Other branches of private law which are not relevant to this handbook include:
- The Law of Trusts
- Land Law
- Law of Landlord and Tenant
- Law of Succession and Family Law.

Sources of law

The main sources of law are statutes and decided cases based on precedents. However, there are three further sources of law:

Delegated legislation

Parliament often passes an Act which is a general framework, giving government ministers or other bodies the power to fill in the details by making 'Rules', 'Orders', 'Statutory Instruments' or 'Orders in Council', which are technically made by the Queen, although in practice made by the government.

Trade custom

A further source of law, of particular importance to the exporter, is how things are done in a particular trade, generally defined as 'trade custom'. Somewhat surprisingly, such practices can be adopted into law through common usage and frequently supersede the general rule of law in that trade. As an example, no one in their right mind would normally suggest that an insurance broker is responsible for the unpaid premiums of their clients, but by trade custom a Marine Insurance broker is held responsible.

EU Law

When the UK joined the EU in 1973 it agreed to accept the European Communities Act 1972 and be bound by EC law which would override any conflicting national law.and be applied by the UK courts. EU law is made by the European Commission, the Council of Ministers and the European Court of Justice. The legislative bodies, the Commission and the Council, make Regulations which pass directly into the national law of member states and issue Directives which are binding on member states but leave each member state with a choice about the method used to achieve the directed result. A transitional period is allowed.

In summary, EU law takes the following four forms:

- Treaties
  Treaties are binding on Member States and EU institutions. In certain circumstances, treaties may create rights for individuals which may be enforceable in national courts.
- Regulations
  Also binding on all Member States without requiring any implementation or adoption by national Parliaments, regulations apply directly and prevail over the national laws. They can also create rights enforceable by individuals in national courts.
- Directives
  Binding but leaving a Member State a choice of the method by which the result required by the directive must be achieved. In the UK the alternative methods are an Act of Parliament or delegated legislation. A directive can also create rights for individuals enforceable in national courts.
- Decisions of the European Court of Justice of the Communities
  Such decisions are binding in their entirety on the highest courts in Member States. The House of Lords in the case of the UK. Decisions are also binding on individuals or companies. The Commission, among other public and private organisations (and even citizens of EU states), can initiate proceedings against a Member State if it believes that steps taken to implement regulations and directives do not achieve the desired results.

3.2

The law of contract

Contract essentials

In essence a Contract is an agreement between two (or more) people which is intended to have the force of law. It can be made in any of the following ways:

- *In writing.* Some contracts, such as Hire Purchase Agreements, must be in writing.
- *Commercially.* contracts involving large sums of money should be written, if only for the sake of clarity. Most large export transactions are the subject of a written contract.
- *Orally.* The method for conducting everyday transactions such as buying food and transport services.
- *By conduct.* Boarding a single-fare bus or buying goods from a vending machine are simple examples of contract by conduct.
- *By any combination of the above.*

Essential ingredients

Certain ingredients are essential for there to be a valid contract. There must be an *offer* and *acceptance* which match. A verbal offer at a price of £10 followed by an acceptance at £9 clearly does not signify an agreement between the parties. The response constitutes a *counter offer* and a rejection of the original offer which is thereby terminated. An acceptance must exactly fit the offer and any attempt to accept on new terms amounts to a rejection of the original offer accompanied by a counter-offer.

There must be *consideration* – something in return. No promise for which consideration in return is not given can be enforced in law. The only exception to this general rule is if a special legal document, called a *deed* is drawn up. Each party must have *capacity to contract* – in other words, the right to enter into legally binding contracts. Making a contract without capacity means that it cannot be enforced against the counter party. It does not mean that it is an offence or in any way illegal for them to make a contract.

The parties must be *ad idem*, which means that they must be making the same contract. Essentially the buyer and seller in a transaction must be intending to deal in the same product or service of the same at the same price and on the same terms and conditions.

True consent. There must be an intention by both parties to create legal relations and for the contract to have the force of law. In commercial situations it is assumed that there is such an intention but an inclusion in the documentation of 'binding in honour only' would likely make the contract void.

There must be true *agreement* to the contract, which means an absence of the following:

- operative mistake
- duress
- misrepresentation
- undue influence

Illegality. The law may refuse to give effect to a contract on the grounds that it involves the execution of a legal wrong: a crime, a tort, or a breach of contract. A statute may make the formation of certain kinds of contracts illegal.

Contracts contrary to public policy. Certain contracts, including those which are void for illegality, are regarded as injurious to society and therefore void. Contracts which restrain trade are an important category unless they can be regarded as reasonable between the parties or as regards the public interest when they were made.

Breach of contract

The remedies for a breach of contract may be categorised as legal remedies and equitable remedies with following sub-classification:

Legal remedies

- *Termination.* Where a breach of an important term of a contract has occurred the innocent party may be entitled to bring the contract to an end, as well as to claim damages. The contract will then be terminated from the date of the breach and the parties will not have been bound by the contracts from that day forward. Following termination the innocent party cannot claim specific performance or an injunction.
- *Rescission and damages for misrepresentation.* Effectively, rescission means cancelling the contract. After rescission for misrepresentation the contract is regarded as having been void from the beginning and the innocent party can be awarded damages for misrepresentation which are assessed differently from damages for breach of contract.
- *Action for an agreed sum.* An action for the price of goods or services sold when the purchaser does not pay is described as an action for an agreed

sum. It is not an action for damages and is only available if the contract subsists. One cannot terminate for breach or rescind for misrepresentation and then sue for price.

Equitable remedies

- *Specific performance.* In certain very limited circumstances where damages would not be enough to compensate the injured party, the court may award an order against the party in breach of a contract to carry it out.
- *Injunction.* An injunction is a court order restraining a defendant from carrying out an act in breach of the contract.

Commercial considerations

Very often it is in the interests of a company that is a seller not to sue the buyer, because they are a regular customer. Litigation will have the inevitable consequence that goodwill will be lost and all future orders from the customer will cease. The use of legal remedies should be looked upon as a last resort where the prospects for future profitable business are dim.

Offer and acceptance

As already identified the essential equation behind every contract is:

offer + acceptance = contract

The realities behind each variable in the equation need to be spelt out.

Offer

An offer must be distinguished from the following:

- a declaration of intention
- a supply of information
- an invitation to treat

   In the case of the latter goods displayed in shop windows with price tags attached are held to be invitations for offers, not offers themselves. Advertisements are also usually invitations to treat rather than offers. An offer must be communicated. This means that the other party must know of its existence. An offer can lapse. It can end after a certain time:

- by the death of either party before acceptance
- by non-acceptance within any stated time
- by non-acceptance within a reasonable time if no time is stated. (The definition of 'reasonable' depends on the facts of each individual case).

An offer can be rejected directly or indirectly (by making a counter offer). An offer can be revoked (ie withdrawn) any time before it is accepted. If sent by post revocation takes effect when the notification arrives.

Acceptance

The requirements for a valid acceptance are similarly well defined. Acceptance must be unqualified. It must correspond exactly with the offer. (A counter offer at the same price but in instalments does not qualify as acceptance when the original offer was for 'cash').

Acceptance must be communicated to the other party. Silence does not imply valid acceptance in the case of a seller writing: "If I hear no more from you, I shall assume your acceptance." Communication of acceptance must be actually received by the offeror and the contract will come into existence when and where acceptance is received. Any prescribed method of communicating acceptance must be followed if it is made clear that no other method will do.

Acceptance subject to contract means that the contract does not become binding until certain formalities have been completed. In an option to purchase where the buyer has given the seller something in exchange for keeping the offer open (ie provided consideration) there is a contract. The seller will keep the offer open in exchange for the money.

Tenders

In addition to the standard commercial process of offer and acceptance, there is an alternative process called the 'Tender' of which there are three types:

- A *request for offers*. This kind of tender arises where an authority/state agency requests offers for the lowest price for doing a certain job (e.g supplying a street lighting system to a town in a developing country). The tender is an invitation to treat, and the lowest offer will be accepted.
- A *standing offer to supply goods*. A tender of this type is an arrangement whereby the buyer agrees to order goods from a supplier on a continual basis whenever they are wanted.
- A *promise by the buyer*. An undertaking by the buyer to buy all the goods they need from the supplier is still not an obligation to order any.

However, if supplies are ordered from elsewhere, the buyer can be restrained by injunction from doing so.

Standard form contract

Standard form contracts may be prepared for a business to cover all transactions of a particular type. Details about the particular transaction in hand are entered on the front of the standard form contract document. On the back is a list of terms which apply to that contract and will apply to all similar contracts made by each customer

Theoretically customers agree to the terms, but they are usually in a 'take it or leave it' situation. The Government eventually recognised that consumers were at the mercy of big business through such contracts and passed the Unfair Contract Terms Act and Supply Goods (Implied Terms) Act.

However, these statutes do not apply to international sales. Therefore, the exporter must read the buyer's conditions very carefully and understand to what it is being asked to agree.

The battle of the forms

Most exporters insist on their terms of sale, and they must take particular care not to accept the buyer's terms by accident, which they will do if they:

- Send out the goods on receipt of the buyer's order without countering it with their own terms; even if the buyer's order is not placed on special terms, accepting it without comment will still deny the seller the benefit of their own terms.
- Allow the buyer to be the last party to send their standard form; in that event despatching the goods means accepting their orders by conduct.
- Accept an order from a new customer, or from one who has dealt with the seller on a very few occasions, over the telephone without drawing attention to the fact that the terms exist.

In practice, a seller should consider varying or dropping some of his conditions only if:

- The order he will gain is very substantial.
- His conditions are very harsh and he faces the threat of adverse publicity concerning them.

Consideration

As noted in Chapter 3.1, all contracts must contain consideration except those made in a legal document called a Deed. Consideration is defined as what each party puts into the contract. The law of consideration refers to a 'Promise' being made by one party (the 'Promisor') to the other party (the 'Promisee). There are two types of consideration:

- *Executory consideration* is a promise of benefit to be given in the future (eg 'to be delivered tomorrow'). A promise can be consideration.
- *Executed consideration* is a benefit given at the time the contract is made.
- *Past consideration is not valid as consideration.* The promise by one party of something already done is not sufficient to bind a promisee to perform his side of an agreement.
- *Consideration must be real but need not be adequate.* In law it does not matter that a correct price has not been paid for an item sold, so long as some consideration has been paid. The law concerns itself with ensuring that some consideration is given – typically set at £1 in agreements concerning intangibles.

Composition with creditors

A composition with creditors is a particular form of agreement where the consideration is less than full value. It is an agreement made by a business or individual with all its creditors whereby each creditor agrees to take so much in the £ (ie less than the full debt). The creditors are legally bound by this contract because if any of them sued for the rest of the debt, the others would get less.

Part-payment by someone other than the debtor

If part-payment from a third party is accepted in full settlement, the debtor is released from the rest of the debt. Therefore, in business, it is essential that whenever an offer of part-payment is received from someone other than the debtor, to write to him to state that it is accepted purely as part-payment and not to cash the cheque until he has agreed.

Terms of a contract

By definition, a 'term' is one of the promises made by one of the parties to the contract – ie it is what that party has agreed to do. It follows that the sum total of all the terms is the contract in its entirety.

Terms are classified into:

- Express and implied terms; and
- Conditions, warranties and innominate terms.

Express and implied terms

An 'Express Term' is one which is agreed orally or in writing between the parties. An 'Implied Term' is one which is impliedly agreed between the parties without express words.

Terms can be implied into contracts in any of four ways:

1. *By statute.* Certain Acts of Parliament impose compulsory terms in all contracts of a certain type. Some are absolutely compulsory and cannot be excluded, whether the parties like it or not. Others can be excluded by mutual agreement between the parties. For example, in the Sale of Goods Act (1979) the compulsory term that the seller must have the right to sell the goods cannot be excluded. But other terms, absolutely compulsory when a business sells goods to a consumer, (eg statsfactory quality, correspondence to description and fitness for purpose) can be excluded by the parties in a contract of sale between two businesses having regard to the circumstances .
2. *By the courts.* The courts are reluctant to imply terms into contracts retrospectively. However, they are prepared to imply a term which is so obvious that no reasonable man would make the contract without it. (eg the lease of a mooring in a harbour which is without water when the tide goes out).
3. *From previous dealings.* When the parties have made the same contract so many times that they must be taken to know what the terms are, the terms will apply to all future contracts of that type between them, whether they agreed to them or not when they made that future contract.
4. *By trade custom.* The courts will give the force of law to common practice if things are done in a certain way in a particular trade. In certain contracts in certain trade a term is always implied unless the parties agree otherwise.

Conditions, warranties and innominate terms

The courts have classified terms into either conditions or warranties since the Nineteenth Century. The distinction made is that:

- a breach of condition gives the innocent party the right to terminate the contract from the date of the breach on the grounds that the contract has been repudiated by the other party. However, termination is not obligatory; the victim can affirm the contract despite the breach.
- a breach of warranty does not entitle the innocent party to terminate the contract; the victim may only claim damages. The logic is that a minor breach may be adequately remedied by money compensation.
- an innominate term (sometimes called an 'Intermediate Term') is one which is neither exclusively a condition nor a warranty, but one which

can be broken in either a minor or a major way. Depending on which kind of breach occurs, the courts will decide whether or not to allow the innocent party to terminate the contract.

If a term is classified as a condition, the innocent party can terminate the contract for breach even if the actual breach of that term is trivial, leading to the opportunity for an innocent party to terminate for a trivial breach of condition for reasons which have nothing to do with the occurrence of the breach. The possibility that a term described in the contract as a condition may be judged to be innominate and a breach of the term as minor when the issue is tried, is plainly unsatisfactory from a commercial point of view. The courts have therefore taken to 'recognising' certain kinds of terms in advance as conditions so that the business community can rely on that knowledge. For example, time is particularly important in commerce and clauses specifying the time for performance of obligations under contracts are usually classified in advance as conditions.

Of course, the intention of the parties regarding the terms of the contract remains important. Contracting parties are advised to make certain that their intention is clear by expressly and unambiguously stating that the breach of a particular term will give the innocent party the right to terminate the contract. Mere description of a term as a condition is not conclusive and it is then open to a court to hold that the term is innominate giving rise to an outcome which was not intended by the parties when entering into the contract.

Duress

Hitherto the law has ignore most of the pressures which may influence a person's decision to enter into a contract, including commercial pressures, economic pressures and social pressures. However, in recent years, the courts have showed an increased willingness to intervene, even in commercial contracts where people have entered into them without genuine consent because they were acting under duress or undue influence. Undue influence does not arise in commercial disputes and is therefore ignored here. Duress, in order to affect a contract, must amount to a coercion of the will which vitiates consent. A contract affected by duress is voidable and can be avoided by the party claiming duress communicating their intention to the other party. The effect of avoidance is to nullify the contract completely. Threats against the person or property clearly vitiate consent. The courts have also recognised that consent can be vitiated by economic duress, even in commercial contracts.

Mistake

Although the general rule is that it does not matter that there has been a mistake in a contract, there is a certain number of special mistakes, called 'operative mistakes' which do operate to make the contract void. Operative mistakes are categorised as:

- Mistake as to the nature of the contract.
- Unilateral mistake – where just one party make a mistake.
- Common mistake – where both parties make the same mistake.
- Mutual mistake – where the two parties make different mistakes.

Mistake as to the nature of the contract

If someone signs a contract, the general rule is that they are bound by it whether they have read it or not. The only relief is a defence of *'Non Est Factum'* where someone claims that the contract they signed was a of a totally different nature from that which they thought they were signing. However, *Non Est Factum* is no defence if the person signing is negligent and is therefore practically ineffective. There will be very few cases where a person signing a document which they have not read will not be negligent.

Unilateral mistake

A unilateral mistake will seldom affect a contract, since the other party will no know about it, and has no reason to know about it.

Common mistake

At Common Law, a common mistake by both parties will only render the contract void if it makes the contract impossible to carry out.

Mutual mistake

A mutual mistake will usually make the contract void because it will mean that the parties are not contracting the same thing.

Misrepresentation

A misrepresentation which induced a party to enter into a contract has the effect of making the contract voidable (unless rescission is barred for some reason) not void as in mistake. Therefore, the contract remains valid until it is rescinded by the innocent party who must communicate the rescission to the other party. However, the innocent party is not obliged to rescind the contract.

In the Misrepresentation ACT 11967, which gives the right to remedies in the event that a misrepresentation is proved, misrepresentation is defined as:

- A statement of fact.
  Made by one party to the other before the contract is entered into,
  Which is incorrect, and
  Which is the reason (or one of the reasons) why the innocent party made the contract

A misrepresentation is often something said about a product but it can also be an action which causes the innocent party to have a misleading impression of the product (eg turning back the mileage clock on a car offered for sale).

A statement of fact

Misrepresentations must be distinguished from:

- An opinion that is honestly held.
- A sales or trade 'puff'.

The law allows sellers some latitude to make claims about their wares, such as a generalised claim about the product which does not say anything specific (eg 'the best on the market') or a claim that is obviously an advertising stunt which no reasonable person would ever believe.

A statement of law

If the seller of an item simply tells the buyer some incorrect information about the law, the buyer is deemed to know the law and cannot sue. Nevertheless, if the misrepresentation is deliberate it may constitute a criminal offence of obtaining the buyer's money by deception.

Types of misrepresentation

In civil law a misrepresentation need not be a deliberate lie. A person can sue if they have made a contract as a result of any of the following types of misrepresentation:

- *Fraudulent misrepresentation*
  Also known as deceit, fraudulent misrepresentation is a statement which the seller knows is untrue or suspects might be untrue but is unsure.

- *Negligent misrepresentation*
  This is a statement which the seller does not realise is incorrect, but which they ought to have realised was untrue.
- *Innocent misrepresentation*
  A statement which the seller believed, and a reasonable person would have believed as well, is considered neither negligent nor fraudulent and is classified as an innocent misrepresentation.

Misrepresentation and contract terms

A misrepresentation that induces someone to enter into a contract may have been made either by a person who is not a party to the contract or by a person who is. If it was made by a person who became a party to the contract the misrepresentation may become a term of the contract, depending on the intention of the parties at the time the contract was made. A court would probably not hold the misrepresentation to be an express term of contract if:

- the person making the statement asks the other party to check or verify it;
- the statement did not relate to an important aspect of the contractual deal;
- the misrepresentor and misrepresentee were equally able, with regard to the necessary skill and knowledge, to verify the truth of the statement.

Remedies for misrepresentation

Remedies are available at common law, in equity or under statute. The Misrepresentation Act 1967provides for damages in respect of negligent and innocent misrepresentation. Section 2(1) deals with negligent misrepresentation and section 2(2) with innocent misrepresentation. A Plaintiff can plead more than one cause of action in court in the alternative so that if they fail on one they may succeed on the other. The remedies available different types of misrepresentation are summarised in Table 3.2.5.

Criminal misrepresentations

There are three categories of criminal offence arising from misrepresentation:

- *Offences under the Trade Description Act (1968)*
  Selling goods under a false trade description is basically the same as misrepresentation. Curiously, there is no civil liability attaching to

Table 3.2.5 - Remedies for misrepresentation

	Fraudulent Misrepresentation	Negligent Misrepresentation	Innocent Misrepresentation
At Common Law	Damages in the tort of Deceit	Damages in the tort of negligence, if a special relationship exists	
In Equity	Rescission and damages. If the contract is executory the fraud is a defence if the misrepresentor brings an action for specific performance	Rescission	Rescission
Under the Misrepresentation Act 1967		In addition to rescission, or – at the court's discretion – damages under s.2(1), if, as a result of the misrepresentation the injured party has suffered loss, proof that the Defendant believed with reasonable cause that the statements were true up to the time of the contract will be a defence.	

offences under the Act, a shopkeeper who displays at a false price cannot be force to sell at that price.

* *Obtaining property by deception*
  Fraudulent misrepresentation made to the person who buys an item constitutes obtaining property by deception and enables the innocent party to sue.
* *Obtaining a pecuniary advantage by deception*
  This offence is committed by a person who gets insurance without disclosing all the facts. It carries a maximum custodial sentence of five years.

Discharge of contract

When a contract is discharged it comes to an end. A contract can be discharged by:

* Performance
* Agreement
* Breach
* Frustration

Frequently, the position of one party which has carried out the contract is of concern in terms of what benefits they can get for having done so.

Discharge by performance

Where one party has performed the contract they will look to the other party for performance. Before doing so, they must have completely carried out their side of the bargain. This rule is subject to two exceptions:

1. Where the agreement is so arranged that there is a series of small contracts, payment is due for each small contract completed.
2. The doctrine of substantial performance which states that if a person doing the work has completed it, but done it badly, they can claim the difference between the price of the finished job and what it costs to put that job right.

Time of performance

Common commercial clauses which relate the time of performance of duties under contract are often classified by the courts as conditions in the interests of certainty in commerce. The general rule in commercial contracts is that time is *prima facie* 'of the essence', provided that time for performance can be fixed with certainty, and that breach will be a breach of condition.

Therefore, where a specific date is fixed, failure to deliver on time will be a breach of condition entitling the buyer to reject the goods and terminate the contract. Conversely, where a commercial contract requires delivery 'within a reasonable time', time will not be of the essence; however, the buyer can make time of the essence by giving reasonable notice of a time for delivery. In the case of a dispute the court will have to decide when failure to deliver has been a total failure of consideration and the buyer can get his money back and terminate the contract.

In practice, the buyer will often prefer to accept late delivery rather than terminate in order to preserve good relations with a valued supplier, or because the terms are more advantageous than those offered by others, or because termination and placing an order with another supplier would involve greater delay. Perhaps the buyer will be able to negotiate a reduction in price in return for acceptance of late delivery.

However, the buyer should be aware that if he does not terminate the contract in response to delay but acts in a way which leads the supplier to believe that he intends to continue to perform the contract (by continuing to press for delivery) a court will see this as a waiver of the right to terminate. The buyer should give reasonable notice of a new date on which delivery is expected and time will again be of the essence with respect to the adjusted date. From the seller's standpoint, although the right to terminate may be waived in respect of any late delivery, the seller will still be liable in damages for loss arising from delay.

Discharge by agreement

If one party has completely carried out their side of a contract and is willing to release the other party, they can only discharge the other party by deed, because they will be getting no consideration for their agreement.

Novation

On the other hand, if both parties have duties left to perform, they can agree to cancel or revise these duties, because each party's promise to revise the duties will be consideration for the other party's promise to revise their duties. Where a contract is modified in this way, there is said to be a 'novation'.

Complete discharge by agreement

By the same principle, where both parties still have duties to perform under the contract, they can discharge each other entirely from the contract, the one's promise to release the other being consideration for the other's promise to release him.

Presumption of discharge by agreement

If a contract is made and remains unperformed for many years this will lead to a presumption that the parties have abandoned the contract.

Discharge by breach

Anticipatory breach

Where one party announces their intention of not performing a contract which they are due to perform in the future, there is said to be an 'anticipatory breach'.

Discharge by frustration

The legal meaning of frustration may be defined as a totally unforeseen event which has the effect of making the contract either physically impossible, or such a different contract that the parties must be taken to have impliedly agreed that they would not go through with it under those circumstances. Frustration is very much a last resort which the court is most reluctant to acknowledge. If the contract is still possible, the court will nearly always enforce it.

Events which do *not* frustrate the contract are:

* increase in cost
* absolute promise to perform, where one party
* has agreed to be bound by it 'come what may'.

However, a contract would be held to have been frustrated when the contract is made impossible by statute, eg Government requisition under emergency powers for war use.

Frustration must not be self-induced

Where the event is caused by the negligence of the party who can no longer perform, the frustration is said to be self-induced, and a party which alleges that a contract has been frustrated must not have caused that frustration himself.

The effect of frustration

Frustration discharges the parties from their obligation to perform the contract in the future. It is not declared void from its inception as in an operative mistake. This means that the rights and obligations of the parties prior to the frustrating event are preserved unless statute law intervenes.

Remedies for breach of contract

When the court has decided that one party is in breach of contract, it has to decide what action to enforce. Bearing in mind that the aim of the civil law is to compensate the plaintiff for their loss rather than punish the defendant for having broken the contract, the court can do one of the following:

Award damages

When awarding money compensation the court will bear in mind the following well-established principles:

1. The aim of damages is purely to compensate. When there is no loss or minimal loss, the innocent party will only get nominal damages.
2. In contracts for the sale of goods, damages are the difference between the contract price and the current market price of the goods. The test is 'What has the innocent party lost?'

When assessing damages, liability to tax is taken into account. Where the party being awarded damages would have had to pay tax on what he lost due to the breach, then his loss should be assessed net of tax.

The mere fact that damages are difficult to assess does not prevent the plaintiff from claiming them.

In cases where the purpose of the contract was to provide enjoyment, relaxation or peace of mind, this principle has been extended to cover damages for injury to the innocent party's feelings, and his sense of disappointment and frustration as a result of the breach.

Damages can be recovered for pecuniary loss resulting from loss of commercial reputation caused by a breach of contract but not for loss of commercial reputation itself.

Damages will not be awarded if the damage is too remote. The 'remoteness of damage' rule is based on the principle that it would be unfair to make the defendant compensate the plaintiff for a never-ending series of losses consequent from the breach of contract.

The plaintiff has a duty to mitigate his loss. This means that he must make his loss as small as possible. This is often an issue in cases of wrongful dismissal from work where a dismissed employee must make reasonable efforts to find himself other work to mitigate his loss.

There are cases in tort (though not for breach of contract) where it is possible for a court to award exemplary damages. In exceptional cases the aim of the award is to show that 'tort does not pay' when:

* the defendant has deliberately committed a tort; and
* he did so calculating that he would make a profit, after paying the necessary damages.

Allow a claim on quantum meruit

'Quantum meruit' means 'as much as it is worth'. Such claims are put forward by persons seeking part-payment for work that they have done, eg:

- Where the party paying for the work stops the work being carried out.
- Where the contract to do work is void.
- Where one person does work for another in circumstances where the parties do not actually agree on payment, but it is obvious that payment is expected.

With a quantum meruit all that the workman is entitled to is reasonable remuneration – not a proportion of the contract price.

Action for money had and received

If one party pays money to the other for which they receive absolutely no compensation, then the payer is entitled to its return under this action which applies to any situation where one person comes into possession of another's money.

Award a decree of specific performance

Such an award is an order of the court to the guilty party to carry out the contract. If the guilty party refuses, they are in contempt of court and liable to imprisonment.

Award an injunction

There are two types of injunction: a prohibitory injunction which orders the defendant not to do something, and a mandatory injunctions which orders him to do something. In the context of breach of contract a mandatory injunction is replaced by a decree of specific performance.

3.3

Sale of goods in international trade

Introduction

Until 1893 a contract for the sale of goods was treated the same as any other contract with the rules applying to it being developed by court decisions. The Sale of Goods Act 1893 was simply a 'codification' of the law, a statement of the rules which the courts had devised in the form of an Act of Parliament.

From then until 1973, apart from evolution through case law, the sale of goods law remained substantially as perceived by the 1893 legislators. However, as a result of the change in economic conditions, it was realised by 1973 that the protection given to the consumer, now a major aspect of sale of goods law, had become outdated. Following a general review of English Law by the 1969 Law Commission, the Supply of Goods (Implied Terms) Act 1973 was passed which stated that merchantable quality condition and certain other conditions could not be excluded in sales to customers (members of the public) and could be excluded only in sales to other businesses where considered reasonable.

The 1973 Act was followed by the Unfair Contract Terms Act 1977 which sought to extend consumer protection to all contracts entered into by members of the public. A new Sale of Goods Act combining the 1893 Act and the 1973 Act into a single Act was passed in 1979.

The 1979 Act has been amended further by:

* The Sale and Supply of Goods Act 1994
* The Sale of Goods (Amendment) Act 1994
* Sale and Supply of Goods to Consumers Regulations 2002

The term 'Merchantable Quality' introduced as a qualifying condition for merchandise sold under the 1893 Act was amended to 'Satisfactory Quality' in the former of the new Acts unless the parties to the sale agree otherwise.

Exporters should note that the protection given to consumers in England and Wales under these Acts is not extended to overseas buyers. Therefore, the exporter need not be concerned about consumer protection legislation unless they sell to a merchant in this country who is going to resell abroad, in which case the protection will apply.

In the case of export sales through an Agent, who never becomes the owner of the goods but is simply receiving commission for arranging the sale, the transaction remains an export sale and the protection does not apply.

The law relating to the sale of goods

The main elements of current sale of goods law and some of the reasons why the Sale of Goods Act 1979 was amended are discussed in this chapter.

Quality and suitability

Although merchantable quality and suitability (or fitness) for purpose were defined by statute in the 1979 Act the following criticisms of the implied terms as to quality under Section 14 were identified by the subsequent Law Commission Report on the Sale and Supply of Goods (1987).

- The term 'merchantable' related to merchants and trade and was inappropriate to consumer transactions.
- There was some uncertainty about whether the 'suitability' test contained in the statutory definition covered minor defects which did not interfere with the use of the goods. eg a scratch on the paintwork of a new car.
- The standard of quality was linked to the expectation of the buyer. A fall in manufacturing standards could result in a fall in consumer expectations which would result in a lower legal standard of quality.
- No express reference was made to the qualities of durability or safety.

The implied terms of fitness for a particular purpose were not criticised. The Law Commission recommended that the implied term of merchantable quality should be replaced by a new definition of quality expressed as a basic principle sufficiently general to apply to all goods and all transactions, and a non-exhaustive list of aspects of quality which would include fitness for purpose, safety, durability, etc. These recommendations are incorporated in the Sale and Supply of Goods Act 1994.

The new definition of quality applies to all contracts for the sale and supply of goods including agreements to transfer property in goods, such as barter, work and materials, hire purchase, hire and exchange of goods for trading stamps.

According to Section 14(2), goods are of satisfactory quality if they meet the standard that a reasonable person would regard as satisfactory, taking into account any description of the goods, the price (if relevant) and all other relevant circumstances.

There is an implied condition that the goods supplied are of satisfactory quality except to the extent of defects which :

- Are brought specifically to the buyer's attention before the contract is made; or

- Ought to have been noticed by the buyer if he or she has examined the goods.

In Section 14(2B) which explains that the quality of goods includes their state and condition, the following non-exhaustive aspects of quality are identified:

- Fitness for all purposes for which goods of the kind in question are commonly supplied;
- Appearance and finish;
- Freedom from minor defects;
- Safety; and
- Durability.

Section 14(2) does not impose absolute standards of quality with which all goods must comply. It recognises that, from a practical point of view, it is likely that a reasonable person will find the quality of new goods satisfactory even if they have minor or cosmetic defects.

A buyer is not obliged to examine goods before he buys them and, if he chooses not to do so, will still be entitled to protection under Section 14(2). A buyer's right to complain is lost in two situation:

- Where the seller specifically points out that the goods are faulty; and
- Where he decides to check the goods but fails to notice an obvious defect.

Delivery of wrong quantity

Under Section 30, Sale of Goods Act 1979, the buyer has a number of choices open to him depending on whether the seller delivers more than ordered or less than ordered.

In non-consumer contracts the buyer is not entitled to reject the goods where the deviation is so slight that it would be unreasonable to reject the whole [section 30(2A)].

Delivery by instalments

Unless otherwise agreed, the buyer is under no obligation to accept delivery by instalments [section 31(1)]. His right to repudiate the contract will depend upon whether the contract is indivisible or severable.

Where a buyer has accepted some of the goods, he will not lose the right to reject the goods because of the acceptance where there is a breach in respect of some or all of the goods [section 30(4)].

Acceptance of goods

Qualifications were added in the 1994 Acts to the three basic methods of acceptance.

- A consumer cannot lose his right to reject the goods by agreement unless he has had a reasonable opportunity to examine them. Therefore, an acceptance note will not deprive a consumer of his right to examine the goods.
- A material factor in deciding whether goods have been accepted after the lapse of a reasonable time is whether the buyer has been given a reasonable opportunity to inspect the goods.
- A buyer is not deemed to have accepted the goods because he has asked for or agreed to a repair or where the goods have been sold or given to a third party.
- Where a buyer accepts goods which are part of a larger commercial unit he is deemed to have accepted all the goods which make up the commercial unit.

Rejection of goods

Provided that the goods have not been accepted, the buyer has the right to reject the goods for any breach of the implied conditions, no matter how slight the breach may be.

This right is absolute for consumers but is subject to qualification in the case of a commercial buyer. The new section 15A of the 1979 Act made a distinction between consumers and commercial buyers in relation to remedies. A consumer's right to reject goods is retained but a commercial buyer's right to reject is now subject to qualification.

Where a seller can show that the breach of Sections 13-15 Sale of Goods Act 1979 is so slight that it would be unreasonable for a non-consumer buyer to reject, the breach is to be treated as a breach of warranty and not as a breach of condition.

Other consumer protection aspects

Two other pieces of legislation, outlined below, relate to consumer protection and have a direct bearing on the supply of goods:

- General Product Safety Regulations 1994
- Unfair Terms in Consumer Contract Regulations 1999

The General Product Safety Regulations 1994

The 1994 Regulations implement the provisions of the European Directive on General Product Safety which was adopted by the Council of Ministers in

1992. The Regulations which came into effect on 3 October 1994 imposed new requirements concerning the safety of products intended for consumers, or likely to be used by consumers, where such products are placed in the market by producers or supplied by distributors. A consumer is defined as a person who is not acting in the course of a commercial activity which, in turn, is defined as any business or trade.

The regulations apply whether the products are new, used or reconditioned. Products used exclusively in the context of a commercial activity, even if for or by a consumer, are not subject to the Regulations.

Regulation 7 provides that a producer may not place a product on the market unless it is a safe product. It is an offence to fail to comply with the general safety requirement and for a producer or distributor to offer, agree to place or supply a dangerous product or expose or possess such a product for placing on the market.

Regulation 2 defines a 'safe product' as one for which , under normal conditions of use (including duration) there is no risk or the risk has been reduced to a minimum. The fact that higher levels of safety can be achieved or that there are less risky products available will not, of itself, render a product unsafe.

Products which comply with UK legal requirements concerning health and safety are presumed to be safe products, but if no specific rules exist the safety of a product will be assessed according to:

- voluntary UK standards which give effect to a European standard; or
- EU technical specifications; or, in their absence,
- UK standards or industry codes of practice relating to health and safety, or the state of the art or technology, and the consumer's reasonable expectations in relation to safety.

Under Regulation 8, a producer is required to provide consumers with information so that they can assess inherent risks and take precautions, where the risks are not immediately obvious without adequate warnings.

A producer must also adopt measures to keep himself informed of any risks which his products present and must take all appropriate action to avoid risk, which may include withdrawal of the product from the market.

A distributor will commit an offence if he supplies dangerous products [Regulation 9(a)]. He must also take part in monitoring the safety of products, including passing on information about product risks and co-operating in action to avoid them [Regulation 9(b)].

Regulation 15 provides a by-pass provision to enable the prosecution of any person whose act or default, in the course of a commercial activity, causes another to commit an offence.

The penalties for offences under the Regulations are a maximum period of imprisonment of three months and/or a maximum fine not exceeding £5,000 on conviction.

Unfair Terms in Consumer Contracts Regulations 1999

These Regulations replaced the previous 1994 Act which implemented a 1993 EU Directive on Unfair Terms in Consumer Contracts and supplement the statutory restrictions on the use of exemption clauses contained in the Unfair Contract Terms Act 1977. There is some overlap between the 1977 Act and the Regulations and similarity between the test of reasonableness within the Act and the test of fairness in the Regulations. However, there are important differences between the two, illustrated in Table 3.3.1.

For the application of the Regulations, a consumer is defined as a natural person who is acting for the purposes outside his trade, business or profession. A business includes a trade or a profession, or any government department and local and public authorities.

Contracts excluded from the scope of the Regulations are those relating to :

* employment;
* succession rights;
* family law rights;
* the incorporation or organisation of companies or partnerships.

Also excluded are terms which have been incorporated to comply with or reflect statutory or regulatory provisions of the UK or the provisions or principles of international conventions to which either the UK or the EU is a party.

Schedule 3 of the Regulations sets out an indicative non-exhaustive list of terms which may be regarded as unfair. Terms which define the main subject matter of the contract or concern the adequacy of the price of the goods or services are not subject to an assessment of fairness provided that they are in plain and intelligible language.

Where there is any doubt about the meaning of a term, the interpretation which is most favourable to the consumer must prevail.

The Unfair Terms in Consumer Contracts (Amendment) Regulations 2001 have also added references to external regulatory bodies ie the Financial Services Authority.

Exclusion of liability

Sometimes referred to as an exemption clause, an exclusion clause in a contract is one which is designed to exclude, or cancel out, the liability to damages (civil liability) to which one party to the contract would otherwise be liable.

Up to 1973, all liability for almost any breach of contract could be excluded, following the logic that the buyer of the goods was deemed to have agreed to the conditions excluding liability by buying the goods. In practical terms, if

Table 3.3.1 - Comparison of the Unfair Contract Terms Act 1977 and Consumer Contracts Regulations 1999

Unfair Contract Terms Act 1977	Unfair Terms in Consumer Contracts Regulations 1999
Mainly exemption clauses	All unfair terms
Business and consumer contracts	Only consumer contracts
Negotiated and non-negotiated contracts	Only non-negotiated contracts
Exemptions in contracts and notices	Only terms in consumer contracts
Exemptions are either automatically void or rendered void if unreasonable	Unfair terms are rendered voidable
Individual right of civil action	Individual right of civil action and administrative control by the D-G of Fair Trading, who may seek an injunction to prevent the continued general use of an unfair term

he did not agree to the conditions that were imposed on him, he did not get the goods. The more recent Acts have developed a number of rules to minimise the effect of exclusion clauses, but the courts have always been aware of their unfairness. There is a body of case law where the exclusion clauses in contracts were held to be unenforceable or void.

Exclusion clauses in sale of goods

The following rules apply to contracts for the Sale of Goods and no others (by virtue of the Unfair Contract Terms Act 1977).

*   S12 (which states that the seller must have the right to sell) cannot be excluded in any contract of sale.
*   S13-15 cannot be excluded in a consumer sale, but can be excluded in a non-consumer sale if the court thinks that the exclusion is reasonable.

A consumer sale is :

*   one made by a seller in the course of a business;
    sale of goods ordinarily bought for private use or consumption;
    sale to a buyer who does not buy the goods for resale in a business, or make it look as if he is buying the goods for such a resale.

A private sale is a sale by one individual to another, where neither person is in business or where only the buyer is a business. S14 of the Sale of Goods Act does not apply to private sales. There is no implied condition as to quality, although an express term as to quality will be effective and may be a warranty, condition or innominate term according to the court's construction of the contract. If there is no express term, a buyer may be able to rely on a misrepresentation made by the seller. Other statutory implied terms do apply to private sales but can be excluded if the exclusion clause is reasonable.

Effect of guarantee periods

A guarantee period may be construed as an exclusion clause in the sense that the seller is stating that he will not be responsible for the goods after the period has expired. In a consumer sale, such a clause is void. The goods must serve their intended purpose for a reasonable period of time.

However, it may be costly to prove that the goods should have served their purpose for longer than they did and will involve calling outside experts. In the case of goods which develop a major fault after some time (not within the first few days of service), it will be very difficult for the buyer to prove that they were defective when he received them. Defects which arise after the sale do not count, but a buyer is entitled to have all his money back, and need not accept a credit note, if the breach of condition occurred before he accepted the goods.

Unfair Contract Terms Act (1977)

This act was passed to extend the consumer protection provided in the area of Sale of Goods to services also. The Act contains a number of provisions designed to strengthen consumer rights of which the following two are the most important:

1. Section 2 states that no person can exclude liability for death or personal injury caused by negligence. It also provides that a person cannot exclude liability for damage to property caused by negligence unless the court thinks that it is reasonable.
2. Section 3 provides that if one party contracts as consumer or on the other party's standard terms of business, the other party cannot claim by virtue of a term of the contract :
3. to exclude liability for his own breach of contract; or
4. to be entitle to perform the contract in a way totally different from that expected; or
5. to render no performance at all, unless the court thinks that the terms in the contract are reasonable.

Non-application of The Unfair Terms Act 1977 to international sales

International Supply contracts are exempted from the Act's provisions so that parties to such contracts must rely on the common law rules alone.

The Act defines an international supply contract as a contract for sale of the goods, or a contract under which the ownership of goods otherwise passes and which is made by parties whose places of business are in the territories of different states (the Channel Islands and the Isle of Man are treated as different states from the UK).

The contract must also satisfy one or more of the following criteria:

*   contract goods are being carried or will be carried from the territory of one state to that of another; or
*   the acts constituting the offer and acceptance have been done in the territories of different states; or
*   the contract provides for the goods to be delivered to the territory of a state other than that within whose territory the acts of offer and acceptance were done.

Under this definition, the Act would apply where a company in the UK buys goods from a UK seller with the intention of reselling them to a foreign buyer. The Act would not apply where the UK company buying the goods is an agent of a foreign buyer and either or both of the first and third criteria above are satisfied.

A very important consequence of this for UK exporters is that the conditions implied by S12-15 of the Sale of Goods Act 1979 in all contracts of sale can be excluded by appropriately worded exclusion clauses where the contract is an international supply contract.

Supply of goods to consumer regulations 2002

The above legislation has made a number of small amendments to The Sale of Goods Act 1979 particularly relating to the situations where the buyer also deals as consumer and where transferees are involved in the process. It has also added additional implied terms in relation to public statement not being the seller's responsibility.

The regulations have also made minor amendments to Section 9 of the Supply of Goods and Services Act 1982 , The Supply Of Goods (Implied Terms) Act 1973 and the Unfair Contract Terms Act 1977 particularly in relation to consumer guarantees.

The law in practice in sale of goods in international trade

Effect of trade custom

If in the custom of a particular trade, or in an established course of dealing where many transactions have taken place, title passes at a different time from that laid down by the Sale of Goods Act 1979, the time of passing of title laid down by the custom will prevail.

Although widely used in international trade, Incoterms have not been recognised as the custom in the trade by the courts, and if the parties wish to use them they must expressly include them in their contract using the words *'This contract is subject to Incoterms 2000 CIF Terms'*, for example.

The price of the goods

Of course, the price is the single most important term of a contract for the sale of goods, and will be agreed normally by the parties at the time of sale. However, the Act does provide for the situation where the price is not agreed. S8 provides that the price may be:

- Fixed by the contract (the usual method).
- Left to be fixed in the future in a manner provided by the contact (e.g 'at a price to be determined by an independent valuer').
- Determined by a course of dealing between the parties (ie the price established in previous transactions for the same goods applies now and in the future unless the parties agree otherwise).

Failure to carry out agreed valuation

S9 of the Sale of Goods Act 1979 provides that if the parties to the contract have agreed to fix the price by independent valuation, but no such valuation is in fact made, the buyer must pay a reasonable price for those goods if all or part of them have been delivered to the buyer, and he has appropriated them to his use. If either party was at fault that the valuation was not made (eg if the seller refused access to the valuer), the party at fault must compensate the other party for any loss he suffers as a result.

Acceptance and rejection of the goods

Acceptance is used in sale of goods law in a technical rather than a colloquial sense, in that acceptance of goods under the Sale of Goods Act (1979) only occurs in certain carefully defined cases and has an important legal effect.
   Acceptance occurs when the buyer:

- Intimates to the buyer that he has accepted the good.
- Does any act inconsistent with the seller's ownership of the goods.
- Keeps the goods for more than a reasonable time, without informing the seller he has rejected them.

Intimation of acceptance

Plainly, 'intimation of acceptance' could occur in a variety of circumstances. A discussion of the goods with the seller after examination without a clear statement of rejection would suffice. If the buyer retakes possession of the goods after a repair, he has certainly accepted them.

Acts inconsistent with the seller's ownership

The resale of the goods or pledging them as security to a third party are clearly acts inconsistent with the seller's ownership. Forwarding the goods to a second buyer would also qualify as acceptance.

Keeping the goods for more than a reasonable time

It seems common sense that if a buyer keeps the goods for more than a reasonable time, he is deemed to have accepted them. However, the issue is more complex than it at first appears.

Under Ss.34-35 of the Sale of Goods Act (1979), the buyer is given an absolute right to examine the goods before acceptance. But the buyer must have a fair opportunity to examine them, not just an opportunity to examine the goods in very difficult circumstances. For example, he would not be expected to examine them fully in a warehouse at the docks if they were inside crates because it would be very costly to open all the crates at the docks, examine the goods, and then repack them.

Acceptance is inevitably extended, if the parties have expressly agreed to there being no inspection at all by a buyer because he has resold the goods and does not intend to use them himself; in these circumstances examination will be postponed until the goods reach the ultimate buyer.

Effect of acceptance

Like the legal concept itself, the effect of acceptance is also technical. Acceptance reduces breaches of condition to breaches of warranty, thus entitling the buyer only to damages, and depriving him of the right to reject.

Rejection of the goods

The circumstances where the buyer has the right of rejection are:

- Where there has been a breach of a condition of the contract of sale, either a condition agreed expressly by the parties, or one of the implied conditions under the Sale of Goods Act 1979 (where applicable).
- Where there has been late delivery.
- Where there has been delivery of the wrong quantity. Section 30 of the Act enables the buyer to either accept or reject what the seller tenders to him, or to accept that part which corresponds with the contract and reject the rest. (If he accepts more or less than he ordered he must pay at the contract rate).

Rejection of instalment deliveries

A frequent problem in export arises where a buyer orders goods to be delivered by instalments, or if the seller starts delivering by instalments, and some of the instalments are faulty or do not correspond with the contract in some other way.

The rules in the Act are:

- No buyer is bound to accept delivery by instalments unless provided for in the contract.
- If the buyer accepts instalments where they have not been previously agreed, he has not accepted them in law but he has waived late delivery

of the rest of the contract goods. Unless the seller has given consideration for the buyer's promise to accept instalment delivery, he has not varied the contract. The buyer can insist on delivery on any future date so long as he gives the seller reasonable notice of the new date of delivery.

- If delivery by instalments is agreed at the outset, it must be decided whether the contract is one contract for all the goods ordered, or whether each instalment is a separate contract.
- If there is a series of separate contracts, the deliveries are not interrelated and there is no special problem.
- Where there is one overall contract, the Act offers no definitive solution to the problem which arises if instalments are delivered which do not conform to contract. Whether the breach is serious enough for the innocent party to repudiate the contract will depend upon the facts.

The rights of the unpaid seller

The rights of a seller who has sold goods for which he has not been paid are clearly stipulated by S38-48 of the Sale of Goods Act 1979.

The seller's lien

A lien is the right to hold on to goods until some charge or debt due on those goods has been paid. A seller's lien on goods arises where the seller is still in possession of the goods and the money outstanding is immediately due. Therefore, if the seller has given the buyer time to pay in the original contract and that time has not yet expired, the seller has no lien.

It is not a necessary condition that the buyer should be insolvent before the seller exercise his right of lien, but if the seller learns that that the buyer has become insolvent and he still has possession of the goods, he may exercise the power of lien [S.41 (1) (c) of the Act]. The power of lien is merely a power to hold on to the goods until payment. The seller may not resell the goods unless he can do so under his power of resale (see below).

The lien is lost if:

- The buyer or his agent gets possession of the goods with the seller's consent; or
- The goods are delivered to a carrier, who is not the seller's or buyer's agent, for transmission to the buyer without reserving title; or
- If the seller waives his right (eg by assenting to a resale before payment); or
- The buyer uses a bill of lading unlawfully in his possession to resell the goods to an innocent third party who gives valuable consideration for the bill.

Stoppage in transit

If the seller can show that the buyer is insolvent, he can exercise the right to reclaim the goods, and have them returned to him, while they are 'in transit'.

Transit is a legal concept, and means that the goods have left the possession of the seller, and are not yet in the possession of the buyer – ie they are currently in the hands of an independent carrier. The transit ceases when the goods are 'delivered' to the buyer or someone authorised to take delivery on his behalf.

When properly exercised, the right of stoppage returns physical possession of the goods to the seller and title also if it had passed to the buyer. If the seller exercises his right of re-sale, the buyer under the re-sale gets good title.

The seller exercises his power of stoppage by notifying the carrier who must then deliver the goods, at the seller's expense, to a place appointed by the seller.

The right of stoppage in transit is lost if:

• The seller issues his stoppage instructions after the Bill of lading has been sold by the buyer to an innocent third party in the case of goods being shipped by sea;
• The seller assents to a sub-sale and the sub-sale has been effected.

Right of re-sale

After exercising the rights of lien or stoppage in transit the seller will want to re-sell the goods as quickly as possible. S48 of the Act authorises the seller to re-sell the goods if:

• He reserved the right to do so in the original contract in the event of the buyer defaulting;
• The goods are perishable;
• The seller has notified the buyer of his intention to re-sell and the buyer has not tendered the price in a reasonable time.

The effect of re-sale, carried out in accordance with the Act, is to rescind the seller's contract with the buyer, but to preserve the seller's right to damages from the buyer.

The Romalpa clause

The rights of the unpaid seller described above were laid down in the Sale of Goods Act and are largely unchanged since 1893. A more recent and more powerful weapon available to sellers is the Romalpa Clause which the seller may put into his sale contracts reserving title to his goods until they are paid for. The effect of such clauses is to place the seller at the top of the list of creditors in the event of the insolvency of the buyer. In this way, the seller's unpaid debt will take precedence over the secured loans of banks and other financial institutions in liquidation proceedings.

A clause reserving title to goods in their raw state does not have to be registered and means that the goods are not part of the buyer's property in insolvency. However, a clause which purports to preserve title to goods when mixed with other goods in a manufacturing process will only be effective when the seller's goods are still identifiable and can be returned to their original nature.

Remedies of the seller

An action for non-acceptance

If a buyer refuses to take delivery for no valid reason, the seller may bring an action for non-acceptance of the goods. The measure of damages is the estimated loss directly and naturally arising from the buyer's breach of contract.

If there is an available market damages will be the difference between the market price and the agreed contract price. However, the seller has a duty to mitigate his loss and, if he deliberately sells the goods for less than he could reasonably be expected to do, or even if he does so negligently, his damages will be reduced by the amount he has thereby lost.

An action for the price

The proper remedy where title to the goods has passed and the buyer has accepted delivery but has not paid for the goods is an action for the full price. There is no question of the seller reselling the goods because they are no longer in his possession.

If the buyer has become insolvent, the seller will simply have to join the queue of his unsecured creditors, unless a Romalpa Clause was included in the sale contract.

Choice of actions

If title has passed but the buyer refuses to take delivery the seller can choose either:

- To sue for the price which does not require the buyer to have taken delivery if title has passed; or
- To sue for damages for non-acceptance.

In practical terms, however, there is often no point in suing the buyer because he either hasn't got the money or, in the export field, is in a country where suing him would be such a costly, complex and uncertain business that it is not worth the effort.

Of course, this is the reason why English exporters use confirming houses when dealing with buyers in such countries, or, in appropriate cases, secure credit insurance, such as ECGD.

Remedies of the buyer

Damages for non-delivery

This is the converse of the seller's action for non-acceptance. The buyer is quite willing to accept the goods; his complaint is that they have not been delivered.

His remedies are very similar to seller's for non-acceptance – damages calculated on the basis of the difference between the contract and the market price.

Generally, the courts do not award a buyer loss of profit on a resale, so long as there is a plentiful supply of the goods on the market. Damages will cover the buyer's cost of getting alternative goods to fulfil his resale contracts in most cases.

If the seller announces in advance his intention not to deliver, the buyer can sue immediately and the court will have to estimate the market price at the time the goods should have been delivered in order to calculate damages.

If the seller is the only supplier, or if the goods are to a specification which is hard to come by elsewhere, the buyer can claim not only his lost profit on his resale, but also any damages and costs claimed by the people who were buying from him for breach of his contract with them.

Specific performance for non-delivery

Wherever possible the courts will award damages only, but the buyer can obtain specific performance if the item is unique or very hard to obtain elsewhere. In practice, it may be awarded for the purchase of capital equipment (such as a ship) which is unique.

Action for return of buyer's money

S54 of the Sale of Goods Act 1979 gives the buyer a statutory right to sue for the return of his money if he has paid for goods that he has not received.

Action for non-compliance with contract

The following actions are open to the buyer in the event of the seller's non-compliance with the contract:

- If the seller delivers the goods late, and a specific delivery date has been agreed, the buyer can reject the goods altogether.
- If there is no set delivery date, the buyer may reject the goods if they are not delivered in a reasonable time.
- If the buyer decides not to reject for late delivery, but to sue instead for damages, the amount of damages will be the difference between the market price at the date of delivery and the market price when the goods should have been delivered, plus any other which he has suffered which the seller ought reasonably to have foreseen.

Action for damages for breach of S13-15 of the Act, or rejection of the goods for such breaches if the buyer has not accepted them. (The buyer can elect to keep the goods and sue for damages even where he has not accepted them. The buyer can claim more than repair costs of the goods if the defects in them have caused other damage including injuries).

Conflict of laws

In negotiation with an overseas customer, the prudent exporter will wish to ensure that there is complete clarity as to the respective responsibilities and obligations of both parties. To that end, he stipulates that his acceptance of the buyer's order is 'subject to our conditions of sale'.

The exporter's legal position is as follows:

- The exporter's catalogue, price list, quotation, etc. represent 'an invitation to treat', unless stated to be a firm offer.
- The buyer's order is 'an offer to conclude a contract of sale' unless it is made as an unconditional acceptance of the seller's offer.
- The seller's unconditional acceptance of the order constitutes a binding contract between the parties.
- If the seller's acknowledgement is qualified (eg stated as 'subject to our conditions of sale'), the buyer's offer is rejected and replaced by a counter offer from the seller.
- For absolute legal safety the seller would insist that the buyer sends an unqualified confirmation before the order is put in hand.
- In practice where the two parties are on regular trading terms and familiar with their rights and duties under these terms, this final safeguard is not normally necessary.

For the avoidance of any legal ambiguity, exporters often include the following general terms in their 'conditions of sale', together with any others peculiar to their particular industry or products:

- Every contract is subject to the seller's conditions of sale.
- The seller retains the property in the sold goods until he receives payment in full.
- The seller is entitled to add costs to his quoted price equivalent to any variations between date of quotation and date of delivery.
- All warranties, guarantees and conditions other than those stated by the seller shall be expressly excluded.
- The contract of sale shall be governed by the law of England, and, in the event of disputes arising out of or in connection with the contract, they shall all be submitted to the arbitration and rules of the London Court of Arbitration.

Such clauses are often found on the reverse of lettered correspondence sheets, pro-forma invoices, order acceptances, etc., and should always be brought to the attention of the buyer.

Of course, the buyer's standard conditions of purchase are also frequently found on the reverse of his lettered correspondence, pro-forma orders, etc. which conflict with the seller's standard conditions of sale. In this 'battle of the forms' the terms which are cited on the final document in the chain of correspondence which receives unqualified acceptance from the other party will prevail. In order to achieve a compromise, the parties may have to enter into a contract drafted for transactions between them which overrides both parties' standard conditions of sale.

Jurisdiction

The exporter will want to know when and how English courts will assume jurisdiction in civil matters where the defendant is not normally resident in this country. There are three sets of rules in English law which govern this question:

The Civil Jurisdiction and Judgement Acts 1982 where the proposed defendant is domiciled in a member state of the European Union (EU).

English Common Law rules which apply where the proposed defendant is not domiciled in a member state of the EU or a member state of the European Free Trade Area (EFTA).

Rules in the Civil Jurisdictions and Judgement Act 1991 where the proposed defendant is domiciled in an EFTA member state.

The admiralty jurisdiction of the English courts is unaffected by the EU rules or the EFTA rules.

The Civil Jurisdiction and Judgements Act 1982

This statute enacts the rule of the Brussels Convention 1968 which aims to promote 'a free movement of judgements' between EU states. It applies to civil and commercial matters with the important exceptions for international traders of admiralty, bankruptcy, revenues, customs and arbitration proceedings.

The Convention provides for the parties to make an express choice of jurisdiction which must be evidenced in writing or in a form which accords with practices in that branch of international trade or commerce of which the parties were, or ought to have been, aware. Failing choice of jurisdiction, the following rules apply:

- So far as individuals or companies domiciled in the EU are concerned, the general rule is that the state in which the defendant is domiciled has jurisdiction. (The nationality of the defendant is irrelevant).
- The general rule is qualified for issues of specific kinds: In contract matters the courts of the place of performance of the contractual obligation which has been breached can also accept jurisdiction. The plaintiff can choose.
- In tort matters, the plaintiff may alternatively choose the courts of the place where the negligence occurred or the place where the resulting damage occurred.
- In disputes arising out of the operation of the branch or agency of a defendant company, the plaintiff may choose the place in which the branch or agency is situated as an alternative jurisdiction. (For these purposes an agent who solicits orders but does not make contracts on behalf of the company is not included).
- In insurance matters, the plaintiff can choose either the courts of the place of domicile of the insurer or the courts of the place where the policy holder is domiciled.
- If proceedings involving the same cause of action between the same parties are pending in the courts of more than one member state, the rule is 'first come first served'. The court in which proceedings were issued last in time must stay the proceedings until the court of the state in which proceedings were issued first has either accepted or rejected jurisdiction.
- A judgement of a court of a member state is recognised by the courts of all member states without any special procedures being required. Such judgements cannot be reviewed by the courts of another member state but are not precedents for them. There is an exception for judgements which are contrary to public policy in the state where recognition is sought.
- Where appropriate, appeals can be made to the European Court of Justice (EUJ); decisions of the EUJ are binding precedents in all member states. A judgement given in one member state can easily be enforced in another member state.

- A company is domiciled in the member state in which it was incorporated or formed under the law of that state and has its registered office or some other official address in that state or its central management and control is exercised in that state. A company may therefore have a 'seat' in more than one state.

The English Common Law rules

These rules apply when a writ is served on a defendant who is present or has presence within England and Wales or where the claim exhibits such connections with England and Wales as are defined in Order 11 of the Rules of the Supreme Court and the court has exercised its discretion in favour of permitting such service on a defendant outside the jurisdiction.

The court has jurisdiction to hear a case in the following circumstances:

A case brought by anyone in the world, as long as the defendant was within the jurisdiction, however fleetingly, at the time of the service of the writ. The dispute need have no connection with the jurisdiction and neither the plaintiff nor the defendant need be domiciled in England or Wales. The action may be stayed, however, by the court deciding that the courts of another state are a more appropriate forum for the case to be heard.

The court will hear the case if the defendant accepts the jurisdiction of the English courts, even though the defendant remains outside the jurisdiction. Where the defendant remains outside the jurisdiction and does not accept the jurisdiction of the English courts, Order 11 of the Supreme Court allows the English courts to hear the case by ordering a writ to be served outside the jurisdiction in the following situations:

- if the defendant is ordinarily resident in England;
- if the case concerns a contract which was made in England by the defendant himself or by an agent on his behalf, or where the contract is covered by English law;
- if the case concerns a breach of contract which took place in England, whether or not the contract was made in England;
- if the case concerns a tort committed in England or where the damages resulting occurred ion England;
- if the purpose of the case is to claim an injunction to stop the defendant from doing something within the jurisdiction;
- if the case has been brought against by another person in the country and the person it is now sought to serve is a necessary third party;
- if the claim is under the carriage by air or road legislation.

In such cases, English court officials do not have to serve a writ personally on a defendant in a foreign country but public notice is given that the writ has been issued.

The English courts will not act in vain, and obvious consideration in deciding whether or not to allow the writ to be served are whether the defendant has any assets in England against which any judgement could be enforced, or whether the English courts have any arrangement with the courts of the state in which the defendant is normally resident regarding mutual enforcement of judgements.

Other relevant considerations will be whether the case can be fairly tried and that any evidence needed can be obtained by the court.

The Civil Jurisdiction and Judgements Act 1991

The Act ratified and gave the force of law in the UK to the Lugano Convention on the Jurisdiction and Enforcement of Judgements in Civil and Commercial Matters 1988,. The aim of the Convention is to extend the 'free movement of judgements' in Europe by extending the scheme in the Brussels Convention to EFTA member states. The effect of the Act is to amend the Civil Jurisdiction and Judgements Act 1982 so that its rules apply whenever an action started in an EU or EFTA state and the defendant is domiciled is domiciled in an EFTA or EU state.

The Admiralty jurisdiction of the English courts

Where the claim arises out of a collision at sea, the ship in question, or any other ship owned by the same person or company, can be arrested in British Territorial Waters, and if the defendant will not submit himself voluntarily to the court's jurisdiction, it can be sold and proceeds of sale used to pay the debts in question. The admiralty jurisdiction will only be needed where the defendant is not domiciled with an EU or EFTA state or is so domiciled but has left with all his assets to a place outside EU/EFTA jurisdiction.

Note that this procedure is only available for claims against the owner of a ship for collisions at sea; an exporter cannot proceed in this way against ship owners who happen not to have paid for goods they have purchased.

Sovereign immunity as a defence

The State Immunity Act 1978 has greatly limited the defence of claiming sovereign immunity which had been much abused by the nationalised industries of foreign states. A state now has immunity only in its full official capacity. This immunity does not extend to commercial transactions made between the government of that state and companies in England and Wales. Ships owned by the state are equally liable to seizure by arrest as privately owned ships.

Regarding enforcement, assets owned by that state and used for commercial purposes are liable to seizure. Only official assets used for diplomatic purposes are immune.

Addressing a broken contract with an overseas buyer

The following practical issues commonly arise:

- It is difficult and time-consuming for an exporter to sue the buyer in a foreign country. It may be so difficult that it is not worth bothering.
- There will be little point in suing in the English courts if the buyer has no assets in England and is not resident there.
- If the buyer is a foreign government, it may plead Sovereign Immunity, even before an English court.
- If these considerations do not apply, or if the exporter feels that the sum of money involved is so great that he must proceed, he must first study the following questions:
  - which court has jurisdiction to hear the case?
  - which Law will that court apply when it hears the case?

The question of jurisdiction has already been discussed. The point at issue here is that, just because English law applies to the contract, it does not necessarily follow that the case will be heard in England. Conversely, the fact that foreign law applies does not prevent English courts from hearing the case if they have jurisdiction to do so.

Which law applies?

English courts can, and frequently do, decide contractual disputes on principles of foreign law. The law governing contracts entered into after 1 April 1991 is governed by the Rome Convention which harmonises the rules on the subject throughout the EU. The Convention was given the force of law in the UK by the Contracts (Applicable Law) Act 1991.

The rules of the convention are broadly similar to the English common law rules. Where the convention applies, the contract is governed by the law chosen by the parties. The choice of law must be expressed or demonstrated with reasonable certainty by the terms of the contract or by the circumstances in which the contract was made. The parties may expressly or impliedly choose a different governing law for different parts of their contract.

Where no express or implied choice of law can be found, then the contract is governed by the law of the country with which it is most closely connected. In international sale of goods contracts, English courts frequently decide contractual disputes on principles of foreign law. In such cases, principles of foreign law must be proved as fact by expert witnesses who are usually lawyers from the relevant state.

The Contracts (Applicable Law) Act 1991 applies to disputes concerning contractual obligations where a decision must be made as to the law governing a contract that comes before the English courts, whether or not it has an EU connection. The law chosen as the law governing the contract may be that of a non-EU state.

The rules of the Rome Convention and the Act do not apply to the following types of case or issue before the court:

- Non-contractual obligations (eg actions in tort or trust law);
- Obligations arising under cheques, promissory notes, bills of exchange and other negotiable instruments (eg bills of lading) where the issue in dispute arises out of their negotiable character. (The Bills of Exchange Act 1882 governs the proper law where negotiable instruments are concerned);
- Arbitration agreements or choice of jurisdiction clauses;
- Questions of company law;
- The question of whether an agent is able to bind a principal (other aspects of agency contracts do fall within the convention);
- Matters of evidence and procedure (other than matters pertaining to limitation period) which are always governed by English law before an English court;
- Insurance contracts which cover risks situated within the territories of the EU member states; (Reinsurance contracts are always governed by the convention);
- Issues of the capacity of the parties to contract are governed by English law;
- Where the contract is a nullity (eg where the contract is void from the beginning due to an operative mistake).

Where the convention does apply, the parties may subsequently agree to change the governing law except where that would prejudice the rights of third parties affected by the contract or the validity of the contract itself.

The country of closest connection

In the absence of an express or implied choice of law, the court has to decide with which country the contract is most closely connected in order to determine the governing law. Events occurring after the contract is entered into are relevant in determining this question.

Without evidence to the contrary, there is a presumption that a contract is most closely connected with the country where the party who is to effect the performance which is characteristic of the contract has, at the time of conclusion of the contract, his habitual residence or, in the case of a company, its central administration. If the contract is entered into in the course of that party's trade or profession, its principal place of business will be the country of closest connection. Alternatively, if under the terms of the contract the performance is to be effected through a business other than the principal place of business, the country in which that other place of business is situated will determine the governing law.

In a sale contract, the 'characteristic performance' will be that act or acts for which payment is or will be due (ie delivery of the contract goods) so that the governing law will be the law of the place of business of the seller. In an agency contract, the characteristic performance is that of the agent.

Contracts of affreightment are guided by a special presumption, in place of the general presumption, that if the country in which the carrier has his place of business, at the time the contract is entered into, is also the place of loading or the place of discharge or the principal place of business of the consignor, then the contract is more closely connected with that country.

Finally, if the result of the application of a foreign law would be manifestly incompatible with the public policy of English law or EU law, then the English courts (like other courts of member states of the EU) can refuse to apply it, even if by the above rules it is the governing law. Moreover, where the effect of applying the governing law would prevent the application of international conventions to which the UK is signatory, then again it would not be applied and some other connected law would be applied in its place.

3.4

EU competition law

The European Economic Community came into being following the signing of the Treaty of Rome in 1957 by the, then six, member states of the European Coal & Steel Community with the aim of creating a common market in Europe and, by thus pooling their resources, preserving and strengthening peace and liberty. These members were: France, West Germany, Italy, Belgium, Netherlands and Luxembourg

The UK joined in 1972 with the passing of the European Communities Act of that year, together with Denmark and the Irish Republic

* In 1981: Greece
* In 1982: Spain & Portugal
* and in 1995: Sweden, Austria and Finland

to make a current European Union of 15 members.

An important development came in 1986 with the signing, by the then 12, of the Single European Act (SEA). The aim of the SEA was to eliminate the remaining barriers to the single internal market before the deadline of 31 December 1992. The establishment of the 'Four Freedoms' ie a free movement of :

* Goods
* Persons
* Services
* Capital

was achieved, in most areas, before the deadline.

The following articles of the Treaty of Rome were added by the SEA. The Treaty of European Union signed by the 12 at Maastricht in December 1991 should be distinguished from the SEA and was the next step towards full economic and political union involving in the economic sphere a single currency by 1999. By the same treaty the EEC was renamed the European Union (EU) in 1993.

The European Monetary Union duly came into being with effect from 1 January 1999, together with the European Central Bank (ECB) based in Frankfurt and the launch of the new euro currency was executed smoothly with 12 of the 15 EU members joining. Only Denmark, Sweden and the UK have held back from joining. Denmark and Sweden have both rejected the euro for the time-being through national referenda. There is no immediate prospect of the UK joining the Eurozone.

In December 2002, after intensive preparation and negotiation, 10 further countries were judged to have made sufficient progress towards harmonization with the EU and were invited to join on 1 May 2004. The 10 admission candidates were :

- The Czech Republic,
- Cyprus,
- Estonia,
- Hungary,
- Latvia,
- Lithuania,
- Malta,
- Poland,
- Slovakia and
- Slovenia

During the first nine months of 2003 a national referendum was held in each country. All 10 countries voted in favour of entry on the terms negotiated.

The Internal Market is defined in the Treaty of Rome as "an area without internal frontiers in which the free movement of goods, persons, services and capital is ensured."

To that end the completion of the internal market entails:

1. customs union which involves the prohibition between member states of customs duties on imports and exports and of all charges having equivalent effect and the adoption of a common customs tariff in their relations with non-EU countries;
2. the elimination of quantitative restrictions on imports and exports and all measures having equivalent effect;
3. states are required to adjust any State monopolies of a commercial character so as to ensure that no discrimination, regarding the conditions under which goods are procured and marketed, exists between nationals of member states;
4. states are prohibited from applying discriminatory taxation and from granting state aid which threatens or distorts competition.

Competition law consists of :

- EU Competition Law; principally Articles 81 and 82 of the Treaty of Rome.
- The English Common Law on contractual terms which restrain trade.
- The Fair Trading Act 1973.
- The Restrictive Trade Practices Act 1976.

- The Resale Prices Act 1976.
- The Competition Act 1980.
- The Competition Act 1998.

Just because a person is an exporter, he obviously cannot have better rights than anyone else, unless they are specifically provided for in legislation. Thus the exporter is prima facie just as subject to the legislation against anti-competitive practices as anyone else. Furthermore, he can only justify a restrictive practices agreement before the courts if a substantial volume of his business is export and likely to be affected if the restrictions he has agreed were not allowed.

But the exporter does have one very important concession in the Restrictive Practices legislation. Any agreement which contains restrictions which would otherwise be registrable is exempt from registration if the restrictions apply exclusively:

- To the supply of goods for export from the UK.
- To production or any process of manufacture outside the UK.
- To the acquisition of goods outside the UK for sale abroad.
- To any sales which take place wholly outside the UK (ie sales of goods purchased and sold abroad).

The only requirement regarding such agreements is that they be notified to the Director General of Fair Trading (but they do not have to be validated by the court). The exporter should study these exceptions carefully, because they may not cover all his trade. Thus although agreements governing the supply of goods by export from the UK are covered by the exemption, the acquisition of goods on the home market for export are not covered. Thus companies which buy up goods for resale abroad must comply with the domestic legislation. Further, even if the agreement is exempt, particulars of it must be furnished to the Director General.

Finally, if an exporter carries on some business in the home market and sells abroad as well, he should negotiate separate agreements - one for his export sales, which will simply need to be notified to the Director, and one for his home sales, which will have to be registered and validated by the court.

EU competition law is contained in Articles 81 and 82 of the Treaty of Rome and is administered and enforced by the European Commission which can impose fines and sanctions and has extensive investigatory powers. Decisions of the Commission can be challenged in the Court of First Instance of the European Courts of Justice (ECJ).

EU competition law has direct effect in the UK (and in other Member States) and operates in parallel to UK competition law (with the exception of the "Merger Regulation" examined below) so that both bodies of law may apply to an arrangement. Indeed the UK's national competition authorities may take action under UK provisions while EU action is pending providing such action does not prejudice the effectiveness of the full application of EU law should it be applied.

EU competition law is an "effects" based system, which is triggered by an arrangement's effect on competition, while the UK legislation tends to looks to the form of an arrangement regardless of its actual effect. However, The Competition Act 1998 has effectively adopted EU competition law by banning any anti-competitive agreement and outlawing abuses of a dominant market position. The Director General of Fair Trading is empowered to police this legislation and to impose stiff financial penalties of up to 10% of turnover.

EU competition law only applies to arrangements which "may affect trade between Member States". Consequently, a body of English law is necessary to cover arrangements which cannot affect trade between Member States.

Note the wording of ARTICLE 2 of the Treaty of Rome: "The Community shall progressively bring about the conditions which will of themselves ensure the most rational distribution of production at the highest possible level of productivity, while safeguarding continuity of employment and taking care not to provoke fundamental persistent disturbances in the economies of Member States." EU decisions on competition law must take this Article into account. It may become more important as the inevitable political tensions caused by the effect of the single market emerge in the future.

Article 81 of the Treaty of Rome

This Article is worded as follows:

1. The following shall be prohibited as incompatible with the common market: All agreements between undertakings, decisions by associations of undertakings and concerted practices which may affect trade between Member States and which have as their objects or effect the prevention, restriction or distortion of competition within the common market and in particular those which:
   o Directly or indirectly fix purchase or selling prices or any other trading conditions;
   o limit or control production, markets, technical development, or investment;
   o share markets or sources of supply;
   o apply dissimilar conditions to equivalent transactions with other trading parties, thereby placing them at a competitive disadvantage;
   o make the conclusion of contracts subject to acceptance by the other parties of supplementary obligations which by their nature or according to commercial usage, have no connection with the subject of such contracts.
2. Any agreements or decisions prohibited pursuant to this Article shall be automatically void.

3. The provisions of paragraph 1 may, however, be declared inapplicable in the case of
    ○ any agreement or category of agreements between undertakings;
    ○ any decision or category of decisions by associations of undertakings;
    ○ any concerted practice or category of concerted practices
4. which contributes to improving the production or distribution of goods or to promoting technical or economic progress, while allowing consumers a fair share of the resulting benefit and which does not:
    ○ Impose on the undertaking concerned restrictions which are not indispensable to the attainment of these objectives;
    ○ afford such undertaking the possibility of eliminating competition in respect of a substantial part of the products in question."

Art. 81(1) defines what is prohibited and a number of examples (a) to (e) are given.

Art.81(2) provides that any agreement or decision in breach of Art.81(1) is automatically void.

However, under Art.81(3), Art.81(1) may be declared inapplicable to agreements or decisions fulfilling a number of specified criteria.

Thus Art.81(1) provides a very broad base of liability subject to the possibility of exemption under Art.81(3).

The European Commission has the sole power to grant exemption under Art.81(3). To obtain exemption parties must "notify" their agreements or decisions to the Commission. Notification gives immunity from fines should the agreement or decision eventually be found to breach Art.81(1) and to be ineligible for exemption under Art.81(3). Notification cannot, however, prevent an agreement or decision from being void from its inception under Art.81(2). This could prove extremely expensive in lost expenditure. An agreement can be held partly void

Alternatively or in addition to notification parties can seek negative clearance from the Commission, ie a decision that their agreement or decision does not infringe Art.81(1) at all. It is common for parties to apply both for notification and negative clearance simultaneously. Both applications are made by completing and submitting the same form.

The combination of stiff penalties for breach and the breadth of Art.81(1) resulted in a heavy workload for the Commission and long delays. Delay had the tendency to deter business from entering into agreements beneficial to Community goals for fear of the consequences. The Commission tackled this problem by: (1) issuing "Notices" providing non-binding guidelines as to the kinds of agreements which do not breach Art.81(1), and (2) by enacting Regulations creating "Block Exemptions" on Art.81(3) grounds, and (3) issuing "comfort letters".

1. What is the field of application of Art.81(1)?
    Note the following points:
    1. Art.81(1) applies to agreements or decisions of associations or

concerted practices which are "vertical" arrangements (ie between manufacturer and dealer) as well as those which are "horizontal" arrangements (ie between manufacturer and manufacturer). The undertakings must, however, be independent of each other. An agreement between a parent and its subsidiary will not be a breach of Art.81(1) unless the subsidiary enjoys full independence of action; otherwise they are not in competition with one another.

2.   The rules in (a) above apply to the relationship of principal and agent so that an agent is not viewed as independent of its principal. The Commission will scrutinise the nature of a relationship in order to ascertain its true nature; the parties use of the term "agency" will not be conclusive.

3.   An undertaking or association of undertakings situated outside the EU may be liable under Art.81(1) provided that the agreement is implemented or partially implemented within the Community.

2.   What are the elements of an infringement of Art.81(1)?
There must be:

1.   An agreement between undertakings, or a decision by an association of undertakings or a concerted practice, which may affect trade between Member States, and which must have as its object or effect the prevention, restriction or distortion of competition within the common market.

2.   Agreements between undertakings, decisions by associations of undertakings and concerted practices.

▪   *"Agreements between undertakings"*
"Undertakings" is not defined but has been interpreted widely by the ECJ as including any legal or natural person engaged in some form of economic or commercial activity whether the activity is pursued with a view to profit or not. A local authority acting commercially is acting as an undertaking but when acting executively in a governmental capacity it is not acting as an undertaking. Such "Agreements" include non-binding "gentleman's agreements".

▪   *"Decisions by associations of undertakings"*
This applies to decisions of trade associations which may co-ordinate behaviour amongst undertakings without any need for actual agreement. A "decision" need not be a binding decision of an association. A recommendation from an association to its members is considered to be a decision of an association of undertakings. Members of an association complying with an offending decision are liable for fines if they comply whether willingly or unwillingly. Of course the association will also be liable.

▪   *"Concerted practices"*
A concerted practice was defined in Imperial Chemical Industries Ltd. v Commission (1969) as "a form of co-operation between

undertakings which, without having reached the stage where an agreement properly so called has been concluded, knowingly substitutes practical co-operation between them for the risks of competition". A concerted practice does not require a concerted plan. It is sufficient that each party should have informed the other of the attitude they intended to take so that each could regulate his conduct safe in the knowledge that his competitors would act in the same way. Such practices are clearly harder to prove than agreements or decisions of associations.

- *The 'de-minimis' rule*
  In *Volk v Etablissements Vervaecke sprl* (1969) the ECJ ruled that in order to come within Art.81(1) competition must be affected to a noticeable extent; there must be a sufficient degree of harmfulness. This involves consideration of the market for the product in question and the position of the parties to the agreement in that market. Thus even agreements which have as their object the prevention, restriction or distortion of trade entail some investigation of their potential or actual effect. If the agreement is "de-minimis" then it will not be caught under Art.81(1) no matter how blatantly anti-competitive it is. The Commission has issued a *Notice on Agrements of Minor Importance (1982)* which states that as a general rule agreements between undertakings engaged in the production and distribution of goods and services which do not represent more than 5% of the total market for such goods and services in the EU area affected by the agreement, and with an aggregate turnover of no more than 200 million EUROs, will not fall within Art.81(1). If, contrary to the Notice, an agreement within the parameters of the Notice is found not to be "de-minimis" and in breach of Art.81(1) then the parties will not be fined. The agreement will nevertheless be void from its inception effect.

3. Art.81(1) (a) to (e), agreements capable of preventing, restricting or distorting competition, specifically referred to.
   (a) to (e) comprise a non-exhaustive list of examples of the type of agreements LIKELY to infringe Art.81(1). Provided that the other elements of Art.81(1) are infringed by an agreement, and the agreement is not "de minimis", if it falls within (a) to (e) then it is very likely that the agreement is void.
   From the cases it is possible to discern that the Commission's and the ECJ's approach is that restrictions are either inexcusable or excusable. Inexcusable restrictions always breach Art.81(1) and are not exempt under Art.81(3). Excusable restrictions either (i) breach Art.81(1) but are exempt under Art.81(3), or (ii) do not breach Art.81(1).

4. Agreements which directly or indirectly fix purchase or selling prices or other trading conditions.

5. Price fixing

This is almost always inexcusable.
6. Minimum price agreements
   These are regarded in the same light as price fixing.
7. Maximum price agreements
   Recommended maximum prices do not breach Art.81(1) since they do not affect competition.
8. Other trading conditions
   These fall under two heads: (a) agreements partitioning markets on national lines (dealt with above) which will always breach Art.81(1); and (b) Franchise agreements (Franchising in distribution and services is the subject of a block exemption under Art.81(3) leaving only a few cases as relevant only to franchise agreements in manufacturing). In such cases it has been upheld that selective distribution systems will not breach Art.81(1) provided that franchisees are chosen on the basis of objective criteria of a qualitative nature relating to the technical qualifications of the franchisees staff and suitability of his premises and that such conditions are laid down uniformly and not applied in a discriminatory manner. Such qualitative criteria must not go beyond what is necessary to protect the franchisees intellectual property, name or trade mark.

Art.81(1)(b) "Agreements which control production, markets, technical developments or investments"

These are usually horizontal agreements and are always in breach of Art.81(1) but block exemptions operate where the agreement supplements an agreement on specialisation or research and development.

Art.81(1)(c) "Agreements to share markets or sources of supply" These are horizontal agreements and are always in breach of Art.81(1).

Art.81(1)(d) "Agreements which apply dissimilar conditions to equivalent transactions with other trading parties, thereby placing them at a competitive disadvantage". These will only breach Art.81(1) if the transactions in question are "equivalent". Thus an agreement to charge different prices to different customers would not breach Art.81(1) if the prices genuinely reflected different (eg transport) costs; it would if they were based on what the market would bear. Similarly, discounts for bulk purchases, will not breach Art.81(1) if they genuinely reflect cost savings, whilst "loyalty rebates" which are tied to the volume of business transacted are a breach of the Art.81(1).

Art.81(1)(e) "Agreements which make the conclusion of contracts subject to acceptance by other parties of supplementary obligations which, by their nature and/or according to commercial usage, have no connection with the subject matter of such contracts". These always breach Art.81(1) but exemptions are made under Art.81(3). If a clause has sufficient connection with the subject matter of the contract then the clause is not one to which Art.81(1)(e) refers; though it may still be held to breach Art.81(1). Sufficient connection is a matter of judgement. Consider the following examples:

Agreements within (a) to (e) which nevertheless are not found to breach Art.81(1) point to the use of the "rule of reason" by the Commission and the ECJ at the initial stage of considering whether an agreement infringes Art.81(1) . The rule of reason applied in this context allows those restrictions which constitute an essential element of the agreement, without which the agreement would be emptied of its substance, and which pose no real threat to competition or to the functioning of the common market. There must be some benefit to the common market in the agreement to justify its anti-competitive aspect.

Of course Art.81(3) enshrines the rule of reason in the Article itself at the exemption stage of deliberation. However, the existence of Art.81(3) means that the scope of the rule of reason in Art.81(1) deliberations is necessarily constricted and policy dependant.

Art.81(3): Exemption

Only the Commission can grant exemptions. The phrase "or category" allows the Commission to make block exemptions. An agreement MUST be notified if it is to be exempted. Therefore an agreement which is not notified risks losing the possibility of exemption. When the Commission decides that a particular agreement should be exempted it issues a Decision to that effect. The parties concerned must be given an opportunity to be heard and the Commission will also hear people with a "sufficient interest". The Decision must be published in the "Official Journal". Appeal is to the Court of First Instance of the ECJ.

In order to gain exemption under Art.81(3) the agreement or decision must satisfy four criteria:

9. It must "contribute to improving the production or distribution of goods or to promoting technical or economic progress"
   The agreement as a whole must show positive benefits of the above kind and one or more of the above kinds of benefit must be shown.

10. "Production"
    Benefits in production are most likely to accrue from specialisation agreements. These are horizontal agreements. Specialisation enables each party to concentrate its efforts on what it can do most efficiently and to achieve the benefits of economies of scale. These are now subject to block exemption.

11. . "Distribution"
    Benefits in distribution occur mainly through vertical agreements in the form of exclusive supply or dealership or distribution agreements. The benefits result from the streamlining of the distribution process and

concentration of activity on the part of the distributor, whether it be in the provision of publicity, technical expertise, after sales service or simply the maintenance of adequate stocks. Students should note that exclusive distribution agreements are subject to block exemption.

12. "Technical progress"

This benefit is most likely to result from specialisation agreements, particularly those concerned with research and development. Research and development agreements are subject to block exemption.

13. "Economic progress"

All the other heads are covered by this head. However, it serves as a catch all to cover beneficial arrangements not covered by (a) to (c).

14. "While allowing consumers a fair share in the resulting benefit"

Provided that there is sufficient inter-brand competition ie from other producers in the relevant market the improvements achieved will inevitably be passed on to the consumer either in the form of a better product, or a better service, or greater availability of supplies or a lower price. If the benefits are not passed on to consumers the parties risk losing market share to their competitors. The Commission will therefore be interested in the parties market share.

15. The agreement must not "impose on the undertakings concerned restrictions which are not indispensable to the attainment of these objectives".

This is the proportionality principle enshrined expressly within Art.81(3). (See Lesson 6.) The Commission will examine each offending clause in an agreement, to see if it is necessary, and no more than is necessary, to the objectives of the agreement as a whole. Where the economic benefits of an arrangement are great even a clause preventing parallel imports may be justified. Price fixing will rarely be indispensable. If without the restriction the beneficial objectives of the agreement could not be obtained or would only partially be obtained then the restriction is proportionate and should be exempted under Art.81(3).

16. The agreement must not "afford such undertakings the possibility of eliminating competition in respect of a substantial part of the products in question".

In all the cases in which exemption has been granted, the parties have been subject to a substantial inter-brand competition whether from producers inside the EU or from outside.

17. Block Exemptions

Block exemptions are Regulations made by the Commission to solve the twin problems of uncertainty (for business people) and excessive work-load (for itself). If parties tailor their arrangements to fit one of the block exemptions then there is no need to "notify". Because the block exemptions are Regulations they can be applied in national courts. A complainant can bring an action in a national court and that court can decide whether the arrangement complained of is within a block exemption or not. This reduces the number of references to the ECJ from national courts (though the parties may appeal to the ECJ). However, parties should make sure they are within a block exemption and if in doubt they should "notify"; if they do not and they are outside the relevant block exemption they will be fined.

The areas selected for block exemption are those which, although restrictive of competition within Art.81(1), are on the whole economically beneficial, and pose no real threat to competition. The Regulations are technical and only general scope is dealt with here. Where a block exemption does not apply individual exemption may be granted. The format of a Regulation lays down a "white list" of the kinds of restrictions which are permitted under it as essential to agreements of the type to which it applies, and this is followed by a "black list" of the kinds of clauses not permitted. With the exception of Regulations (a), (b) and (f) below the Regulations also have a "grey list" of restrictions which are subject to a special procedure known as the "opposition procedure". Grey restrictions must be "notified" but if they are not opposed within six months they are deemed to be exempt.

The following are the most important block exemptions:
- Exclusive distribution agreements
- Exclusive purchasing agreements
- Specialisation agreements
- Research and development agreements
- Patent licensing agreements
- Motor vehicle distribution agreements
- Franchising agreements
- Know-how licensing agreements
- (7) Comfort Letters

  The Commission has further attempted to reduce delays and its work load by the issuing of "comfort letters". These are letters from the Commission to the effect that in its opinion, the agreement either does not infringe Art.81(1) at all ("soft" negative clearance) or that it infringes Art.81(1) but is of a type that qualifies for exemption. Though these letters are not formal Decisions the file is normally closed. Authoritative legal opinion is that so long as parties act in good faith in reliance on a letter then they would not be fined and would be compensated for any loss resulting from a contrary subsequent Decision of the Commission.

Article 82 of the Treaty of Rome

Article 82: "Any abuse by one or more undertakings of a dominant position within the Common Market or in a substantial part of it shall be prohibited as incompatible with the Common Market in so far as it may affect trade between Member States. Such abuse may, in particular, consist in:

- directly or indirectly imposing unfair purchase or selling prices or other unfair trading conditions;
- limiting production, markets or technical development to the prejudice of consumers;
- applying dissimilar conditions to equivalent transactions with other trading parties thereby placing them at a competitive disadvantage;
- making the conclusion of contracts subject to acceptance by the other parties of supplementary obligations which, by their nature or according to commercial usage, have no connection with the subject of such contracts."

There is no provision for exemption from liability under Art.82 so that a party cannot notify and get exemption from fines. The difference between Art.82 and Art.81 is one of degree rather than kind. The existence of a dominant position makes the conduct more dangerous and that is why there is no possibility of exemption from Art.82. However, parties can apply for negative clearance in order to obtain a Decision that their proposed action does not breach Art.82.

Art.82 contains a prohibition with three essential ingredients:

(a) There must be an abuse by one or more undertakings;
(b) of a dominant position within the Common Market or a substantial part of it, and;
(c) the abuse must affect trade between Member States.

The prohibition is followed by a non-exhaustive list of examples of abuse.

Art.82 is aimed at the dangers to competition in the common market from individual undertakings and at the special problems raised by market power. Undertaking has the same meaning it has in Art.81(1).

The scope of Art.82 is not limited to monopolies enjoying substantial market power but covers groups of undertakings within the same corporate grouping and also parent companies acting in conjunction with their subsidiaries. Art. 82 can also apply to the activities of undertakings which are independent of each other, though the degree of co-operation must be distinctively high. There is an overlap with Art.81(1).

This was defined in *United Brands Co. v Commission* (1976) as "a position of economic strength enjoyed by an undertaking (or undertakings) which enables it to prevent effective competition being maintained on the relevant market by giving it the power to behave to an appreciable extent independently of its competitors, customers, and ultimately of its consumers". In a subsequent case the Commission added that "the power to exclude effective competition is not in all cases coterminous with independence from competitive factors but may also involve the ability to eliminate or seriously weaken existing competitors or to prevent potential competitors from entering the market". Ascertaining whether an undertaking is dominant within this definition involves:

1. identifying the relevant product market which includes a temporal aspect (i.e. time period);
2. ascertaining whether that market is geographically within the common market or a substantial part of it; and
3. ascertaining whether the undertaking is dominant within that market.

The Relevant Product Market

The relevant product market in any particular case is determined using the economists' notion of "product substitution". Seasonal considerations affecting opportunities for product substitution may be a factor in determining the relevant product market.

The Relevant Geographical Market

To fall foul of Art.82 an undertaking must be dominant "within the common market or in a substantial part of it". Thus the "relevant geographical market" must be determined so that it can be decided whether it is a substantial part of the common market.

Proof of Dominance in the Relevant Product Market

The question of dominance requires a wide ranging economic analysis of the undertaking concerned and of the market in which it operates. The Commission thought in UNITED BRANDS that an undertaking's market share, either in itself or when combined with its know-how, access to raw materials, capital or other major advantage such as trademark ownership, were the relevant considerations. Thus market share is not the only factor. From the Decisions and case law the following guidance can be given:

4. Market Share
    This is the first consideration but a high figure is not essential. Where the market share is less than 50% the structure of the market will be important, particularly the market share of the next largest competitors. Where the market is highly fragmented a 20% to 40% share may constitute dominance.
5. Duration of Market Strength
    A firm cannot be dominant unless it is dominant over time.
6. Financial and Technological Resources
    These enable a firm to adapt its market strategy in order to drive out competition by for example selling below cost in order to undercut rivals. Technological resources enable a firm to keep ahead of potential competitors.
7. Access to Raw Materials and Outlets
    The greater the degree of vertical integration the greater a firm's power to act independently of the market.

8. Behaviour
    If a firm acts independently of the market then that is evidence of dominance. A discriminatory rebate system would be accepted by the Commission as evidence going to dominance.

    Dominance must be accompanied by abuse if Art.82 is to be activated. Art.82 (a) to (d) is a non-exhaustive list of examples of abuse.
    Abuse under Art.82 can be divided into (a) exploitative abuses and (b) anti-competitive abuses.

(a) Exploitative Abuses
    An exploitative abuse occurs when an undertaking seeks to take advantage of its position of dominance by imposing oppressive or unfair conditions on its trading partners, such as :
(b) Unfair Prices
    The Commission has defined an excessive price as "one which bears no reasonable relation to the economic value of the product". Problems inevitably arise over the question of "economic value". Though economists and accountants do disagree on the principles to be applied in answering such a question the courts take a practical commonsense approach taking the arguments into account.
(c) Discriminatory Treatment
    Charging different prices in different common market countries, not, apparently, according to objective criteria, but according to what the market would bear would constitute discriminatory treatment of trading partners.
(d) Refusal to Supply
    A refusal to supply which was not retaliatory would fall into the category of anti-competitive abuses.
(e) Anti-Competitive Abuse
    This type of abuse is not in itself unfair or oppressive but is damaging because it reduces or eliminates competition. This arises under (b) and in some cases under (d) of the Art.82 list. The Commission takes a hard line on import and export bans.

An Abuse must affect trade between Member States

As with Art.81 there must be some effect on trade between Member States for Art.82 to apply; but the cases indicate that this is not difficult to establish. Consider the following cases:
    Under UK law the decision to investigate a monopoly situation under the Fair Trading Act 1973, or anti-competitive practices under the Competition Act 1980, is a discretionary one and does not give rise to rights or remedies to individuals. Art.82 on the other hand is directly effective and gives rise to rights and remedies for individuals.

Mergers under EU Law

A Regulation known as the "Merger Regulation" came into effect on 30th October 1990. It applies to "concentrations" with a "community dimension"; which are

(a) mergers;
(b) acquisitions (ie of shares); and
(c) joint ventures which create an autonomous economic entity (i.e. "concentrative" joint ventures not "co-operative" joint ventures);
(d) between undertakings
(e) with a combined world-wide turnover of more than 5,000 million EUROs;
(f) where at least two of the undertakings have a combined turnover of more than 250 million EUROs within the EU; but
(g) do not earn more than two thirds of their turnover in a single Member State (i.e. their combined turnover).

Concentrations falling within the (i) to (iii) threshold have a "community dimension". "Concentrations" falling within the Regulation must be notified to the Commission which has exclusive jurisdiction. That is to say national courts have no jurisdiction at all and cannot apply national or EU law. The Commission has taken exclusive jurisdiction in order to create a "one stop shop" which enhances "certainty in commerce".

Where the market share of the undertakings concerned does not exceed 25% either in the common market or a substantial part of it then undertakings can presume that the Merger Regulation is not infringed. This is a non-binding guideline of the Merger Regulation but notification is still required.

Concentrations falling outside the Regulation will be subject to:

(a) national law on such activity, and
(b) possibly Art.82 applied by the national courts of Member States, where the "concentration" affects trade between Member States. Here national courts may refer a point of EU law with which it has difficulty to the Commission. Any decision of a national court on EU law can be appealed to the ECJ.

3.5

The law of agency

Definitions

An AGENT is a person employed by their PRINCIPAL to make contracts on the principal's behalf with THIRD PARTIES.

Agency is a CONTRACT, and can therefore be created in the same way as any other contract (orally, in writing, etc.).

In the agency situation there are two contracts in force: one between the principal and the third party, negotiated by the agent on the principal's behalf, and one between the principal and the agent, called the 'contract of agency'.

The special methods of creating agency are:

- By conduct
  Where Party X does something on Party Y's behalf on a regular basis, they will be appointed Party Y's agent by law, although they were never actually told that that they were an agent by Party Y. (eg a clerk going to the bank each week to collect the firm's wages is the firm's agent for that purpose).
- By necessity
  Where a person not appointed an agent takes urgent steps to protect someone else's property. (eg your neighbour's house is burgled and
- the back door smashed while he is on holiday. In arranging for the door to be replaced or repaired you are his agent of necessity and can recover the cost of restoring security).

The commercial agents regulations 1993

On 1 January 1994, *The Commercial Agents Regulations 1993* came into effect in order to implement the EU Directive on Commercial Agents. For the purpose of these regulations, commercial agents are defined as agents engaged in transactions involving goods rather than services. A commercial agent can be an individual or a company.

Important provisions of the regulations

The Regulations introduce a number of important provisions:

- A duty on the part of the agent to comply with the principal's reasonable instructions, and on the part of the principal to provide necessary documentation and information to the agent to enable the agent to carry out their work and to inform the agent when a transaction is not to be executed. These duties are in addition to any common law duties. The duties under the Regulations cannot be excluded from any contract.
- An agent's entitlement to commission where a transaction is concluded either as a result of the agent's action, or where the transaction is made with a previously acquired customer. This allows for commission payments on repeat orders, even if the agent does not undertake ay work in securing the repeat order. The right to commission terminates if it is clear that the contract between the principal and the prospective customer will not proceed, provided that this is not due to the fault of the principal.
- Regulation of the conclusion and termination of agency contracts. The provisions for conclusion and termination are complex but may be summarized as follows:
- either the principal or the agent can request a signed written contract setting out the terms an conditions of the agency;
- if fixed term agency continues beyond the term it is converted to an agreement of indefinite period;
- the minimum period of notice of termination of an agency is one month for the first year, two months in the second year and three months for the third and all subsequent years. (Note that some agreements incorporate much longer notice periods).
- the agent has the right to claim damages as compensation if the agency agreement is terminated. The right arises where age, illness or infirmity makes it no longer reasonable for the agent to continue. A prudent principal is likely to stipulate that the agent, if an individual must take out insurance against illness at their own expense and for the principal's benefit. It is not clear what the measure of compensation is likely to be on termination.
- Compensation is not payable where the principal has terminated the agency agreement on grounds of breach by the agent.

Authority of the agent

The agent's power to make contracts depends on what type of agent they are. There are the following types of agent:

Special agent

A special agent has authority to do only one act. They can perform that act many times, but that act is the limit of their authority. If they exceed that authority in any way, the principal is not bound by the agent's action. (eg the clerk going to the bank weekly to draw out £500 for the firm's wages is a special agent only for that amount. If one week the clerk draws out £10,000 and disappears, the bank cannot take that amount from the firm's account).

General agent

A general agent (eg the manager of a business) has authority to do a whole range of acts for their principal. The principal is bound by any act the agent performs which is within the agent's *ostensible* authority, which is the authority that they appear to have to a reasonable third party. It must be emphasised that ach case depends on the evidence as to what is the apparent authority of the agent.

Universal agent

A universal agent is a person who has power to do anything that the principal could have done. Such an agency is usually created by deed and is called a 'General Power of Attorney' – not to be confused with a general agent.

Confirming houses

Confirming houses find suppliers for foreign buyers and make contacts as an agent of the buyer. However, they do confirm or guarantee the sale to the seller so that if the buyer does not pay then the confirming house in the UK will be liable for the price.

Del credere agents

Del credere agents guarantee that, in consideration of additional commission, they will pay to the principal any amounts not paid by the buyer within the agreed credit period. They differ from confirming houses in that they do not guarantee the sale itself. They are not liable if the buyer refuses to take delivery of the goods, only if they do take delivery but do not pay.

Freight forwarders and combined transport operators (C.T.O.s)

A C.T.O. may act as principal or agent depending on the contract agreed with the seller or buyer. When acting as legal carrier for the seller or buyer they will contract as principal, being legally responsible under the contract of carriage to the seller or buyer even though, as is usual, they will make contracts with the actual carriers performing the physical transport. When acting as forwarding agents they will act as agents of the seller or buyer, making a contract of carriage and other related contracts on the seller's or buyer's behalf. When acting as principal they will have different duties and obligations than when acting as an agent.

Breach of warranty of authority

An agent who purports to act for a principal, knowing that they have no authority to do so, even if they believed that the principal would ratify their actions, is liable to the third party in deceit. The following rules apply in an action brought by the third party against the agent:

- If the third party knows or has reason to suspect that the agent is exceeding their authority, the implied promise that they had authority is overridden.
- If the agent misinterprets ambiguous instructions, they will not be liable for breach of warranty of authority.
- Even if the agent has the authority of one of two principals, that is not enough.
- The agent must pay damages to the value of the amount of loss sustained.

Effect of contracts made by agents

The general rule is that the contract is between the principal and the third party, and that the agent has neither rights nor duties under it. However, the agent is exceptionally liable in any of the following circumstances:

- If they sign a deed for their principal and their own appointment was not by deed.
- Where they sign a Bill of Exchange if the words 'per pro' or 'for and on behalf of' are not used.
- Where the agent contracts as the principal (see further below).
- Where trade custom makes the agent liable. (eg it is trade custom that an insurance broker will pay a marine insurance premium if the client does not do so).

Where the agent contracts for an unnamed but disclosed principal

In such cases the agent will not be liable provided that they make it clear that they are acting as agent.

Where the agent does not disclose the principal's existencey

In this situation the principal can reveal himself at any time. The third party also has a choice: if breach of contract occurs and they sue, they will discover the principal. They can elect to sue either the principal or the agent, but not both. Once they have made the election they cannot change their mind.

Rights and duties of principal and agent

The overriding duties of the agent are as follows:

- Not to disclose confidential information, or information specially collected for the principal's use. Confidential information comprises information that no one else has, such as a secret industrial process.
- Any information that is specially collected by the agent for the principal's use must not be disclosed.
- Not to let their interest conflict with their duty.
- Not to serve more than one principal. This does not mean that an agent cannot have masses of clients – it merely means that they must not represent more than one side in the same case.
- Not to delegate their authority, except where: the principal allows delegation; delegation is obviously essential. For example, solicitors cannot do all the work personally, and are permitted to delegate it to clerks.

Sometimes an agent may be appointed, with exclusive rights to commission on sales in an overseas territory, simply by means of a verbal agreement. However, in most cases a written agency agreement is desirable.

Key clauses in an agency agreement

A typical agreement would need to include the following clauses:

- Statement of parties to the agreement;
- Definition of purposes of the agreement;
- Description of goods (either the whole or a part of the principal's range);
- Definition of territory (not always a whole country);
- Duties of the principal (where not expressed elsewhere.) eg promotional literature, samples, training visits, pre- and after-sales service levels, levels of commission and payment terms, etc;
- Duties of the agent:
  - must not handle, sell or have any interest in competitive goods;

- not to sell goods outside the territory;
- sell under the principal's description only;
- access for the principal to agent's books, offices, warehouse, etc;
- maintain books/records;
- provide periodic reports etc;
- Commission - methods of calculation and payment;
- Exceptions, reservations or restrictions eg house accounts, buying houses, etc;
- Method of quoting by principal, method of purchase by agent (if applicable), consignment stock details eg stock levels, records, warehouse costs, resale price levels, discounts, etc;
- Allocation of costs eg telephone/fax., administration, promotion, etc.
- Limitation of powers; agent shall not, unless agreed:
  - sell goods under warranty;
  - pledge principal's credit;
  - commence legal proceedings;
  - release confidential information.
- Force majeure.
- Duration of agreement, termination, period of notice.
- Reasons for breach of agreement.
- Law governing agreement; method of arbitration.
- Assignment; benefits and obligations cannot be passed on.
- Del credere clause.

Part 4

The Export Order Process

4.1

The export office

The fundamental functions of an export department may be broken down into just two areas:

Sales	ie order getting
Shipping	ie order filling

Add to these specific functions the need for overall management control and the whole department can revolve around those three.

It is perhaps easier to identify what particular things are done within each of these areas if we identify the duties of the individuals responsible for their operation. See Table 4.1.1

Table 4.1.1 defines a simple structure of a Sales and a Shipping Manager directly responsible to an Export Manager. Of course, it is always possible that there could be an Export Director, or that the Export Manager could report to a Marketing Director.

Also, it is not unusual that an Export Marketing Manager should run the office and an Export Sales Manager handle the field sales operations. There are no rules which can apply to every company because all will be different in terms of size, product range, type and number of markets, channels of distribution and even their stage of development.

In particular, the size of the export office will have a great effect on its organization. Some companies' export departments will consist of one man or woman, perhaps with secretarial support, in which case any division of labour is somewhat irrelevant. At the other extreme is the company with major ex-port business which employs many hundreds of people within its export department. In such a case it is essential that the functions are defined down to very specialised levels of responsibility.

Whatever the size of the operation there is a logical sequence of tasks which are necessary to develop and initial enquiry into a profitable payment, virtually all of which are examined in detail in the chapters which follow:

The export order process

- Enquiry
- Quotation

Table 4.1.1 - Duties of export, sales and shipping managers

EXPORT MANAGER

Liaison with Directors

Negotiation of Budgets and Targets

Market Selection

Product Development

Pricing Policy

Promotional Strategy

Channel Management

Cost & Credit Control

Staff Selection & Development

Control of Major Accounts

SALES MANAGER

Order Negotiation

Price Calculation

Quotation Production

General Sales Correspondence

Order Processing & Progress

Maintenance of Records

SHIPPING MANAGER

Assist with Price Calculation

Check Letters of Credit

Transport Negotiations

Document Production

Payment Collection

Maintenance of Records

- Order
- Order acknowledgement
- Order process and progress
- Packing and marking
- Space booking
- Documents prepared
  - ○ Transport
  - ○ Customs
  - ○ Insurance
  - ○ Payment
- Goods despatched
- Payment received

Companies will develop internal procedures to deal with this process which will vary enormously from one to another depending on the nature and size of their business, number of shipments, number and expertise of staff etc.

There are a number of systems available to manage the process and the sequencing of functions, the simplest of which are based on tracking files or folders which can be completed manually, and the more complex of which are software packages that can produce all export documentation and be linked with internal production and inventory systems. The computer based packages are covered in Chapter 9. Examples A and B, illustratd in Figures 4.1.1 and 4.1.2 respectively, are typical manual folders.

The enquiry

It is pretty obvious that the beginning of the process is the enquiry from a potential overseas buyer. This may have been instigated from many sources such as personal contact, advertising or recommendation or it could simply be a regular buyer coming back for more. The enquiry will take almost as many forms as there are overseas buyers; it could even be a verbal request, but is often a simple piece of correspondence, either post or e-mail, detailing their requirements or it could be a more formalised tender document.

Careful examination of the initial enquiry could be facilitated by the use of a check list:

- Does the enquiry require translating?
- Is it a new or regular customer?
- Are there any restrictions by the UK authorities eg export licensing
- Are there any restrictions by the buyer's authorities eg import licensing
- Does the enquiry match our own product/service specifications? If not, what modifications are required?
- Can we produce the quantity required in the time required?
- What delivery terms are requested?
- What payment method and terms are requested?

Export Order No. . . . . Customer's Order No. . . . . Date.	Order Approved Date. . . . . . . Signature.	Customer XYZ Imports New York, USA	Delivery Date. . . . . Confirmed. . . . .
Product		A/C Approved	
Price Currency		Value	
Quantity		Credit Insurance Cover	
Incoterm		Agent . . . . Commission	
Terms of Payment		Bank	
Sub: File to Works/Production/Stores			
Works Delivery Date			
Assembly and Packing Completion Date		Documents to Bank . . . . Advice to Customer . . . . Payment Received	
Transportation Method Dispatch to Port/ICD, etc.		Invoices: Documentation Requirements Bill of Lading/Waybill	
Vessel Closing Date		Insurance Documents	
Documentation Closing Date		Consular Invoice	
L/C Expiry Date Weight Lists, etc.		Contents Note	

Figure 4.1.1 - The oder action file (example 'A')

CUSTOMER	DESTINATION		ORDER NUMBER			CONTRACT DELIVERY DATE	L/C RECEIVED...... CHECKED......
PACKING type						MARK......	GOODS DESCRIPTION
Stores Promise	Packing Date	Closing Date	Insurance Date	Dispatch Date	L/C Shipping Date	B/L/Waybill Required by	

Figure 4.1.2 - The order action file (example 'B')

- Has a status report been taken up on the buyer?
- Can the delivery period be met?
- What is the most suitable mode of transport?
- Are there any special packing and marking requirements for the market in question?
- Are there any special documentation requirements?
- What insurance is required?
- What ancillary (third party costs) need to be built into the price eg freight, insurance, packing, documentation etc.

4.2

The export quotation

The quotation in response to an export enquiry may be just as informal as an original verbal enquiry, or could be an extremely formalized completion of tender documents. Of course, it is advisable that all communications are in writing and recorded

Many of the problems which exporters face could be avoided by an improved understanding of the nature of export quotations, the correct procedures for their production and the contractual consequences of the information they contain.

Various formats exist in practice and will be examined in this chapter, but it may be useful to first identify the range of information which would need to be included in a simple export quotations. The essentials are listed in Table 4.2.1 and would include:

Goods

As the description of the goods is directly relevant to the range of tariff and non-tariff barriers that they might attract at destination then we should carefully consider the wording even at this early stage of the process. If choices exist, it could be advantageous to be selective as to product descriptions. (More on this point later in this chapter).

Price

Perhaps the most important element of the quotation and one which many exporters actually get wrong.

Firstly, the price makes no sense without a specific Incoterm, such as FCA, FOB, CIP or CIF, and the importance and meaning of these terms is not always understood.

Secondly, the actual process of calculating an accurate export price is one which causes problems for many exporters. The worst scenario being that the relevant costs are underestimated. Most exporters can get an Ex Works (EXW) price correct but additional costs are often closer to guesstimates.

Table 4.2.1 - Essential information in typical quotation

Goods:	:-	Rubber hammers as per attached specification
Quantity:	:-	2,000
Price:	:-	€ 26.00 per unit FCA Manchester International Freight Terminal
Terms of Sale:	:-	Except where otherwise specified this quotation is governed by INCOTERMS 2000
Packing:	:-	Each unit carton packed (in five extra strong fibre board containers, 20 per container)
Delivery: (lead time)	:-	12 weeks from receipt of an acceptable order.
Terms of Payment:	:-	Cash against documents by means of a Sight Bill of Exchange presented through Chase Manhattan Bank, New York.

Delivery

One of the most common mistakes made at this stage is the habit which exporters have of suddenly becoming super optimists as far as delivery times are concerned. Whilst it is tempting to quote short lead times in order to make the quotation more attractive to the customer, the long term consequences of subsequent late deliveries really make the exercise pointless. It is far better to promise 12 weeks and deliver in 10, than to quote 10 but deliver in 12. From a purely practical point of view the deadlines imposed by carrier's schedules and Letters of Credit mean that the consequences of late delivery can be far more severe than simply an unhappy customer.

Terms and method of payment

The exporter's estimate of the risks involved with certain customers and certain markets should lead to sensible choices regarding the method of payment and the credit terms granted. A brief point here; the credit risk in international trade is now perceived as being worse than it has ever been, and this does not just refer to developing countries. Many nations of the world are bankrupt in strict business terms, and as businesses would have been liquidated long ago. Credit risk management is essential to all exporters and starts at the beginning of the process, not at the end when attempting to collect money. (See Risk Assessment below and Part 7 – Risk Management).

Order acknowledgment (acceptance)

It is important to understand that a simple quotation made by a UK exporter is seen in English law as an *invitation to treat*. That is an invitation for the buyer to offer to buy. The order from the buyer is therefore an offer to buy which can be accepted, or rejected, by the acknowledgement or acceptance of the seller. This means that the terms and conditions of the contract can be defined in the order acceptance and are therefore the seller's term and conditions. (See Chapter 3.)

Forms of export quotation

Verbal

This speaks for itself - in many cases price and delivery information may be given during personal meetings or over the telephone. It is very important that such quotations are con-firmed in writing as soon as possible so as to avoid any possible misunderstanding. Don't forget, a verbal contract isn't worth the paper it's written on.

Standard letter/e-mail

The most common form of quotation which requires no specific format as long as it contains the relevant information mentioned above. Many companies use pre-printed letterheads or templates, and these may merely cover price lists, and not state any quantities or specific requirements.

Tender documents

Particularly when dealing with overseas governments or state buying agencies, it is common for the enquiry to be received in the form of a tender document. These are also often related to large projects, but not exclusively to large companies, as smaller exporters may tender for parts of a large tender.

There are a number of problems related to tender documents:

1. There is no standard format and the exporter is required to complete the tender document. This involves some quite time-consuming investigation of the tender itself in order to complete it correctly and to ensure that the stated terms are acceptable.
2. The requirement for Bonds or Guarantees.

A *Tender Bond* must be provided by the seller along with the completed tender document. This will need to be issued by a bank and promises an amount of money (a percentage of the tender value) payable to the potential buyer in com-pensation should the tenderer withdraw the tender before expiry or refuse the order when placed. This compensates the buyer for the expenses involved with the complex process of examining all tenders. It may also be seen as a sign of good intent by the tenderer. A typical example of a Tender Bond is shown in Figure 4.2.1.

When the order is placed and accepted it will then be necessary for the seller to produce a *Performance Bond* which again guarantees an amount of monetary compensation should they not perform according to the contract conditions. (See Figure 4.2.2 .)

The problems associated with these Bonds relate to the fact that the banks make a charge for their issue, and regard any monies guaranteed as being unavailable to the exporter. That is to say, the seller's facility at the bank will be reduced. When one considers that Performance Bonds can be valid for six years or more, then this can be quite restrictive.

Also, most overseas governments insist on unconditional, sometimes referred to as 'on demand', guarantees. This means that the buyer simply has to call on the bond and the bank will pay, there being no requirement for any explicit proof of the seller's breach. The only possible solution to this, assuming that conditional guarantees are not acceptable, is to arrange, through a credit insurance company, for Unwarranted Calls cover. The other solution is, of course, not to give them, but this almost certainly means that the tender would not be considered.

Fig. 4.2.1 - Example of a Tender Bond

GUARANTEE NUMBER:

We understand that   (APPLICANT'S NAME) (the Applicant')

(APPLICANT'S ADDRESS)

are tendering for the (DESCRIPTION OF GOODS) under your invitation to Tender (TENDER/CONTRACT NUMBER etc.) and that a Bank Guarantee is required for ...% of the amount of their tender.

We, (NAME OF APPLICANT'S BANK) hereby guarantee the payment to you on demand of up to (AMOUNT IN FIGURES) say, (AMOUNT IN WORDS) in the event of your awarding the relative contract to the Applicant and of its failing to sign the Contract in the terms of its tender, or in the event of the Applicant withdrawing its tender before expiry of this guarantee without your consent.

This guarantee shall come into force on (COMMENCEMENT DATE) being the closing date for tenders, and will expire at close of banking hours at this office on (EXPIRY DATE) ('Expiry').

Our liability is limited to the sum of (AMOUNT IN FIGURES) and your claim hereunder must be received in writing at this office before Expiry accompanied by your signed statement that the Applicant has been awarded the relative contract and has failed to sign the contract awarded in the terms of its tender or has withdrawn its tender before Expiry without your consent, and such claim and statement shall be accepted as conclusive evidence that the amount claimed is due to you under this guarantee.

Claims and statements as aforesaid must bear the confirmation of your Bankers that the signatories thereon are authorised so to sign.

Upon Expiry this guarantee shall become null and void, whether returned to us for cancellation or not and any claim or statement received after expiry shall be ineffective.

This guarantee is personal to yourselves and is not transferable or assignable.

Fig. 4.6 - Example of a Performance Bond

GUARANTEE NUMBER:

We understand that you have entered into a Contract (TENDER/CON-TRACT NUMBER etc.) ('the Contract') with (APPLICANT'S NAME & ADDRESS) ('the Applicant') for the (DESCRIPTION OF GOODS) and that under such Contract the Applicant must provide a Bank Performance Guarantee for an amount of (AMOUNT IN FIGURES) being ...% of the value of the contract.

We (NAME and ADDRESS OF APPLICANT'S BANK) HEREBY GUAR-ANTEE payment to you on demand of up to (AMOUNT IN FIGURES) say, (AMOUNT IN WORDS) in the event of the Applicant failing to fulfil the said Contract, provided that your claim hereunder is received in writing at this office accompanied by your signed statement that the Applicant has failed to fulfil the Contract. Such claim and statement shall be accepted as conclusive evidence that the amount claimed is due to you under this guarantee.

Claims and statements as aforesaid must bear the confirmation of your Bankers that the signatories thereon are authorised so to sign.

This guarantee shall expire at close of banking hours at this office on (EXPIRY DATE) ('Expiry') and any claim and statement hereunder must be received at this office before Expiry and after Expiry this guarantee shall become null and void whether returned to us for cancellation or not and any claim or statement received after Expiry shall be ineffective.

This guarantee is personal to yourselves and is not transferable or assignable.

This guarantee shall be governed by and construed in accordance with the Laws of England.

Pro-forma invoice

The primary function for this document is as a form of quotation and it is intended to demonstrate what the final invoice will look like should the order be placed. That is, it is an advance copy of the final invoice. In this case it is obvious that the quantity and type of goods required will have to be clearly specified. It is laid out in invoice format, and invariably contains a breakdown of the ancillary charges, such as freight and insurance premiums, commonly being prepared as a CIF or CIP quotation.

This type of quotation is extremely common when dealing with developing countries and is specifically related to their requirement for a specific Import

Licence and/or to comply with Exchange Control regulations. The buyer will use the pro-forma to provide detailed information to the authorities before an order can be placed on the supplier. It is not, as is often thought, needed for the buyer to raise a Letter of Credit.

Import Licensing controls are used by all countries but the developed countries tend to issue Open General Licences covering most goods and use specific licensing very selectively. However most developing countries use specific Import Licensing control regimes, which require the potential importer to obtain a licence for each consignment.

The information on the pro--forma invoice is essential to the buyer's licensing authorities and the licence will be issued for the exact amount. In some cases the importer will be granted an annual licence, for certain goods and a limited value, but the value of each consignment will be deducted from the floating balance of the licence. This means that the exporter will have to he very sure of the accuracy of the price quotation as any cost increases before delivery cannot be passed on.

The other major function of a pro-forma invoice is to obtain advance payment, sometimes referred to as cash with order or pro-forma payment. Some years ago advance payment was quite unusual, and only occurred where the buyer had little, or no, choice as to supplier. So, for example, a company like Unipart could insist on cash with order in risk markets, and Marlboro operated on the same basis in West Africa.

Most suppliers are not in such a strong position but nevertheless the incidence of advance payment has increased. The reason for this is that many UK exporters perceive the risk of non-payment, or delay in payment, as being so great in many markets that the only basis on which they will do business is cash in advance.

The buyer has no alternative, and in many cases is not unhappy, to deal on such a basis. This is not uncommon when dealing with African, Near and Far Eastern and sometimes Latin American markets. When the eventual shipment is made the exporter must still produce a final invoice which should be identified as being for 'Customs Valuation Purposes Only', and should, of course, be for the full amount paid.

Risk assessment

The comments above regarding the increased incidence of cash in advance in international trade introduces one other essential consideration for an exporter at the time a quotation is being prepared. In order to decide what is the most appropriate method (how) and term (when) of payment we should carry out some informed risk assessment.

So what choices do we have as to method of payment. Viewed from the point of view of risk to the seller we could produce a 'ladder' as illustrated in Figure 4.2.1.

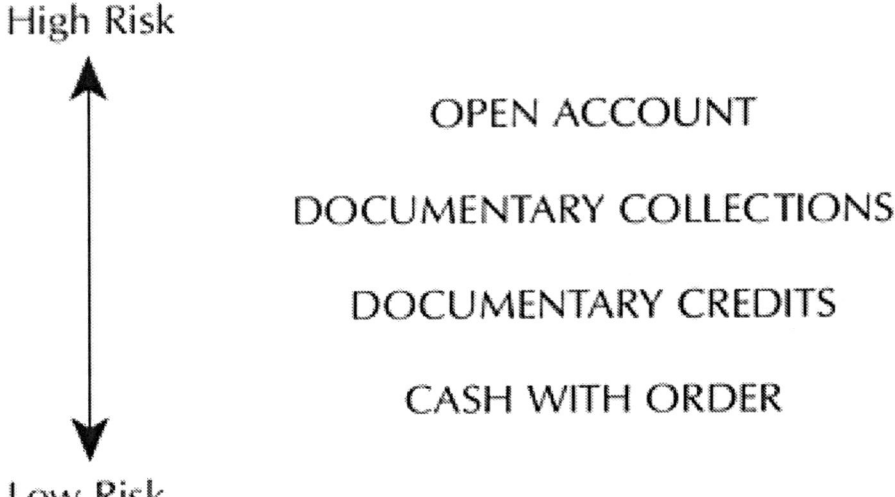

Figure4.2.1 - The risk ladder

The detailed operation of each of these methods is covered in Chapter 8. For now, we need to consider what sources of information are available to allow us to make some informed judgments about the credit risk inherent in a particular market and a particular buyer ie country risk and buyer risk.

Country risk

Certain methods of payment are clearly more common in particular markets than are others; so the exporter invariably has a 'rule of thumb' as to the usual method for a particular market. In this context it is no surprise that for the high risk markets, for example West Africa, cash in advance is not uncommon and Letters of Credit are very common. On the other hand, in a developed market like Germany, Open Account contracts are the most common.

There are sources of information available which can help make an objective estimate of country risk and normal payment methods. Rating agencies like Standard & Poor's and Moodys produce long term gradings of countries and large corporations, including banks, in a sort of league table descending from AAA (triple A) down. These gradings are of concern to organisations looking to make direct and long term investments in overseas markets but the typical exporter is concerned about short term risk , up to a maximum of 180 days.

Such short term country risk is assessed by organisations such as Dun & Bradstreet who produce the International Risk and Payment Review. They not only grade countries on a scale:

DB1(a,b,c,d)	Highest Creditworthiness
DB2	Good
DB3	Creditworthy
DB4	Adequate
DB5	Questionable
DB6	Poor
DB7	???

but also recommend a minimum method of payment for each.

Buyer risk

Irrespective of the traditional and accepted method of payment in a particular country, the seller's perception of the particular buyer risk, or lack of it, can override any 'rule of thumb'.

The seller's perception may simply be based on a trading history with a buyer over a period of time which has established an element of trust which allows for methods of payment, such as Open Account, in what are regarded as Letter of Credit markets.

However, for newer buyers we need other sources of information:

- *Trade references* – from other UK companies with which they do business
- *Bank report* – which will at least tell us that they exist
- *Credit report* – from specialist agencies and more expensive but more detailed
- *Credit risk insurers* – for the smaller exporter the use of a specialist export credit insurer not only provides a safety net for non-payments but also provides the ability to request written credit limits on new buyers.

Whatever decisions are made they should be the result of the operation of a credit management system which takes a pragmatic approach to the calculation of country and buyer risk and establishes operative credit limits based on the methods of payment in use.

There is one other essential element of our export quotation and it is one which can be seen as the cornerstone of the contractual obligations which each party accepts.

International delivery terms

The major elements of the export quotation have been discussed earlier, but it is obvious that the price(s) quoted are central to its purpose.

It can also be seen that for an exporter to simply say to an overseas customer that a particular product is, for example, $25.00 per unit does not

Table 4.2.2 - The categories of Incoterms

Group E

EXW   Ex Works (...named place)

Group F

FCA   Free Carrier (...named place)

FAS   Free Alongside Ship (...named port of shipment)

FOB   Free on Board (...named port of shipment)

Group C

CFR (C&F)   Cost and Freight (...named port of destination)

CIF   Cost, Insurance and Freight (...named port of destination)

CPT   Carriage Paid To (...named place of destination)

CIP   Carriage and Insurance Paid (....named place of destination)

Group D

DAF   Delivered at Frontier (...named place)

DES   Delivered Ex Ship (...named port of destination)

DEQ   Delivered Ex Quay (....named port of destination)

DDU   Delivered Duty Unpaid (...named place of destination)

DDP   Delivered Duty Paid (...named place of destination)

really say much, in that the goods could cost them $25.00 each in a warehouse in Manchester or $25.00 each in their warehouse in Tokyo, and there is clearly a big difference between the two.

For the export price to make any sense then there must be some expression as to what is included, and not included, in that price, as in $25.00 per unit FOB. It is here where the use of what are referred to as *delivery terms* or *trade terms* is necessary and this has been the case for centuries.

It is natural that international traders have established, over long periods of time, a range of standard expressions to cover most types of contract, but the most important development was in 1936 when the International Chamber of Commerce (ICC) produced the first version of Incoterms. This publication has been amended and updated on six separate occasions since then and the current version is Incoterms 2000 (ICC Publication No 560), available from your local Chamber of Commerce or direct from the ICC on www.iccbooks.com. And reproduced in this book as Chapter 4.3

What Incoterms does is to provide definitive definitions of 13 trade terms in common use, in the form of a very detailed breakdown of the seller's and buyer's duties. Whilst exporters can invent any term they choose, it is clearly better to use terms for which standard definitions are available. It has to be said that it is also unlikely that terms could be produced which are superior to the ICC Committee's work, or that an Incoterm is not available to suit any requirement.

As the trade term specified on the quotation is such a vital factor in the conditions of the contract of sale between seller and buyer, and as it has such a direct relevance to the price calculation, it is extremely important that all exporters have a firm grasp of the meaning of the various Incoterms.

The 13 terms can be grouped into four categories and are listed in Table 4.2.2.

The listed terms all identify a very specific point, on the journey from the seller to the buyer, for the passing of *costs, delivery and risk*.

Costs

As we have already seen, the export price quoted makes very little sense without some reference to what is included in the price and what is excluded. Each trade term acts as a statement as to what costs will be met by the seller, and are therefore already included in the quoted price, and what costs will have to be paid by the buyer, in addition to the purchase price.

Thus an EXW price means that the buyer will have to pay all the costs of the physical distribution of the goods from the place of collection at the seller's premises, but a DDP price means that the seller has included all those costs in the quoted price.

Delivery

This defines the seller's and buyer's responsibilities for the transport and documentary arrangements for delivery of the goods. In this context it is not enough for an exporter to quote, as in the previous example, $25.00 each, it is also necessary to define a particular geographic location.

Thus the seller needs to be specific, as in $25.00 per unit FOB UK Port, in which case the buyer can request shipment out of any UK port, or even more specific, as in $25.00 per Kilo FOB Liverpool. The point of delivery, once identified, confers obligations on both parties for the transport arrangements and production of the relevant documentation.

In relation to other topics covered in the Handbook it is interesting to ask, 'How would a seller actually prove that they had delivered goods FOB Liverpool'? The answer, of course, is not a photograph of the smiling driver watching his load being lifted onto the vessel with the Liver Buildings in the background. It is documents which will prove performance and, in this case, the relevant document would be the receipt from the shipping line ie a Bill of Lading. The fact that export documents evidence performance of contracts is vital to many of the topics covered in this Handbook.

Risk

One of the most contentious issues in international trade is the relative responsibilities of the parties involved when the goods are damaged or lost during transit. It is important to establish first of all where the risk of loss or damage to the goods passes from the seller to the buyer, which is in fact defined by the trade term, and secondly to attempt to establish exactly where the loss or damage occurred during the transit.

In simple terms, if loss or damage occurs before the point specified by the trade term then it is the seller's problem (they have not in fact delivered in accordance with the contract) but if loss or damage occurs after that point then the seller has fulfilled a contractual obligation and it is the buyer's problem.

Table 4.2.3 shows the points in the journey where risk passes from the seller to the buyer as identified in the Incoterms.

Each of the Incoterms defines the seller's and buyer's duties within a formalised structure.

The definitive version of the seller's and buyer's duties under these terms is, of course, Incoterms 2000 itself. However the following is an overview of the main points of each term.

Ex Works (EXW)

The lazy exporter's term ! This is the easiest term for the seller and it may be that it is perfectly acceptable to the buyer, particularly for EU trade.

Table 4.2.3 - Definiton of seller's and buyer's obligation within Incoterms

THE SELLER'S OBLIGATIONS

A1	Provision of goods in conformity with the contract	B1	payment of the price
A2	Licences, authorisations and formalities	B2	Licences, authorisations and formalities
A3	Contracts of carriage and insurance	B3	Contracts of carriage and insurance
A4	Delivery	B4	Taking delivery
A5	Transfer of risks	B5	Transfer of risks
A6	Division of costs	B6	Division of costs
A7	Notice to the buyer	B7	Notice to the seller
A8	Proof of delivery, transport document or equivalent electronic message	B8	Proof of delivery, transport document or equivalent electronic message
A9	Checking-packaging-marking	B9	Inspection of goods
A10	Other obligations	B10	Other obligations

However to use EXW as a matter of policy is unacceptable when we are dealing with buyers who would have significant problems in arranging collection and shipment from a place in the UK. We often have to do more for the buyer.

The 'named place of delivery' is invariably the seller's loading bay, before the loading of the vehicle. The buyer is responsible for arranging the collection, transport, export clearance and paying all costs from this point.

The risk of loss or damage passes when the goods are *'placed at the disposal of the buyer at the named place'*. The seller has no responsibility for loading the goods, but in practice often does, and does not have to get the goods off their premises or past any 'factory gates'.

An issue which can cause difficulty is export packing. The seller has a duty to pack the goods for the journey only 'to the extent that the circumstances related to the transport (eg modalities, destination) are made known to them'. In order to avoid any problems the seller should be aware of where the goods are going and how they are being transported so that they can pack them suitably for the journey.

Free On Board (FOB)

FOB is a very popular term and has been used by traders for centuries. The seller is responsible for the goods until they ' *have passed the ship's rail at the named port of shipment'*. It is at this point that the costs, risk and responsibility end for the seller and begin for the buyer.

The major issue here is that traders today do not now exclusively use sea freight for their exports but a whole range of air, road, rail, express and courier services. Indeed, even when moving goods by sea the goods are invariably containerised and delivered to a groupage depot for Less than Container Load (LCL) shipments or the shipping line will collect the goods at the seller's premises for a Full Container Load (FCL) movement.

In addition, container ship does not have a ' ship's rail'. This means that FOB, no matter how standard is its use, is inappropriate for most modern, multimodal, forms of transport where, not only does the ship's rail not exist it is also irrelevant to the place at which the seller hands goods over to the carrier.

In fact, the term FOB is really only accurate for traditional but increasingly rare conventional sea freight movements (ie non-containerised). The 2000 revision of Incoterms contains more appropriate terms for container sea freight, air, road, rail, express and courier services.

Free Carrier (FCA)

FCA is one of the new terms incorporated originally in the 1990 revision of Incoterms. Instead of specifying the ship's rail, the FCA term gives the seller the duty to deliver the goods to the *'carrier... nominated by the buyer at the named place'*. This place will invariably be the inland depot (container base, road depot, rail terminal or airport) not unloaded for LCL shipments or the seller's premises when the goods are loaded on the buyer's collecting vehicle for FCL shipments.

This is particularly suited for the multi-modal movements of goods form depot to depot, or door to door, which characterises modern international transport.

Free Alongside Ship (FAS)

The seller must deliver the goods alongside the vessel nominated by the buyer at the named port of shipment. Its main relevance is where vessels may be berthed in deep water and lighters are needed to move the goods alongside, it is therefore very unusual out of the UK.

Cost Insurance & Freight (CIF)

Cost & Freight (CFR – often stated as C and F or C&F)
CFR and CIF are like FOB in terms of longevity but, as is the case with FOB, they are appropriate only to conventional sea freight, where a ship's rail actually exists, and inappropriate for multimodal movements. For CFR the contract for the international carriage will be arranged and paid for by the seller and, for CIF, the seller will additionally arrange and pay for cargo insurance on behalf of the buyer.

Therefore, the costs and arrangements for the seller end when the goods effectively arrive at the port of destination. However it is very important to note that the risk ends for the seller when the goods *' have passed the ship's rail at the port of shipment'*.

It is at this point in the performance of the contract that the seller can produce a set of documents proving full performance of a CIF contract eg Bill of Lading or Waybill, invoice, certificate of origin, insurance certificate etc. Therefore, if the goods are subsequently damaged in transit before they arrive at the destination port this is contractually the responsibility of the buyer. It is perfectly feasible for the overseas buyer to make a claim on insurance arranged by the seller.

These are therefore 'shipment contracts' not 'arrival contracts'.

Carriage & Insurance Paid to (CIP) and Carriage Paid to (CPT)

CIP and CPT can be viewed as the multimodal versions of CIF and CFR respectively. As with FCA they have been introduced to address the irrelevance of the ship's rail to modern international movements. The only difference between CIP and CPT is again the cost of the insurance for the goods in transit.

The critical point where the risk ends for the seller is when the goods have been delivered to ' *the first carrier at the named place*'. The expression 'first' carrier is used because it may be the case, particularly in road freight, that there is a 'subsequent' carrier who completes the delivery.

This means that, in a similar way to FCA, the risk passes to the buyer when the seller has delivered the goods to the carrier at the named place. Damage in transit following this point is again the buyer's responsibility.

These are again ' shipment contracts' not ' arrival contracts'.

Delivered Ex Ship (DES)

The seller arranges, and pays for, the carriage to the named port of destination and must '*place the goods at the disposal of the buyer on board the vessel at the unloading point*'. This term tend to be used for bulk goods only.

Delivered Ex Quay (DEQ)

The seller arranges, and pays for, carriage to the port of destination and must 'place the goods at the disposal of the buyer on the quay (wharf)' at that point. This term also tends to be used for bulk goods only.

Delivered At Frontier (DAF)

The seller arranges, and pays for, the carriage to the named point of delivery at the frontier and must '*place the goods at the disposal of the buyer* .... *not unloaded*' at that point. There is no obligation to arrange cargo insurance and risk passes at the frontier.

Delivered Duty Unpaid/Paid (DDU/DDP)

The opposite of EXW is DDP. The most onerous term for the seller in terms of costs, risks, and responsibilities. The seller must '*place the goods at the disposal of the buyer... not unloaded at the named place of destination*', which is usually the buyers' premises in the country of import.

Under a DDP the seller would have to arrange and pay the costs of Customs formalities at import, ie import declarations, duty, tax, excise etc. whilst under a DDU these would be the responsibility of the buyer. In either case there is no obligation for the seller to insure the goods as they are responsible for loss or damage until goods are delivered to the named place but do not have to insure that liability – however most would. These are therefore ' arrival contracts'.

An examination of these terms will reveal immediately that an Ex Works contract is much easier for the exporter than would be a DDP contract. However the seller must consider what the buyer might prefer in terms of a package deal, rather than simply take the easy way out by quoting Ex Works. Also the exporter should appreciate that for a number of these terms the obligations for transport and insurance, often to an overseas destination, differ from the point at which the risk of loss or damage passes from the seller to the buyer. Figure 4.9 shows the points at which risk passes from the seller to the buyer, although the seller's obligations in terms of costs would be different.

The final point to make about the selection of appropriate trade terms is relevant to the introduction of the, relatively, new terms of FCA, CPT and CIP. Their introduction reflects the in-creased use of electronic messages rather than paper and the changing nature of international movements, in that the tradi-tional port to port transit of goods, where the ship's rail was an important point in the journey, has given way to the depot to depot movement of unitised (mostly containerised) loads.

What this leads to is the, almost, heretical statement that FOB, CFR and CIF are actually obsolete for the majority of exports and imports. The fact that they are still the most commonly used terms is somewhat unfortunate.

The fact is that the only really identifiable points on a modern international transit are the departure and destination depots, rather than the point where the container or road trailer crosses a non-existent ship's rail, and terms which identify the depot rather than the port are far preferable.

In fact it could be argued that there are only four terms (and four places) of any real relevance:

- EXW - at the seller's premises but only when it is the buyer's preference
- FCA - inland depot or seller's premises
- CIP/CPT - destination depot
- DDP - buyer's premises

This is particularly true for trade within the Single European Market. As there are arguably minimal differences between domestic movements and cross frontier movements within the Single Market, it is logical that, just as FOB Manchester or CIF Glasgow make little sense in the UK, then FOB and CIF make no more sense in Europe. The only logical terms in domestic trade are either delivered or not, that is Ex Works or Delivered, and it is also logical that they should apply to the Single Market. Add the UK depot (FCA) and the destination depot (CIP) and that is all you need.

Price calculation

The calculation of accurate export selling prices is clearly dependent on the relevant trade term but, at the risk of stating the obvious, depends on the starting point of an accurate EXW price.

The trade terms directly affect the component, and cumulative, elements of the price which are added on to an EXW base. On the assumption that most companies are able to calculate an EXW price, based on an accurate costing plus a profit margin, then the components of the final quoted price would be as illustrated in Table 4.2.4.

Exactly how costs such as freight and insurance premiums are calculated is covered in detail in other chapters of this handbook.

A final point: there seems to be a perception within some companies, particularly in the sales departments, that export has 'hidden costs'. Of course there are no such thing as hidden costs, only those that we do not choose to find.

Table 4.2.4 - Components of the final quoted price

EXW	PRODUCTION COSTS + PROFIT
	+
	EXPORT PACKING
	+
FCA	INLAND CARRIAGE & INSURANCE TO
FAS	NAMED DEPOT OR PORT
	FOB
	+
CFR	INTERNATIONAL FREIGHT
CPT	TO NAMED DESTINATION
	+
CIF	CARGO INSURANCE PREMIUM
	CIP
	+
DES	DISCHARGE COSTS
	DEQ
	+
	ON – CARRIAGE
	+
	DAF
DDU	CUSTOMS CLEARANCE
	DDP

Part 5

International Transport

5.1

Modes of international transport

In the dim and distant past the UK exporter had an easy job in choosing the mode of transport for an international consignment. It went by sea, or it did not go.

The modern exporter is now faced not only with a range of modes of transport (sea, air, road or rail) but with a wide variety of specialized services within each mode. It is no longer enough to simply decide to send the goods by sea, or air, but decisions need to be made regarding the use of unitised systems, FCL or LCL services, RO/RO or LO/LO, LASH or BACAT, and so on. An understanding of the wide range of modern freight services is essential to the exporter attempting to compete competitively in world markets.

Freight forwarders

Most exporters, and nearly all importers, use freight forwarders. Some use only one, others use dozens, but clearly the freight forwarder plays an essential part in the UK's international trading activities.

Their basic function is to act as intermediaries between shippers, with goods to send, and carriers with space to be filled, as defined in Figure 5.1.1.

The traditional situation represents a clear cut distinction between the range of organisations providing cargoes, either as pure manufacturers,

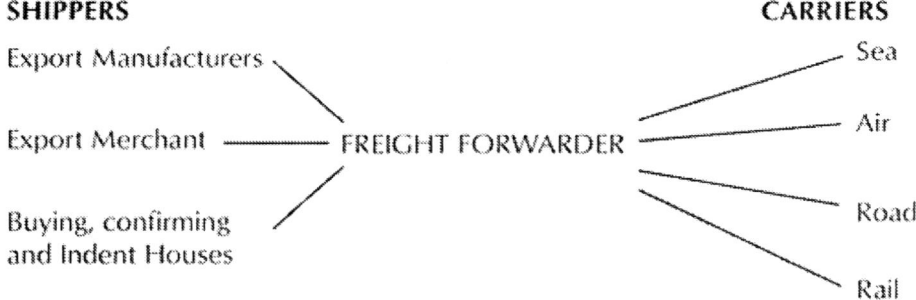

Figure 5.1.1 - The freight forwarder as intermediary

merchants or as representatives of overseas buyers, and the freight forwarder acting as an agent between them and the various shipping and air lines, and road and rail carriers.

However, over the last decade the distinction has become somewhat blurred. The exporter is now more likely to become involved in own account operations; that is, they will carry their own goods. This is perfectly feasible for road freight movements, although much more difficult for other modes of transport, and reflects the increase in the UK's trade with Western Europe, which now represents some 65% of its total exports.

Also the increase in containerised movements, and the growth of Inland Clearance Depots, has made it easier for the carriers to move their operations inland and offer their own groupage and documentation services.

Finally, and most importantly in terms of future developments, the Customs & Excise are proceeding ever faster towards the collection of trade information through computerised systems which provide Customs declarations in electronics form. Whilst this has increased the importance of the forwarder's ability to make direct inputs it has also meant that declarations of European Union trade via the Intrastat system are increasingly produced by traders themselves rather than by agents.

All of these developments have caused the freight forwarder to do one of three things; go out of business, get bigger or become more specialised. There are actually less forwarding agents than there used to be but the range of services which they offer has expanded into almost every area related to the movement of goods or people.

The services of the forwarder

Advice

As a service industry, the major function of all agents is to provide specialist advice. In the case of the forwarding agent this advice will be specific to the complex procedures of inter-national trade. Good agents will have detailed knowledge of Transport and Customs procedures in particular, and can save the trader much time and money, both in terms of legal com-pliance with systems and the selection of optimum procedures.

Documentation

Much of the day-to-day work of the forwarder is concerned with the completion of a range of documents to do with inter-national physical distribution. Some exporters produce nothing but an invoice and leave all other documents to their agent. Others subcontract the more specialized documentation, particularly Customs documents, but complete the remainder in-house.

Customs clearance

In relation to the above, the role of the forwarder in arranging Customs clearance of both export and import consignments is extremely important, and the majority of declarations are completed by agents on behalf of traders. As will be mentioned later, this does not mean that the exporter or importer can abdicate responsibility for the accuracy of these declarations.

Transport booking

Exporters can approach carriers directly and book space on their own behalf, but many find it more convenient to use for-warders who can perhaps make more efficient arrangements for carriage. The agent will also be able to predict accurately the carriage charges for particular transits.

Groupage

The expression 'unitization' describes the growing trend towards the movement of goods in standard size units, the most obvious example of which is the ISO standard container. Since many exporters are not able to produce 'Full Container Loads' then, to take advantage of containerisation, they deliver 'Less than Container Loads' to forwarders who group a number of different exporters consignments into one full load. Containerisation and groupage are covered in more detail later in this chapter.

In addition to the main services mentioned above, the larger forwarders will also be involved in many other functions, which could include any or all of the following:

- packing and marking;
- storage;
- personal and business travel;
- personal effects;
- exhibition goods; courier services.

As most traders make use of forwarding agents to a lesser or greater extent then they are clearly seen to offer advantages to the trade.

Advantages of using freight forwarders

Expertise

As previously stated, the forwarder operates within a service industry which offers specialized knowledge in certain areas. All forwarders should have a good grasp of basic international trade procedures and be able to give advice in a wide variety of areas, not just on physical distribution. Some will also specialize in certain market areas (often having contacts and offices at destination), or specific types of transport (refrigerated, large indivisible, and so on) or types of goods (hazardous, foodstuffs, livestock and even antiques).

Contacts

The contacts forwarders have in the UK and overseas may be official ones with carriers, Customs & Excise, receiving authorities, warehouse keepers and other agents, but just as important are the personal, and informal, contacts that individuals have with other individuals which should not be underestimated, in terms of avoiding problems, and finding quick solutions when they occur.

Facilities

Most forwarders can offer, or arrange, a wide range of physical facilities for traders, including storage, packing and repacking, sorting and checking, as well as the actual movement of goods. Of increasing importance are the computer facilities of the forwarders which take advantage of the growing 'Direct Trader Input' of Customs declarations.

Convenience

Whilst convenience may not seem to be such a powerful advantage in the use of forwarders, it has to be said that for many traders it is the main reason why they use agents rather than do it themselves. The point is that many exporters and importers choose to do what they do well, which is to manufacture or procure goods and sell them overseas, and are very happy to subcontract the physical distribution problems to third parties.

Disadvantages of using freight forwarders

To be perfectly equitable, it has to be said that the use of forwarders may also involve some disadvantages.

Increased cost

Because a third party is involved, which is attempting to be a profit making organisation, then it must cost more for traders to use intermediaries rather than do it themselves. It can be argued that the savings that agents can generate more than compensate for the fees that they charge, but there is still no doubt that a trader, doing the job properly, would reduce costs.

Loss of control

Some exporters find it difficult to accept that a third party should have such control of, and access to, their business, and endeavour to keep everything in-company. Increasingly, bottlenecks can sometimes happen with the typical forwarder representing a very large number of traders

The British International Freight Association (BIFA) acts as a trade association for forwarders in the UK and provides a Code of Conduct and standard contract terms.

A final point regarding the use of freight forwarders should be emphasised. The exporter or importer has a perfect right to delegate the business of physical distribution, and documentation, to an agent but it should never be forgotten that the forwarder is an agent, and the trader remains the principal in any dealings. This is particularly important in respect of the mandatory obligations to comply with Customs & Excise requirements which cannot be abdicated to an agent. The Customs will always hold the trader liable for the accuracy of any declarations, even if they are made by an agent on the trader's behalf.

Modes of international transport

Sea freight

The two basic forms of ocean cargo carriers are identified in Figure 5.1.2.

Figure 5.1.2- Alternative forms of ocean cargo carriers

LINERS	TRAMPS
General cargo and passengers	Mostly bulk cargo
Regular sailing schedules	No schedule (react to demand)
Regular routes	No fixed routes
Firm freight rates	Rates subject to negotiation
Bill of lading	Charter party

The distinction between liners and tramps is based on the nature of the service and not the type of vessel. Tramp vessels are not so called because they are rather scruffy, but because they have no fixed abode. Perhaps the most appropriate analogy is that the liners are the buses of the shipping world, whilst the tramps are the taxis.

Liners offer regular schedules, between the same ports, based on an advertised sailing schedule, and carry the majority of international sea transits (certainly in terms of the number of consignments). Tramps will carry, generally bulk, cargoes from almost anywhere in the world to anywhere else, and negotiate a rate for the job.

Many liner services, operating on the same routes, voluntarily form together into 'Freight Conferences'. They cooperate on both rates and schedules and are, of course, illegal, particularly in terms of European Union Competition law. However, whilst the lines do not compete on rates, they do benefit the shipper in terms of their cooperation on schedules and the exporter is virtually guaranteed a regularity of service. Just like buses, when operating efficiently, there will be one vessel for a particular destination, receiving cargo every seven days, rather than three receiving all at once and then nothing for a month.

There may also be Non-Conference lines operating on some routes, in competition with the Conferences, and this means that the exporter has, basically, three choices

- Conference line;
- Non-conference line;
- Tramp.

The cheapest freight rate per ton of these three will invariably be the tramp, but very few exporters can produce cargoes of sufficient size to interest even small tramp steamers. The choice between Conference and Non-Conference lines is influenced by the fact that the Conferences offer immediate discounts, usually 9.5%, off the freight invoice to shippers who contract to use Conference vessels only. Alternatively, deferred rebates, usually 10%, are given following periods of loyalty to the Conference. It may also be the case that Non-Conference services are either not available on certain routes, or are seen as being less reliable than the Conference services.

The simple consequence is that the majority of exporters use Conference lines for all of their sea freight consignments.

The equivalent distinction in terms of air freight would be between schedule and charter; tramping is also an expression used to describe road haulage operations across national frontiers.

Charter party

Before we examine the range of liner services available to the exporter, it is sensible to briefly look at the arrangements which could be made with a tramp operator, and which could be relevant to larger traders. There are basically three types of charters which can be arranged.

Voyage charter

The vessel is chartered for one specific voyage between specified ports. This may involve more than one port of call but is nevertheless just one voyage.

Time charter

The vessel is chartered for a period of time. During that period the charterers might have a degree of freedom regarding the use of the vessel, or it may only allow a number of repetitive voyages.

Bareboat (Demise) charter

Both of the previous charters depend on the vessel owner operating and crewing the ship, and the vessel owners' own Master will be in control. A Bareboat charter is almost self-explanatory in that the charterers takes over the vessel, often for periods of time as long as 15 years, and operates the vessel as if it were their own. This is not uncommon, for example, in the oil industry, where the tankers carrying oil company's cargoes are crewed by oil company staff, but will revert back to the vessel owners at the end of the charter period.

In all these cases, the contract will be based on the Charter Party, and a Charter Party Bill of Lading will be issued. It should be noted that such Bills are not acceptable to banks against Letters of Credit requiring Shipping Company's Bills, as the banks have no knowledge of the contract of carriage conditions.

On the assumption that the average exporter will be using liner services for most, if not all, sea freight there are still alternatives from which to choose.

Types of sea freight services

Conventional

The traditional, but now less common, service carrying break-bulk, that is non-unitised cargoes. The development of containerisation over the last 30 years has severely reduced the number of conventional vessels in operation.

Containerised

By far the most common sea freight service used by the average exporter. The principle was first developed in the mid 1950s and is based on the concept of moving goods in standard sized units ie unitised loads. The service is sometimes referred to as Lift On/Lift Off (LO/LO) in that the container is lifted from one mode of transport on to another.

The majority of containers are built to the International Standards Organisation specification, basically 6 or 12 metre, and a wide range of different designs are now in common use.

These include:

- insulated and/or refrigerated (reefers)
- open topped
- curtain sided
- liquid and powder tanks
- half height (donkey)
- hazardous cargo tank containers (tanktainers)

There are few cargoes which cannot be containerised, except for the very large indivisibles.

It is also important to note that the standard container is suitable for all surface freight, and not just sea, which yields major advantages.

Multi-modal

The risk of loss or damage to the goods is much reduced because he goods are not handled as they transfer from one mode of transport to another, for example road trailer to vessel. This allows an exporter who can fill a container, that is supply Full Container Loads (FCL), to actually arrange door to door deliveries during which the goods will not be handled at all.

Through documentation

Because containers move goods door to door, or depot to depot, the documentation covers more than just the sea freight part of the journey. This also means that 'through freight rates' are used which cover the greater part of the journey.

Vessel efficiency

There are a number of advantages to the vessel owner, notably the ease of segregation of cargoes which require separation from others and the 'turn-round' time of the vessel, that is the time spent in discharging and receiving cargo, is minimized because of the speed with which the container units can be handled.

Specialist barge services

There is a growing use in mainland Europe, if not in the UK, of vessels which are designed to carry floating lighters or barges. These units are like floating containers but carry up to 600 tonnes of cargo, and their main advantage is that they make use of inland waterway systems, the cheapest means of inland transport. The barges are floated into ports such as Antwerp, Rotterdam and Zeebrugge and the ocean going vessels load them for the deep-sea movement. The most common versions are Lighter Aboard Ship (LASH) and Barge Aboard Catamaran (BACAT) but sea-going barges known as SEABEES, which move as large pontoons of barges, are also available.

Whilst this list does not exhaust the range of sea freight services, others are more appropriate to road or rail modes and are covered below.

Road freight

The function of the international road haulier has become increasingly important to the UK's export business in that over 60% of its exports are to western Europe and a very large proportion of that (over 80%) is moved by road freight.

Since the UK is an island, these road trailer loads are dependent on Roll On/Roll Off (RO/RO) services to cross the North Sea or Channel. In fact RO/RO vessels also offer deep sea services. The load may be accompanied by the driver who continues the journey, or be unaccompanied and a 'subsequent' carrier will collect the trailer and continue the transit to destination.

Rail freight

Only a small proportion of UK exports are shipped by rail freight (approximately 6%) and those that are use the rail equivalent of RO/RO, that is a Train Ferry service, particularly from Dover to Dunkirk. However, the environmental problems of increased road freight usage and the opening of the Channel Tunnel mean that there is great potential for the growth of rail freight

Apart from the specific operation of the Channel Tunnel, European freight movers have, for many years, operated road-rail services, often referred to as 'Piggyback', based on road trailers being carried on specially designed rail wagons.

In particular, French railways have operated so called Kanga-roo services all over Europe. There is also a growing use of 'Swapbodies' which are flat bed wagons, without wheels, carried on rail wagons.

Air freight

The traditional use of air for high value, low volume, cargoes will always exist but there is now a clear trend towards the increased use of air transport for many other cargoes. In fact there has been an average increase in the volume of air cargo out of the UK of almost 9% per annum since 1992.

The benefits of speed and security, very competitive rates and the increased appreciation of the Total Distribution Cost of a transit rather than just the freight cost (see later) have persuaded many exporters that air freight is a genuine and viable option.

Much of this cargo is carried on scheduled passenger aircraft rather than dedicated freight flights and there has also been an increase in combined services, which link either sea or road transits with air freight legs, using combined transport documentation.

Just as many of the shipping lines form together into Freight Conferences, so some 80% of scheduled air traffic is operated by members of the air freight equivalent which is the International Air Transport Association (IATA). The IATA Traffic Conferences operate in the same way in terms of cooperation on rates, but also attempt to promote safe, regular and economical air commerce. Whilst IATA deals with the commercial aspects of airline operations, the International Civil Aviation Organisation (ICAO), which is a branch of the United Nations, governs relationships between member countries.

Groupage

This applies to all modes of transport and describes the group-ing of a number of distinct export consignments into one unitised load. The most typical unit is the ISO container, carrying Less than Container Loads (LCLs), but road trailers and rail wagons are also units which require certain quantities of cargo to fill.

In air freight the expression more commonly used is Consolidation and the standard unit is referred to as a Unit Load Device (ULD), sometimes called an Igloo because of its distinctive shape. These services may be offered by the carriers themselves or by specialized Groupage operators which are often general Freight Forwarders.

Express operations

Express operations are an area of rapid development, specialising in relatively small consignments, up to 40 Kilos, and use large networks of vehicles and aircraft to guarantee deliveries within specified time limits. They may also be linked with courier services which specialize in documents and very light items, again guaranteeing fast and personal delivery.

It will be clear from the above that the international trader has a very wide choice as to the specific transport mode and nature of service for each consignment. So, what factors will need to be considered when making that choice?

Choosing a mode of transport

Destination

The final destination of the goods will clearly have a direct influence on the transport service used. Certain modes of transport become a logical 'rule of thumb' for particular markets, unless there are reasons why other modes should be used.

It is not surprising that over 80% of the UK's exports to western Europe are by road, and that the most com-mon transport mode for our markets in developing countries is sea freight, although there is a growing use of air freight into those countries.

Availability

In relation to the above comments it is generally the case that the most available transport services, in terms of number, regularity and quality, will be those most commonly used for certain destinations.

Type of goods

There are many factors to do with the nature of the goods to be shipped which will affect the mode used. These include:

- Size
  Large indivisibles (which cannot be 'broken down') require very special treatment and routing. It may also be that very dense cargoes cannot be moved as full loads because they will exceed legal weights.
- Segregation
  Some goods are liable to taint others, or be easily tainted them-selves. That is to say they impart on other goods, or pick up themselves, odours or flavours which are not desirable. This may preclude the use of a normal groupage service.
- Fragility
  Not only does this affect the nature of packing but also leads to modes of transport which minimize handling and maximize speed of transit.
- Value
  Likewise, highly valuable goods will require minimum handling and maximum speed. It is also the case that certain services, for example express, can provide greater levels of security and personal care than others.

- Perishability
  Perishable goods need maximum speed of transit and often special stowage.
- Special Requirements
  Apart from the above there are many other special needs which the transport method must accommodate. These include refrigeration, insulation, ventilation and even heating. Plus all the packing, marking and stowage requirements of hazardous goods.

Speed of transit

It is not only perishable or high value goods which are appropriate to fast transit times, but also those for which there is an urgent demand. This would include items such as replacement components for broken down equipment, or vehicles off the road. It should also be borne in mind that a faster transit invariably leads to earlier payment with calculable financial benefits. More on this later.

Cost

A factor which is always of concern whenever choices must be made in business. In the case of international transport it is pretty obviously the case that the freight rate charged will differ from one service to another, and that the fastest method, that is, air freight, will be the most expensive, and the slowest, usually sea freight, will be the cheapest. It is extremely important that the exporter is able to make accurate predictions of the freight costs, not only as an aid to choice of mode of transport, but also to ensure that the quoted prices adequately cover all costs.

Freight calculation

It is an unfortunate fact that many exporter's method of calculating a freight cost is to telephone a freight forwarder and ask them to do it. Some exporters have only a vague idea as to the true cost of international movements, and operate on rough; and often outdated, figures. It is not uncommon that a percentage of the value of the goods is used as an estimate of freight for various destinations. This could work, but not when the percentage has not been checked for the last few years. 'Guesstimates' of a cost per ton, with no reference to current tariffs, represent another way of taking the easy way out, and another way of losing money.

There is no reason why every exporter cannot calculate the freight charge for each individual consignment, without the need to rely on a third party, such as the freight forwarder, and get it right every time. All carriers operate on the basis of open and firm tariffs for the whole of their service, and the principle which governs the calculation is the same for all modes of transport.

Sea freight calculation

An enquiry to a shipping line for a specific freight rate could elicit a response such as

US $285.00 per freight ton – Weight or Measure.

Quite what is meant by a 'freight ton' or 'weight or measure' we will look at soon, but first we should examine the criteria which affect the actual base freight rate quoted.

The rate quoted by carriers is based on:

* Destination

Logically enough, the carrier offering a range of services to different destinations will charge different rates depending on the final point of delivery. Typically lines will operate regular (scheduled) services to specified destinations, and will specialize in certain geographic areas.

Clearly, the further away the destination then the higher the freight rate is likely to be, but distance is not the only criteria affecting rates. The carrier must also consider other operating costs related to specific destinations such as routing costs (canal and inland waterway links), port or harbour dues, berthing fees, lighterage and/or handling charges, and any other costs specific to a particular route and destination.

Many carriers will therefore operate on a tariff which contains a number of basic freight rates per freight ton for the specific points of delivery on their schedule.

* Commodity

In addition to the differing destination rates, which is perfectly logical, carriers also charge a range of different rates dependent on the nature of the goods themselves, which might appear to be somewhat less logical. It is not unusual for lines to have anything up to 22 different commodity rates for each destination.

The explanation is partly to do with the fact that higher value goods do increase the carrier's liability for loss or damage but is mostly to do with the range of cargoes carried by sea, Imagine the situation if all goods attracted the same freight rate. Freight as a percentage of the value of the goods would differ enormously in that high value goods would pay very low percentage freight, whilst low value goods would be paying very high percentages of their value as freight.

A final consideration regarding commodity rates is the carrier's need to accommodate the Stowage Factor of goods. This refers to the weight of a commodity in relation to its volume, that is the density of the goods. Clearly the stowage factor would differ greatly from, say, stainless steel sheet to foam rubber, and this affects the available capacity of the carrier.

As we shall see when we actually look at the calculation of a freight charge for a particular consignment, the method of calculation does directly relate to the Weight and the Measure (or volume) of goods, but some carriers use a tariff which ignores the nature of the commodity but contains perhaps eight classes based on the weight to measure ratio of the goods.

- Box rates

Because of the predominance of containerised movements for modern ocean freight it is not surprising that there is a move towards the calculation of freight based on the standard container load, as opposed to the weight or measure of its contents. The typical situation is that the carrier will apply a small number of broad commodity bands and calculate a 'lump sum' charge for the box. By definition this FCL 'box rate' can only apply to exporters able to supply Full Container Loads as opposed to Less than Container Loads, but it does also allow for large shippers to negotiate very favourable rates for sufficient FCL shipments.

It is also possible that so called Freight of All Kinds (FAK) rates can be obtained. This represents a situation in which a relatively large number of containers, composed of a wide range of different commodities, are shipped as one consignment. The carrier may be prepared to charge an 'averaged' rate rather than be involved in a complex breakdown of the individual commodities. Whilst this is not a common method of charge it can be seen that it has a clear relevance to Grouped or Consolidated consignments and could be negotiated by the groupage operators rather than the exporters.

- Ad valorem

In rare cases the freight rate may be calculated as a percentage of the value of the goods. A quoted rate per freight ton may be followed by a comment such as 'or 3% ad valorem', in which case if 3% of the value of the goods is greater than any weight or measure charge then that percentage is charged. It serves to reflect the increase in the liability of the carrier but is quite unusual in practice.

Whatever the basis of the freight rate the carriers will also operate a Minimum Rate which will be charged should the calculated freight fall below the specified minimum. This clearly applies to relatively small consignments and can be avoided by the use of groupage (LCL) services.

Unfortunately, finding the appropriate freight rate for a particular commodity is not the end of the exporter's problems in that there are often adjustments to the basic rate which have to be taken into account.

Typical adjustments would include:

- Conference Discounts or Rebate. Either 9.5% Immediate Discount (for contract signatories) or 10% Deferred Rebate.
- Currency Adjustment Factor (CAF). As most shipping lines use the US $ as the basis for their tariffs they make adjustments to allow for fluctuations in the value of the $ against the currency in which they earn their revenues. The actual £, sterling rate used will be based on the agreed conversion rate on the sailing date.
- Bunker Adjustment Factor (BAF) Bunkerage is the expression used to describe the fuel used by the vessel and derives from the coal bunkers used on the original steam ships. The BAF therefore reflects any changes, generally increases, in the cost of fuel to the carrier.

Having considered all of the above we should now have a basic freight rate per freight ton which can be applied to an individual consignment to calculate the specific freight charge. As we saw earlier this would often be expressed as US $285.00 per freight ton – Weight or Measure.

The shipping line will charge either on the weight of the consignment or its volume, whichever gives them the greatest return. This is still sometimes referred to as 'W/M Ship's Option'. This is perfectly reasonable as the carrier's capacity is limited both by the space available for cargo and the maximum weight (deadweight) which can legally be carried.

A vessel fully loaded with steel sheet will still have volume unused, and a vessel full of foam rubber would not use anywhere near its deadweight capacity. The process of freight calculation takes into account the different stowage factors of the wide range of commodities carried.

For sea freight the units used are:

Metric Tonne	or	Cubic Metre
(1,000 Kg)		(CBM or M³)

The weight unit is 1,000 kg, commonly known as the metric ton or tonne, and the freight will be calculated on the gross weight of the consignment. That is to say that the weight of the packing (Tare weight) will also be included for freight purposes.

As an example, a consignment of 2 cases each 4,000 Kg would generate a total of 8 freight tons.

The volume, or measure, unit is the cubic metre and is calculated by a multiplication of the length by breadth by height. Thus if our two cases above where each 200 cms x 200 cms x 150 cms then each would be 6 cubic metres (CBM), giving a total of 12 CBM.

This can be calculated by a multiplication of the cms to give cubic centimetres, and then a division by 1,000,000 (1 CBM = 1,000,000 cubic cms) or, more easily by converting cms into metres, by dividing by 100, and then multiplying. Thus, in our example we actually have 2 cases which are 2 m x 2 m x 1.5 m, that is 6 CBM per case.

Given that the freight rate for these two cases was, for example, $285.00, then the freight cost would be:12 CBM x $285.00 = $3,420.00NOT 8 tonnes x $285.00 = $2,280.00the carrier charging on volume, not weight.It should also be noted that the volume must be calculated on.

The Appendix contains a fully worked example of a sea freight calculation, including insurance premium and duty, which is actually a model answer from the international Physical Distribution examiner of The Institute of Export.

Road/rail freight calculation

The other two modes of surface freight are based on exactly the same method of calculation, that is Weight or Measure, but there does tend to be a greater range of rates applied, particularly in the highly competitive area of road haulage.

Also it is very common that the ratio of weight to measure changes, the most common being 1,000 Kg or 3.3 CBM. Sometimes, because the average consignment size may be smaller than 1,000 Kg, the carriers will quote rates based on smaller units of 100 Kg or 0.33 CBM.

Air freight calculation

Just as with surface freight, the principle of weight/volume is applicable to air freight, but the structure of the carrier's tariff is different.

The typical airline will base its tariff on:

- *General Cargo Rates (GC)*
  These apply to non-unitised consignments of mixed commodities
- *Specific Commodity Rates (SC)*
  Shippers of large quantities of specific commodities between specific ports can apply for SC rates which will be much lower than the GC rates.

In the case of both GC and SC rates the lines will often offer quantity discounts once a certain level of business is achieved.

Classification rates

Certain categories of goods, for example live animals, cadavers and bullion attract charges based on a discount or surcharge on the GC rate.

Unit Load Device Rate (ULD)

ULDs are the air equivalent of the ISO container. The ULD rates ignore the nature of the goods and charge for a specific unit up to a specified maximum weight. They are the air equivalent of the 'box rates' which may be available for sea shipments.

Freight of All Kinds (FAK)

There is a growing use of FAK rates as a means of simplifying the rate structure and avoiding SC rates. A rate per kilo is charged subject to a minimum weight requirement.

The actual calculation of air freight charges is again based on a ratio of weight to volume which is somewhat different from sea freight. The most common ratio is 1,000 Kg or 6 CBM.

It will be clear that volume does not become relevant to air consignments unless the cargo is extremely voluminous. So whilst the majority of sea shipments are charged by volume, it is more usual for air cargoes to be calculated on the basis of weight.

In practice the ratio of 1,000 Kg or 6 CBM is somewhat too large for the average air consignment and it is therefore more usual for rates to be quoted per kilogram or per 6,000 cubic cms, that is the volume unit is one thousandth of 6 CBM. A 6,000 cubic cms unit is referred to as a 'volumetric unit' or a 'chargeable kilo'.

Take as an example: a case of 50 kilos, 100 cms x 100 cms x 50 cmsat a rate of £9.00 per chargeable kilo.The freight charge will not be 50 kilos x £9.00 = £450.00but will be   83.33 volume units x 5,9.00 = 5,750.00.(The volume units being the product of 100 cms x 100 cms x 50 cms = 500,000 cubic cms, divided by 6,000 cubic cms.)

In conclusion, each transport mode will generate its own basic tariff, based on factors such as destination, commodity, value and standards units, and will apply that basic rate to the weight or volume of the cargo in order to maximize revenues in relation to the carrier's limits on deadweight and space available. The ratio of weight to volume will differ from one mode of transport to another, but the principle of W/M (weight or measure) is one which applies to all modes.

Total distribution cost

Assuming that we are now in a position to calculate an accurate freight cost we still must accept that the freight itself is not the only cost item which should be considered in comparing one mode of transport to another. The concept of Total Distribution Cost, mentioned earlier in this chapter, is based on the fact that a number of other, transport related factors, in addition to freight cost, can be quantified, in order to make a more realistic choice as to transport mode and route.

A simple comparison of freight costs will always reveal air freight as being far more expensive than surface freight, but a consideration of other cost factors could change that perception.

Elements of the Total Distribution Cost, other than the freight charge, would include:

- Packing
  The need for protection is reduced where the transit time, and level of handling, is reduced.
- Documentation
  A simplified documentary regime, which is offered by air freight, and to a lesser extent road and rail, can lead to savings in ad-ministrative costs.
- Inland carriage
  It is often the case that there are major differences between the costs of transport into the port of departure, and from the port of destination, which will depend on the mode, and specific ports, involved.
- Insurance
  it may be the case that the cargo insurance premiums will differ depending on the mode of transport, the most common dis-tinction being between air and surface freight.
- Unpacking and refurbishing
  With some goods, following, surface movements, extensive renovation of the goods and packing is necessary. This can be minimized by fast transits such as air freight.
- Speed of transit
  Many of the points raised lead to a conclusion that air ship-ments provide a number of advantages as compared with surface freight, many of which are related to the reduction in handling time and the speed of transit. Perhaps the most obvious consequence of a faster transit time is the fact that, whatever the terms of payment, then payment will be received sooner. The higher the interest rates faced by exporters then the greater are the savings from quicker payments.

Taking all these factors into consideration it is possible to prepare a Total Distribution Cost Analysis which compares the transport options available to the exporter for a particular consignment.

Figure 5.1.3 illustrates how a simplistic comparison of sea and air freight might look.

The additional saving from faster payment of the delivered price if we were to assume that the reduction in transit time between air and sea transits was 28 days (which would be perfectly reasonable for any dispatch to a developing country) and if interest rates were, for example, 5%, is calculated n Figure 5.1.4.

Figure 5.1.3 - Comparison of sea and air total distribution costs

	AIR £	SEA £
Ex Works value	26,000	26,000
Freight	1,170	220
Packing	190	530
Inland transport - UK	50	200
Overseas	130	430
Insurance	60	70
Total	27,600	27,450

Whilst this example is not representative of all consignments, it does illustrate the point that a consideration of all the quantifiable factors of physical distribution may well lead to a more objective choice of transport modes which takes into consideration more than just the freight costs. The narrowing of the gap between air and surface freight cost is typical of a genuine and comprehensive comparison which all exporters should attempt.

The calculation of a true Total Distribution Cost can provide great advantages to all exporters and could lead to a more professional approach to the whole area of Physical Distribution Management. This would involve the consideration of all aspects of the physical movement of goods, from the receipt of raw materials, through the whole process of internal handling and storage to the actual delivery to the end-user.

It is not the purpose of this text to examine Physical Distribution Management (PDM), often referred to as Logistics, in any detail but perhaps the example of Toyota's success in PDM could be instructive. Toyota (allegedly) have achieved the ultimate level of efficiency by making Just In Time (JIT) principles actually work.

They claim to hold zero inventory, that is, no stock at all. Components arrive from suppliers JIT to be fitted, JIT to be tested, JIT to be packed, JIT to be dispatched, JIT to be shipped, JIT to arrive and JIT (it is hoped) to be sold.

Well, it is worth thinking about, and is certainly an improvement on the more common British version known as JTL (Just Too Late!).

Figure 5.1.4 - Comparison of total distribution costs adjusted for interest

	AIR £	SEA £
Delivered price	27,600	27,450
Interest saved	- 106	
Total Cost	27,494	27,450

5.2

Packing and marking for export

The vital importance of correct packing and marking of export consignments is often not appreciated by many companies, even though they may take great pains with other elements of the export process. This is particularly short sighted when one realises that in virtually all export sales it is the seller who will be responsible for adequate export packing and correct marking.

Not only can it represent a significant cost element in terms of price calculation but also if the goods get to the customer smashed to pieces, or with half of them missing, or they arrive in perfect condition in the wrong place this can be extremely expensive in terms of direct financial loss, time taken in corrective action and loss of customer goodwill.

What must be accepted is that packing and marking for export is a highly specialised function, and what is considered adequate for domestic dispatches is invariably inadequate for overseas dispatches.

There are a number of reasons why export consignments face greater risks of theft, pilferage and damage than do domestic consignments.

- Distance
  On a purely statistical basis there is more likelihood of loss or damage, the longer the transit.
- Increased handling
  Most loss and damage occurs to goods during handling.
- Quality of handling
  Not only do goods tend to be handled more often when exported but also the quality of handling may leave something to be desired.
- Environmental conditions
  Overseas consignments are often subject to far more arduous conditions than are domestic transits

As a final point, the exporter should be aware that goods need to be prepared for the whole of the journey, not just the easiest part. Even containerised goods are broken down and on -carried towards the end of their journey in conditions which may be much inferior to those prevailing at the beginning. It is a sensible exporter who prepares goods for the worst possible element of the transit, not the best possible.

So what do we expect from our packing? It must:

- Protect;
- Contain;
- Identify.

The packing protects against damage and pilferage, contains the goods so that they can be handled, even when protection may be less relevant, and bears the marks which enable the goods to be identified.

Whilst there is little problem in identifying what export packing is required to do, the actual choice as to how goods will be packed is far more difficult. An increasing problem is the huge choice of methods which exporters now have.

Packing methods

- Cartons
  The carton is the most widely used type of outer packing now used, and available in a range of materials, in particular, double or triple walled cardboard. In most cases, this combines adequate pro-tection, in most cases, with low cost and lightness.
- Cases or crates
  Traditionally made of wood, but less common now because of the ever-increasing cost of timber, the case is a solid box, whilst the crate is composed of a skeleton, or slatted, structure. Apart from the material cost and the added weight (which increases the freight cost) it may also be necessary for the wood to be treated with pesticides and be certified as such for certain markets.
- Bales
  Used regularly in certain trades where goods can be compressed and then wrapped, often with hessian, and banded, the bale is sometimes referred to as a 'truss', particularly when not banded.
- Drums
  Drums are produced in a very wide range of materials apart from the traditional steel variety. They are suitable for many liquid and powder goods.
- Sacks
  Again available in a range of materials, from paper to plastic, sacks are often used when containment is more important than protection.

In addition to the above, there is also a range of highly specialized forms of export packing suitable for specific goods, such as carboys, glass containers for corrosive liquids, steel cases for highly pilferable items, shrink wrap for goods damaged by moisture, and so on.

For advice on the range of packing materials available the exporter can, of course, consult the manufacturers, but must accept that they may be biased. A good forwarder or carrier can also be very helpful. An element of the British Standards

Institution known as Technical Help to Exporters, and the Paper and Board Printing and Packaging Industries Research Association (PIRA) can also offer specialised advice.

Given a fair knowledge of the choices available to the exporter what factors actually impact on the method eventually chosen?

Factors affecting choice of packing

- Nature of goods

   The special requirements of the goods must be considered. They may be bulky, fragile or valuable, or may require special packing, handling and stowage, perhaps to avoid sweating or tainting. The very special requirements of Dangerous Goods are examined in Chapter 5.3.

- Destination

   This relates to the distance to be travelled, the quality of hand-ling and the range of climatic conditions experienced by the goods. Also there may be specific regulations, in the country of destination, regarding the type of packing. Typically, this would be an insistence on the treatment of organic packing with insecticides, or even a total ban. Such regulations would not only affect wooden cases or crates, but also wood wool and straw.

- Mode of transport

   The need for protection, and the particular packing regulations, will differ from one mode of transport to another. As a broad example, it is often the case that packing for air freight needs to be less robust than for sea freight, on the grounds that the transit is shorter and handling more sophisticated.

- Customer's requirements

   In some cases the type of packing the exporter would normally use is replaced by a type requested by the customer. Assuming the buyer is prepared to pay any extra costs which this may involve, then the exporter would normally comply. Care should be taken if the buyer requests inferior packing in an attempt to save money, if only to ensure that the seller has no contractual obligations for damage in transit.

- Cost

   If cost was not a factor in the selection of packing methods then the great majority of goods would be packed in solid wooden cases. Because this is a very expensive method, cheaper, but adequate, alternatives must be found, such as cartons. We should also remember that the freight charge is based on the gross weight of the shipment that includes the weight of the packing, known as the 'tare' weight. Heavy packing is therefore not only a cost factor in its own right, but also increases the freight charge.

The use of second-hand packing as a means of reducing cost may be possible but the exporter should take great care to ensure that the packing is still adequate, and that any previous marks are completely removed. There is a potential risk that the carriers may issue claused receipts if they consider packing to be inadequate (see Chapter 5.3).

Marking for export

Once the goods are packed the exporter must make certain that they are marked sufficiently well to ensure that they get to the intended final destination. In this context, the only rules which apply are those concerning the marking of dangerous goods and these are addressed later.

So far as non-hazardous goods are concerned the only recommendations are available from Simpler Trade Procedures (SITPRO and the International Cargo Handling Coordination Association (ICHCA).

For air, road and rail movements it is not uncommon that the goods simply carry the full address of the consignee, in which case they would be labelled as opposed to marked. The parties involved should seriously consider whether the naming of the consignee poses any security problems in terms of the possible identification of the nature of the goods.

Where sea freight shipments are concerned, it is far more common for the goods to carry identification which is basically coded shipping marks. These have the great merit of being simple and do not clutter the packing with large amounts of, possibly irrelevant, information. SITPRO suggest that the marks should be 'sufficient and necessary for goods in transit'.

A typical mark is shown in Figure 5.2.1

Lead Mark	Identifies the consignee and, maybe, the consignment or order reference number.
Port Marks	It is important that the mark not only contains the final destination but also that the port of discharge is clearly displayed.
Sub Marks	These, for example, include Gross and Net Weights in Kilograms, dimensions in Centimetres, and running numbers which identify the unit number, for example 4 of 8, or 4/8 would identify case number 4 of a total of 8 cases.
Handling Marks	A range of standardized pictorial handling marks Have been established through the International Standards Organisation (ISO) and give clear instructions regarding the handling of goods which are recognized throughout the world.

The more common pictorial handling marks are illustrated in Figure 5.2.2 Exporters should also consider:

- Legibility
  Lead marks and Port marks should be at least 7.5 cms high and Sub marks at least 3.5 cms high. Care should also be taken that any banding does not mask the marks.
- Indelibility
  Obviously the mark needs to be permanent in all conditions. One which washes off in the rain is not particularly effective.
- Position
  It is important that the marks are always visible and this therefore requires at least two, and sometimes three, marks on different sides of the goods.

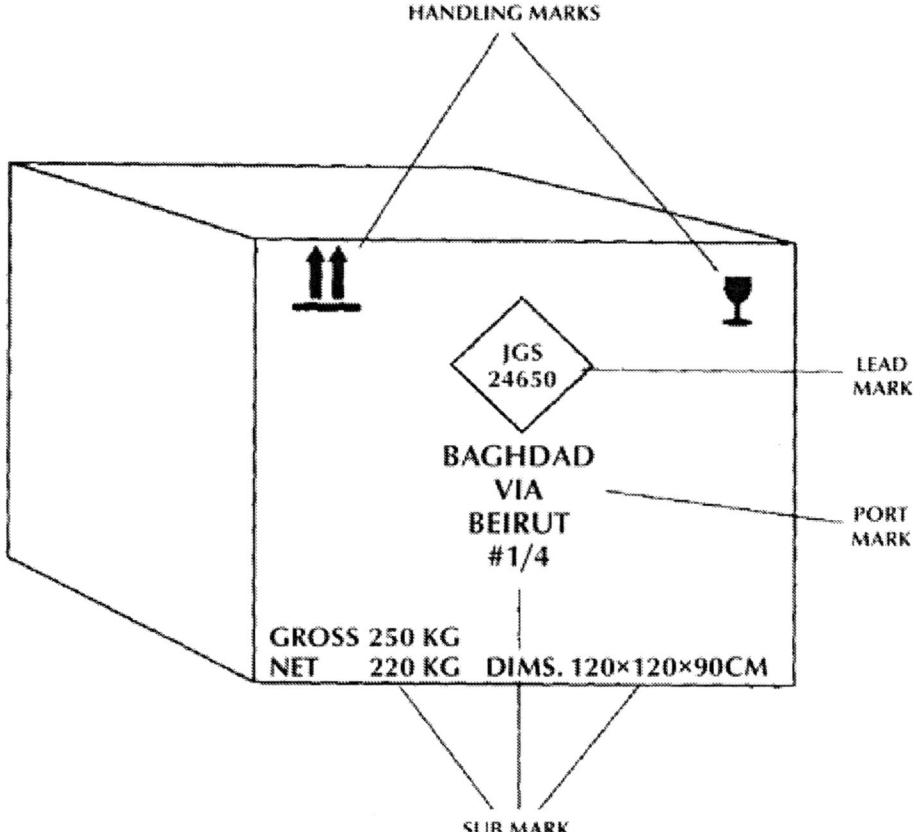

Figure 5.2.1 - Typical coded shipping mark

APPENDIX 5.2

Sample price calculation

A consignments of high quality textiles to be despatched to Ukraine.

Despatch is from Manchester Container base or airport and the terms of delivery are 'Delivered Duty Paid Kiev'. Delivery can be made by either road or air.

Consignment details are as follows:

| Sling here | Fragile | Use no hooks |

| This way up | Keep away from heat | Keep dry |

Centre of gravity

Figure 5.2.2 - Some pictorial handling marks

- Free Carrier (FCA) Manchester value of goods is £50,000.
- Packing - 10 cases, each measuring 150 x 150 x 100cms and weighing 250kgs.

The freight rates quoted are:

- Road - £550 per 1,000 chargeable kilos
- Air - £1.30 per chargeable kilo
- Chargeable weight/volume ratios are:
- Road 3cbm =1,000 kgs
- Air 6cbm =1,000 kgs
- Collection, delivery and other despatch charges total:
- Road -£150
- Air - £250

Insurance charged at a flat rate is:

- Road - £175
- Air - £ 95
- Ukraine Import Duty Rate 10% of landed value

If you wish to attempt the calculation – the answer is on the next page.

Solution

Delivered Duty Paid (DDP) Kiev

10 cases each, 150 X 150 X 100 cms. = 22.5 CBM (M^3)
    250 kgs. = 2.5 metric tonnes

	ROAD £	AIR £
FCA	50,000	50,000
FREIGHT	4,125	4,875
	(7.5 X £550 volume units)	(3750 X £1.30 volume units)
COLLECTION	150	250
Carriage Paid To (CPT) Kiev	54,275	55,125
INSURANCE	175	95
Carriage Insurance Paid (CIP) Kiev	54,450	55,220
DUTY (10 %)	5,445	5,522
Delivered Duty Paid (DDP)	59,895	60,742
	=========	=========

5.3

International transport documentation

Perhaps the biggest problem for companies involved in international trade is the number of bits of paper which are essential to the performance of their export contracts. That is to say that the documentation involved in the administration of their overseas business is perceived as being abundant in quantity, complex in character and designed to hinder rather than help their export effort.

Whilst there is an element of truth in this perception, it has to be said that many companies suffer from the consequences of this complexity because they make very little effort to understand the purposes and functions of the range of documents with which they deal. There is often an element of negligence in their own management, in particular in terms of staff training, which translates itself into a continuous saga of documentary errors and their, sometimes disastrous, consequences.

The fact that something like 70% of document sets, presented to banks against Letters of Credit, are rejected on first presentation due to documentary discrepancies does serve to prove this point.

It is an unfortunate fact that many personnel involved in export documentation have only received what is sometimes referred to as 'standing next to Nellie' training. The administrative procedures are passed on to new operatives by the more experienced ones, so that it is often clear what is to be done, but very rarely is it so clear why it needs to done.

Not only is this an extremely boring way to perform office functions for the personnel involved, it is also an extremely error prone process, simply because there is no real understanding of the consequences of procedures and documents are simply completed or produced by rote. Also, the systems become very inflexible and unable to accommodate anything out of the ordinary. Moreover, just because something works does not make it right, and it can often be the case that company systems incorporate mistakes which become almost 'carved in stone' because they work, despite being incorrect practice.

It could be said, with some validity, that because of the use of forwarding agents and of computerized systems, such an understanding is of less value in modern offices, but agents have to be instructed, monitored and, most importantly, paid; and computer systems have to be set up on the basis of a clear understanding of procedural requirements, all of which work much better with a knowledgeable principal.

This chapter looks at the 'why' of documentary procedures rather than just the 'what', and to show how logical the procedures are (yes, even Customs procedures) once it is clear exactly what they do.

An overview of export documentation

As has already been mentioned, the range of documents encountered by exporters is often seen as intimidating and confusing, and those involved directly in the procedural elements can find it difficult to take a step back and, as it were, see the wood for the trees.

This is aggravated by the, perhaps obvious, fact that it takes more than one piece of paper to move an international consignment. A set of documents is required which may be relatively simple and involve only three or four or may be extremely complex and include a number of specialised documents. Also, the set will differ from one consignment to another depending on the specific collection of variables including the type of goods, method of transport, destination, method of payment and the buyer's requirements.

It is possible to take what is a veritable 'mountain' of documents and to rationalise them into four smaller 'hills'. in that we can categorise any document used in international trade into one of four types depending on its origin or application.

The four categories are:

1. Transport.
2. Customs.
3. Insurance.
4. Payment.

With a little flexibility all international trade documents can be listed under these headings and Figure 5.3.1 lists those documents which will be described in the chapters which follow.

Figure 5.3.1 - International Trade Documents

Transport
Bill of Lading (B/L)
Air Waybill (AWB)
Road Waybill (CMR Note)
Rail Waybill (CIM Note)

Customs & Excise
Intrastat

Single Administrative Document (SAD)
Export Invoice
Certificate of Origin
Status Documents
ATA Carnet

Insurance
Policy
Certificate
Declarations

Payment
Letters of Instruction
Bill of Exchange
Letter of Credit

If any of the titles or abbreviations or not clear or familiar, rest assured that they will be explained in full in the following chapters.

Thus, an international consignment will require a set of documents which can be selected from those listed. As an example, a simple document set could be composed of a Bill of Lading, an Export Invoice, a Certificate of Origin, a Cargo Insurance Certificate and a Single Administrative Document.

This could also be supplemented by a wide range of more specialised documents, depending on each consignment's specific requirements.

The Transport Conventions

There is a fundamental problem associated with international trade which is so obvious that it is often missed. It is the fact that there are always at least two nationalities involved in the export transaction. This is most obvious when one considers the Contract of Sale (see chapter 3) in which the buyer and seller are of two different nationalities, and where the law governing the contract must be established.

These problems are compounded by the fact that the international carrier is often a third nationality.

The problems that this could cause to the exporter can be divided into two areas:

- the contract of carriage, and
- the bill of lading

The fundamental question is, do the carriers impose their conditions of carriage (dependent on nationality) on the shipper, in which case the exporter will potentially be involved in many different contracts of carriage; or do the shippers impose their conditions on the carrier, in which case the carrier, working for a range of different nationalities of shipper, has the same problem?

The same complexities could apply to the transport document, in that many different Bills of Lading could exist depending on the nationality of the shipper or the carrier.

The situation in practice is that a range of international conventions address, and solve, the problem of the mix of nationalities involved in the Contract of Carriage.

Each mode of international transport operates within the scope of a Convention which standardizes the documentation and the Contract of Carriage and which, in practice, mean that the exporter can generally ignore the nationality of the carrier. The International Transport Conventions are (briefly):

Sea	Hague-Visby or Hamburg rules
Air	Warsaw
Road	CMR
Rail	CIM

These are the titles of the major international transport conventions which have been ratified in many countries, including the United Kingdom's Carriage of Goods Acts, and which standardize the conditions of carriage and the documentation. In practice, they mean that an exporter can deal with a variety of nationalities of carrier and still operate with standard documentation. (See Clause Paramount below.)

The bill of lading

Procedure

1. The exporter, or their agent, completes an Export Cargo Shipping Instruction (ECSI) from which the Bills will be produced from the shipping line's computers.
2. The goods are delivered into the port or depot with a Shipping Note.
3. Goods are recorded, compared with the Stowage Plan and Booking References, and entered on to the Ship's Manifest.
4. Once the goods are in the possession of the carrier, the Bills of Lading are produced behalf of the Ship's Master and returned to the exporter/agent. Computer produced Bills may carry facsimile signatures, but are still issued on behalf of the Ship's Master.

Whilst the layout of Bills differs from one carrier to another, the majority are now produced with very similar A4 size layouts and contain broadly the same information. (see example IN Appendix 5.2)

This would include:

1. the parties involved (shipper, consignee and notify party);
2. ports/depots of loading and discharge;
3. vessel name/s and voyage number;
4. number of original Bills;
5. marks and numbers;
6. description of goods;
7. type of packages;
8. gross weight (Kg) and measurement (M3);
9. received and/or shipped dates; and
10. reference to payment of freight, that is prepaid or forward.

and, of course, the important signature on the original Bills on behalf of the Ship's Master. All Bills will contain most of these items and all operate in the same way.

Functions

The Bill of Lading has three major functions:

1. A receipt for the goods.
2. Evidence of the Contract of Carriage.
3. A Document of Title

Receipt for goods

A Bill of Lading will contain the words 'apparent good order and condition' thus obliging the carrier to deliver the goods in the same condition. Such a Bill is known as a clean Bill and acts as a clean receipt for the goods.

However, there may be situations in which the shipping line does not think that the goods are in good order and condition and will say so on the face of the Bill. Such a reference is known as a clause on the Bill which overrides the 'good order and condition' reference. These Claused Bills are sometimes referred to as 'dirty' or foul' Bills of Lading and cause great problems to exporters.

The clauses can be stamped or handwritten and typical examples might be: 'Inadequate packing'; 'second hand packing'; 'one case short'; 'five cases short shipped'; and even 'five cases thought to be short shipped – if on board will deliver'; or 'three drums leaking'.

This reflects the justified attitude of the shipping lines that they will honour their part of the Contract of Carriage, if at all possible, and earn their freight, but protect themselves from the misconduct of the shipper.

The problem for the shipper is that a Claused Bill of Lading clearly provides no evidence of contract performance to the buyer, in fact quite the opposite, and will never be acceptable to a bank against a Letter of Credit.

However, the incidence of Claused Bills has been much reduced over the last few decades because of the widespread use of unitised ie containerised, transport. In fact, the shipping lines very often do not see the goods at all but simply receive the containers which have been loaded in a groupage depot or even the shipper's own premises.

The slight downside to this is that the lines will often issue a Bill which states 'said to contain....', ie a receipt for a container which it is claimed contains a particular quantity of specified goods. Whilst this still generates clean Bills it can make it more difficult to take action against the shipping line for partial loss within containers.

Evidence of the Contract of Carriage

The first point to be made is that the Bill of Lading is not the Contract of Carriage itself, but merely evidence of it. The actual contract is a verbal one made at the time the space is booked and the Bill is produced part way through the performance of the contract. In practice it is rare that the conditions expressed on the Bill do not represent the Contract of Carriage conditions.

As the contract is a verbal one made at the time the space is booked, this also means that the carrier is able to charge freight for space booked even if it is not used by the shipper. This is known as dead freight and is reduced should the carrier obtain alternative cargo to take up that space.

The second point is that the Bill evidences the conditions of the contract and will contain, on its back, a wide range of contract clauses. As has already been mentioned the majority of contracts for the carriage of goods by sea are carried out by shipping lines whose national legislation has ratified the appropriate convention (either the Hague-Visby or the Hamburg Rules) and the clause which specifies this is known as the Clause Paramount or Paramount Clause. Thus the carrier is committed to the standard rules, which which will take precedence over the rest of the carrier's conditions should there be a conflict. The fact that these rules are ratified in legislation also means that carriers cannot contract out of such obligations.

A typical Clause Paramount is shown below.

Typical clause paramount *'The Hague Rules contained in the International Convention for the unification of certain rules relating to Bills of Lading, dated Brussels 25th August 1924, or in those countries where they cre already in force the Hague-Visby Rules contained in the Protocol of Brussels dated February 23rd 1868, as enacted in the Country of Shipment, shall apply to all carriage of goods by sea and, where no mandatory international or national law applies, to the carriage of goods by inland* *waterways also, and such provisions shall apply to all goods whether carried on deck or under deck.'*

Document of title

This is the most relevant, and unique, feature of the Bill of Lading and one which has important implications in terms of its functions and applications in practice.

The first point to make is that Bills are issued in sets containing two or three originals and any number of Copies. The Originals are signed on behalf of the Ship's Master and are referred to as 'negotiable' as they contain, and are able to transfer, property in the goods.

The copies are unsigned, and non-negotiable, and merely convey information. The availability of at least two Original Bills means that they can be dispatched to the destination port separately to ensure that at least one is available.

The reason why this is so important, and an explanation of the practical importance of the Bill of Lading's status, is the fact that one Signed Original Negotiable Bill must be presented back to the Shipping Line at destination in order for them to release the goods.

The Bills may be sent direct, or through the banks, and once one is accomplished (by presentation to the Line) the others are void. Facsimile or photocopy versions are not acceptable.

The relevance of this to the exporter should not be underestimated in that it is possible to restrict the buyer's access to the goods at destination, by withholding the Bills of Lading. Thus payment terms can be arranged which require buyers to pay not for goods but for documents, and this does create some security for the seller.

The relationship between documents and methods of payment is examined in Chapter 8.

The negotiability of the Bill is effected by the manner of its completion, in that the title may be addressed to a specific consignee, in which case it is not freely negotiable. The consignee may then endorse the back of the Bill which can then transfer title.

More commonly, the Bill is made out to order, rather than to a named consignee, endorsed by the exporter (signed on the back), and naming a notify party which the carriers will advise of the arrival of the goods. In this case the Bill is drawn up as a negotiable instrument' as in Figure 5.3.2

Figure 5.3.2 - Bill of Lading completion

	EITHER	OR
SHIPPER:	Exporter	Exporter
	(or Agent)	(or Agent)
CONSIGNEE:	Importer	'Order' or

| NOTIFY PARTY: | ---------------- | 'To Order'
Importer
or
Agent
or
Bank etc: |
| | Title addressed to
a specific party.
No endorsement.
Named consignee may
endorse and transfer. | Title open to bearer;
Endorsement needed. |

It is clearly important for an exporter to be careful in the handling of Bills of Lading as a 'To Order Blank Endorsed Bill of Lading' confers title in the goods to the bearer.

The face of the Bill will always show how many Signed Originals there are and the banks will invariably require the Full Set of Bills, which may be expressed as 2/2 (that is, two of two) or 3/3.

From a purely practical point of view it is obviously necessary to ensure that Bills are available at destination in order to clear the goods on arrival. Should the goods have arrived but not the Bills, they are then known as *Stale Bills of Lading*, and this will inevitably lead to delays in clearance.

In some cases extra charges for such a delay may be imposed which are known as *Demurrage* and can be expensive, particularly in congested ports and depots.

Banks dealing with Letters of Credit will describe a Bill as being Stale when it is presented outside of the days allowed for presentation of documents against the credit. This will often be seven or 15 days, and if no time period is specified, the bank will assume 21 days.

A Bill of Lading glossary

Received

Confirms that the goods are in the possession of the carrier, but not that they have been loaded. The increase in containerised, depot to depot, movements has led to the increased use of Received Bills which are issued as the goods arrive at the Inland Container Base.

Once the goods are loaded the Received Bill can be stamped with a 'Shipped on Board' notation and date and therefore become a Shipped Bill of Lading.

Combined Transport

This refers to the fact that the typical, containerised, sea freight consignment will move from one inland depot of departure to another at destination. The whole transit will be organized under one contract of carriage evidenced by the Bill of Lading, and therefore covers, for example, a road-sea-road transit. Most Bills issued by container lines are Received Combined Transport Bills of Lading. A Bill showing an inland destination may also be referred to as a *Through Bill of Lading*.

Transhipment

In the case where the goods are not shipped direct to the port of discharge, but via a third port, using two vessels, it is possible to obtain a Bill covering both vessels. These may be referred to as the Feeder vessel and the Ocean vessel and the transhipment port will be shown as well as the ports of shipment and destination.

Letters of Credit may not allow transhipment but as long as there is one single transport document the banks will not regards it as a transhipment.

Groupage

It is common that exporters who cannot provide full loads, for either containers and/or road trailers, will make use of Groupage operators. The Groupage operator will group or consolidate a number of exporter's consignments into one shipment which will be covered by a set of Groupage Bills of Lading issued by the Shipping Line.

The Groupage operator may issue a *Certificate of Shipment* which simply acts as a Freight Forwarder's receipt or a *House Bill of Lading*, which is often referred to as a Non Vessel Owning Common Carriers Bill (NVOCC) and is inferior in status to a Shipping Company's Bill of Lading.

FIATA

Issued on behalf of the Federation Internationale des Associations de Transitairies et Assimiles (International Federation of Freight Forwarders Association) and acceptable as an Ocean Bill of Lading against a Letter of Credit. It is perceived as being issued by an agent of the Shipping Line.

Common

Sponsored by SITPRO (Simpler Trade Procedures), the Common Bill of Lading and intended to replace the range of individual Bills produced by the Lines. The carrier's name is not pre-printed on the Bill but a space is left for the name to be added. Unfortunately, the Common Bill of Lading is not in common use.

Short Form

The detailed clauses on the reverse of many Bills are omitted and instead the carrier's 'standard conditions of carriage' are referred to along with the Clause Paramount on the face of the Bill.

Both Common and Short Form Bills are acceptable against Letters of Credit, unless the Credit says that they are not.

Lost or destroyed Bills of Lading

In this case delays are inevitable but can be reduced by the use of a Letter of Indemnity. This will allow release of the goods at destination without presentation of a valid Bill. The original, or replacement, set will be produced at a later date. The indemnity is invariably required to be countersigned by a bank and should not be accepted at destination without the approval of the shipper.

Waybills

Waybills, used for Air, Road and Rail transits, have a number of characteristics in common with the Ocean Bill of Lading but have one very important difference as shown in Figure 5.3.3.

Figure 5.3.3 - Comparison of Ocean Bill of Lading and Waybills

BILL OF LADING	WAYBILL
Receipt for the goods	Receipt for the goods
Evidence of the contract of carriage	Evidence of the contract of carriage
Document of Title	Not a Document of Title
Goods released in exchange for an original Bill	Goods released to named consignee

Where Waybills are issued the carriers will release the goods at destination. It is not necessary to produce a transport document to obtain possession of the goods . The advantage of this is one of convenience in that the availability of a document at destination is not related to the release of goods.

However it should be realised that a Waybill is not a Document of Title and cannot be used to transfer property in the goods as part of the payment procedures. The most obvious problem area is associated with air freight into high risk markets.

Air Waybill procedure

The exporter, or agent, completes a Letter of Instruction to the Airline. In the great majority of cases air freight is arranged through agents rather than direct with the Airline. Because of this it is not uncommon that House Air Waybills are issued as opposed to the carrier's Air Waybill. However, as long as the carrier countersigns the House Air Waybill, it will be accepted as a carrier's receipt against a Letter of Credit.

The Air Waybills are issued in sets of anything up to 12 copies but will contain at least three originals:

1. retained by Airline;
2. forwarded to consignee;
3. returned to exporter;

and any number of copies for internal control and information. The Air Waybill does not protect ownership of the goods but it may be possible to arrange Cash on Delivery (COD) in certain markets.

In cases where the exporter perceives a risk and is looking for some security then it is possible for a party other than the buyer to be named as consignee. If you do not entirely trust the buyer, then do not name the buyer as the consignee, name a party that you do trust, that is, a bank. It is not uncommon that banks are named as consignees for air, road and rail shipments, and subject to specific instructions will collect payment against release of the goods as opposed to release of documents

Road Waybill

Covered by the CMR Convention. (Convention des Merchandises par Route) the road waybill provides a standard, non-negotiable, consignment note used by most nationalities of international road haulier.

Rail Waybill

Covered by the CIM Convention (Convention Internationale des Merchandises par Chemin de Fer) the rail waybill again acts as a standard consignment note for international rail carriers.

Both of the road waybill and the rail waybill act as receipts and evidence of the contract of carriage but not as a Document of Title.

As will be seen from an examination of the sample documents, they all contain their equivalents of the Clause Paramount in terms of the references to the Warsaw Convention (Air), CMR (Road) and CIM (Rail).

Sea Waybill

As we have seen, the Bill of Lading is specifically a sea freight document and is unique in that it operates as a Document of Title. This confers great advantages in terms of the security afforded to the exporter in controlling physical access to the goods, but can be very inconvenient where the Bills become stale due to late arrival at destination.

This is a particular problem where short sea transits are concerned, in which case it is very difficult to get Bills to destination before the goods arrive. In these cases it is not unusual for a Sea or Liner Waybill to be issued by the Shipping Line. This document serves as a receipt for the goods and evidence of the Contract of Carriage but not as a Document of Title.

Such Waybills are now being used for deep-sea transits to low risk customers and markets such as the USA, Australia, S. Africa etc. and are sometimes referred to as Express Bills in that the goods are subject to express release without the presentation of a Bill of Lading.

Carrier's liability

It is not the intention of this book to examine the complex articles of the Transport Conventions but it is important to highlight a potential problem regarding the liability of the carrier for loss or damage to the goods whilst in their charge.

The Conventions basically define liability as 'the value of the goods at place and time of collection', but it should be noted that this is subject to a maximum which protects the carrier. The ceiling will differ from one convention to another but the current versions all use a unit of account known as a 'Special Drawing Right' (SDR), the value of which is published in the national financial press.

Very approximately the maximum carrier's liability for the current conventions (based on an SDR of £0.86) are:

SEA	(Hague-Visby)	£570 per package or £1,720 per tonne
(Hamburg)	£720 per package or £2,150 per tonne	
AIR	(Warsaw)	£14,500 per tonne
RAIL	(CIM)	£14,500 per tonne
ROAD	(CMR)	£7,095 per tonne

It should be noted that these figures represent the maximum liability of the carrier, but exporters of high value goods may well find it worthwhile to negotiate higher limits with the carrier.

Dangerous goods

The exporter of dangerous goods is responsible for taking the actions listed in Figure 5.3.4.

International regulations

The United Nations Committee of Experts on the Transport of Dangerous Goods produce revised 'recommendations' every two years in a publication known as the 'Orange Book'. This is then incorporated, with adaptations. in the published regulations of each of the authorities involved with the major modes of international transport. These separate authorities are:

SEA   International Maritime Organisation (IMO)
International Maritime Dangerous Goods Code (IMDG Code)

ROAD   Economic Commission for Europe (ECE)
Accord Dangereux Routier (ADR)

RAIL   Central Office for International Rail Transport (OCTI)
Reglement International Dangereux (RID)

AIR   International Civil Aviation Organisation (ICAO)
Technical Instructions
   Fundamental requirements for all dangerous goods procedures are.

1.   Identification of goods
2.   Packing and Marking requirements;
3.   Documentary declarations.

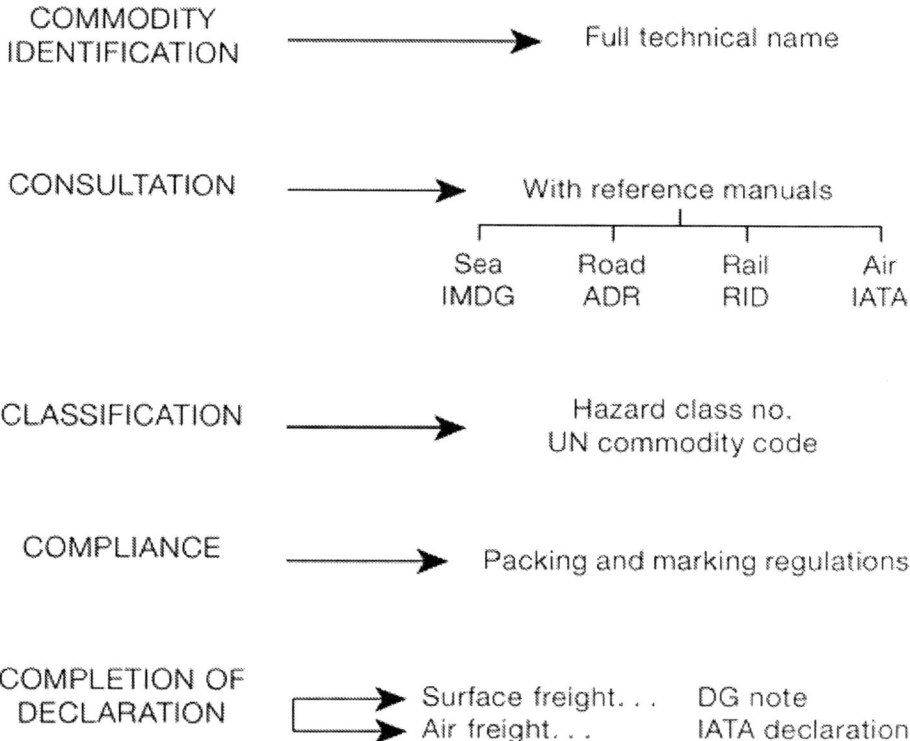

Figure 5.3.4 - Exporter's responsibilities for dangerous goods

Identification of goods

The correct technical name of the product or substance must be used and not brand or proprietary names. Thus 2,000 litres of 'Gramoxone' would be unacceptable because that is a brand name; these goods should be described as 2,000 litres of Paraquet Dichloride in Solution.

However, word descriptions of goods are not specific enough for the detailed identification necessary and more precise classification systems are needed. The broadest classification is the United Nations Commodity Classification system which covers all goods, including dangerous ones. The UN 4 digit code must be included in the written declarations. In addition hazardous goods are classified into nine hazard classes.

This is the basis of the IMDG and other modal classifications (with amendments for air freight) and also leads to a standardised hazard warning labelling system.

The classes are:

1. Explosives
2. Gases
    ○ Flammable (same meaning as Inflammable)
    ○ Non-flammable
    ○ Toxic
3. Flammable Liquids
    ○ Flash point below 18°C
    ○ Flash point 18° to 23°C
    ○ Flash point 23° to 61°C
4. Flammable Solids
    ○ Liable to Spontaneous Combustion
    ○ Emit flammable Gas in Contact with Water
5. Oxidising Substances
    ○ Organic Peroxides
6. Toxic Substances
    ○ Infectious Substances
7. Radioactive Materials
8. Corrosives
9. Miscellaneous Substances (not covered by other classes)

Packing and marking requirements

There is a simple UN classification of packing groups which is based on the broad level of hazard. They are:

Packing Group	I	High Hazard
	II	Medium Hazard
	III	Low Hazard

For international road and rail freight the group numbers become (a), (b) and (c).

Each transport mode also specifies more detailed packing types for each class. Most packing also needs to be approved by the Paper and Board, Printing and Packaging Research Association (PIRA).

Documentary declarations

It is essential that any exporter shipping hazardous goods makes a written declaration certifying that the goods are properly classified, packed, marked and suitable for carriage. The document used for surface freight movements is the Dangerous Goods Note (DGN). The DG note not only identifies the exact nature of the goods but also replaces the Shipping Note, which is not appropriate to dangerous goods, and should act as a written application for shipping space rather than the usual informal verbal booking.

For air freight consignments the declaration is not the DG Note but the International Air Transport Association's (IATA) Shipper's Declaration. The above are requirements which broadly apply to all modes of transport but each individual means of international transport has adapted and extended these procedures.

Dangerous goods by sea

The International Maritime Dangerous Goods (IMDG) Code has been ratified in the UK by the Merchant Shipping (Dangerous Goods and Marine Pollutants) Regulations. It is important to note that the operational manual familiar to many and known as the *'Blue Book'* (Report of the DTI's Standing Advisory Committee on Carriage of Dangerous Goods in Ships) has now been replaced by the IMDG Code, which will be regularly updated. In addition to the four volume Code there is a supplement which contains Emergency Procedures, Medical First Aid Guide, Reporting Procedures and Guidelines for Packing Cargo in Freight Containers.

This means that the information needed from the exporter also includes the EmS number (Emergency Schedule) and MFAG number (Medical First Aid Guide). Finally, exporters should never attempt to identify goods with the IMDG page number. The IMO publications exist in various languages and therefore page numbers may differ and amendments may alter the page running order.

Dangerous goods by road

The Accord Dangereux Routier (ADR) is ratified in the UK as the 'European Agreement concerning the International Carriage of Dangerous Goods by Road the *'Green Book',* which is available from HMSO. This provides provisions which govern the goods and the vehicle. Annexe 1 covers goods classification, packing and marking; Annexe 2 covers vehicle type, loading, stowing, safety equipment and driver training.

The nine IMDG classes broadly apply but ADR does make a distinction between 'restrictive' goods which cannot be moved without special arrangements with the transport authorities of the countries of transit and 'non-restrictive' goods which can be moved. so long as they meet ADR provisions. Within the classifications ADR groups goods under item numbers which are expressed as 1°, 2°, 3° and so on, for example Benzine is ' 3.3 ° (b) ADR'.

The standard hazard warning diamonds are acceptable under ADR but, in addition, the vehicle must be placarded with rec-tangular orange plates (sometimes referred to as Kemler plates) which not only identify the hazard but also carry a telephone number for specialist advice. A final and very important requirement under ADR is the need for *Transport Emergency Cards* (Tremcards) to accompany the goods in the languages of the countries of transit.

Dangerous goods by rail

The Reglement International Dangereux (RID) is the rail freight equivalent of ADR. The requirements are very similar to the ADR because of the deliberate co--operation between the two regimes. In the UK, RID is entitled 'The Regulations Concerning the International Carriage of Dangerous Goods by Rail' and has force of law through the ratification of the 'Convention concerning the International Carriage by Rail' (COTIF).

Dangerous goods by air

In the UK the Air Navigation Order and Air Navigation (Dangerous Goods) Regulations that ratify the 'Technical Instructions for the Safe Transport of Dangerous Goods by Air' are published by the International Civil Aviation Organisation (ICAO) which is the air version of the International Maritime Organisation (IMO).

However, in practice, the operational manual is the International Air Transport Association's (IATA) Dangerous Goods Regulations which are published annually and which can be more restrictive than the ICAO in some areas. The written declaration is not the Dangerous Goods Note, which is specific to surface freight, but the IATA 'Shipper's Declaration for Dangerous Goods' which *must* be signed by the shipper and not the agent.

The nine hazard classes also apply to air freight, with special additions such as Magnetised Material, and a distinction between cargoes which can be carried on passenger aircraft and those that are only permitted on pure freight flights. Specific packing and marking conditions are also specified in the regulations, particularly a restriction on the size of packing units.

An element of the ICAO legislation is that regular shippers of dangerous goods by air must be trained on an official CAA approved IATA course. This is a three day course involving a course examination to qualify. The delegate must also attend a refresher every two years to validate the certificate. Approved courses are offered by a number of organisations including PIRA, BIFA and Croners.

Air freight poses unique problems, particularly with regard to possible changes in temperature and pressure which the goods may experience. This means that goods which are non-hazard or low hazard for surface freight may be declarable, and potentially high hazard, for air freight. Examples of this would include barometers, manometers and other electrical equipment which contains mercury, solid carbon dioxide (dry ice) and even toys if they are made from cellulose-based material.

The one other problem relating to air freight is that of security. Following the Lockerbie disaster the problem of cargo checking was addressed by the Aviation and Maritime Security Act 1990. Not only did this tighten up the definitions of *'known'* and *'unknown'* shippers but also required certifications as to the security of shipments. In addition, the Aviation Security (Air Cargo Agents) Regulations 1992 makes it possible for agents, and regular shippers, to be *'listed'*, based on the quality of their security systems, and thus avoid the more stringent checks, and related delays, experienced by other cargo providers.

Following the events of 11 September 2001, cargo security measures have become increasingly stringent, around the World, for all modes of transport. The Department of Transport, 2 Marsham Street, London SW1 P 3EB can supply specific information.

Part 6

Customs Controls

6.1

Export procedures and documents

All exporters and importers must comply with Customs regulations and cannot abdicate that responsibility to a third party. That is not to say that agents cannot be used, and in fact the great majority of Customs declarations are made by agents on behalf of traders, but that the exporter and importer always bears the ultimate responsibility for the accuracy of the information provided. It is this fact, coupled with the need to instruct and pay agents, that should persuade traders generally to at least attempt a basic understanding of Customs requirements.

It is vital to understand that compliance with Customs requirements is mandatory and the consequences of non-compliance can be very expensive, in terms of time as well as money. Link this to the fact that ignorance is *never* an excuse and it is obvious that all traders should be concerned with understanding those procedures which apply to them.

It may seem hard to believe but there is a logic to Customs controls. There is no document or procedure which is there simply to make your life more difficult. They all exist for good reasons and, in many cases, they actually simplify rather than complicate. In fact, it is probable that an improved understanding of Customs procedures will actually present great opportunities to reduce the time spent and the costs of compliance. The Customs even give money back on occasions.

An overview of customs controls

Just as it is possible to rationalise the range of export documents into four basic categories (see Figure 6.1), so it is possible to take the wide and complex range of Customs procedures and to rationalise them into three categories, or, more accurately, sources. These are:

- EXPORT (DEPARTURE)
- TRANSIT
- IMPORT (DESTINATION)

A little simplistic, perhaps, but it does allow some logical rationalisation of the 'mountain' of Customs procedures into three smaller 'hills'. It also makes an important, although perhaps obvious, point that goods moving internationally must move through Customs controls for the whole of the journey. The same, of course, applies to people.

Goods depart from their country of export from a Customs post of departure (where some form of export declaration will be required) through Customs posts of transit (if applicable) and into a Customs post of destination (where an import declaration will be needed). For some international movements only the departure and destination posts will be relevant, such as a sea or air freight movement between two ports or airports. However for road and rail movements it is perfectly possible that the goods will cross a number of countries of transit, in between the departure and destination countries, and therefore move through posts of transit into and out of these countries.

So what sort of controls result from these movements?

Export

All countries are interested in goods leaving their territory but invariably it is only because they wish to count them. Developed countries operate highly sophisticated systems designed to collect trade statistics, such information being considered, quite rightly, as being vital to economic planning. Whilst less sophisticated levels of collection may operate in other parts of the world, all countries still count and analyze their exports. In fact, the great majority of exports are only of statistical interest and are described by Customs as 'Non-Controlled' goods (even sometimes as 'innocent' goods).

However, certain types of goods are subject to export controls as well as being of statistical interest. Thus, you cannot send your Chieftain tanks off to Iran without encountering some controls; in such a case, export licensing control. The range of Customs regimes which could apply controls to exports are examined later in this chapter (see Pre-entry).

Import

Just as logically, Customs authorities throughout the world are interested in goods entering their territories. In fact, they are invariably a lot more interested in their imports than their exports. This is due to the fact that, whilst most exports do not attract controls, there is no such thing as a 'Non-Controlled' import. Imports are of statistical interest in the same way as exports but many other controls may also apply. These can be broken down into:

TARIFF BARRIERS	duty, tax, excise, levy
	licensing
	quotas
NON-TARIFF BARRIERS	standards – technical, medical, health & safety, etc.

and a wide range of specialised control duties affecting specific goods such as veterinary and phytosanitary regimes.

These will be examined in greater detail later, but it should be quite clear that all imports will be affected by a number of these control regimes. Even if goods are entering duty free they are probably subject to VAT. We should also remember that when the first teams of Excise men were formed in the 16th century in the UK to collect revenue on behalf of the Queen on, for example, French brandy, the UK coastline was divided up into 'Collections' and, to this day, each Customs region in the UK is referred to as a Collection. Their job is to collect and they collect almost 65% of central government revenues because it is imports which generate revenue, not exports.

Transit

As mentioned earlier, it is not unusual for goods to actually move through other Customs territories between their departure and destination points. This is, in fact, quite common for international road and rail movements. In such a case, it would be nice for the road trailer driver to say to the first Customs post en route that he was only passing through their country and did not intend to stop, and for the Customs to take his word for it and allow the goods to enter. It would be nice, but you can guess that it cannot happen. We have to remember that those goods, if they remain in that country, are potentially subject to all of the import controls mentioned above. The countries of transit need some way to ensure that goods allowed in actually leave, or that they collect whatever revenues are due if they stay.

Also, consider the fact that the vehicle is quite a valuable commodity in its own right, irrespective of the goods. A driver allowed in, simply on the promise that he would leave, could sell the goods, sell the vehicle, even sell the diesel in the tanks, and there is a lot of revenue, in the form of duty, tax and excise, at stake. It may even be that the goods are subject to other controls in addition to these fiscal ones. The result of all this is that Transit procedures have been established to protect the countries of transit and these are examined later in this chapter.

The European Union (EU)

Before we can actually look at these procedures there is one other broad overview necessary to put them into context. The UK is a member of not just a free trade area but a Customs Union. The distinction is of great significance. A simple free trade area such as the North American Free Trade Area (NAFTA, comprising the USA, Canada and Mexico) is based on an agreement between its members that they will give duty free entry to each others goods. Thus, Canadian origin goods will be allowed in duty free into the USA, but UK origin goods will attract tariff controls. However the controls which UK goods attract into the USA will not necessarily be the same as those applicable if the same goods were to enter Canada or Mexico. They do not cooperate on the treatment on non-member country's goods, only on each other's. The distinction is that the EU not only has free trade between it members but also operates a Common Customs tariff against non-members.

A useful map of the EU, although clearly not a geographic one, is shown in Figure 6.2.

This reveals some very interesting facts regarding the UK as a Customs authority.

1. The distinction between INTERNAL and EXTERNAL frontiers. The borders between member states being Internal and those with non-members being External.
2. Goods entering the EU from outside, ie from non-members, cross a

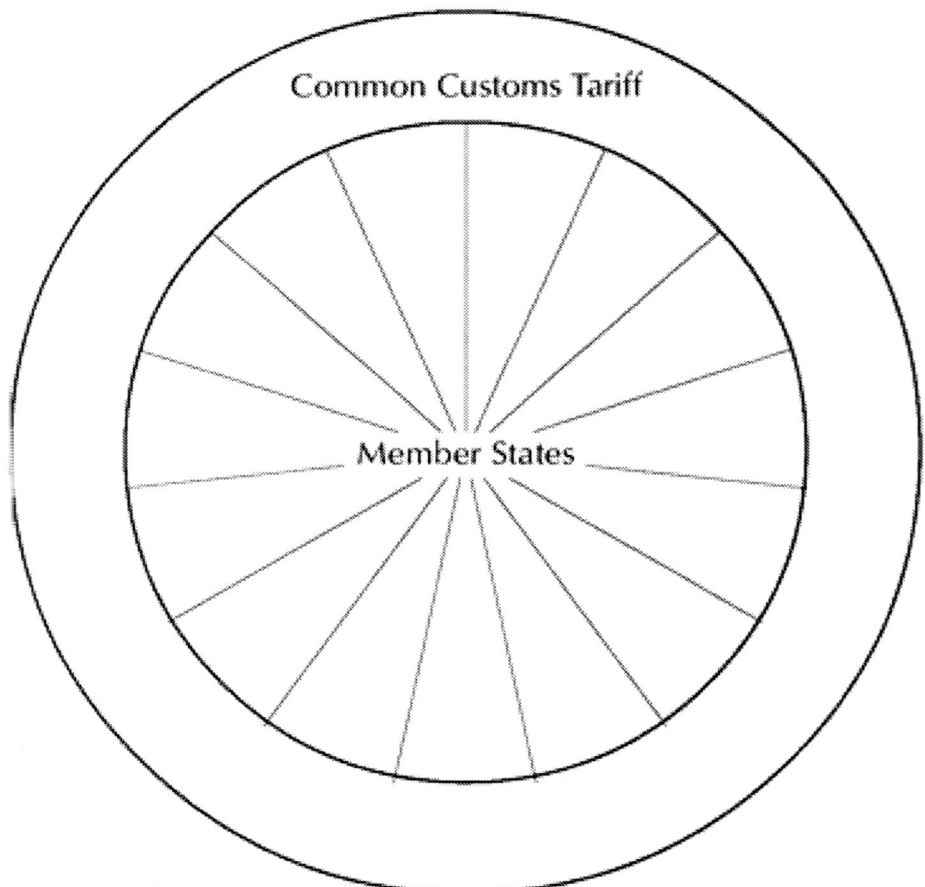

Fig. 6.2 - EU tariff status pre-1993

common Customs frontier which means that they should attract the same tariff controls whichever member state they enter; in particular, the duty rates will be identical in every member state.

The changes which occurred on 1 January 1993 in creating a Single European Market are clearly based on this distinction and the situation now is that the internal frontiers have been removed allowing the 'Four Freedoms': Free movement of goods, people, services and capital.

However the Common External frontier remains intact. So a more accurate picture of the EU tariff status might look like this Figure 6.3.

What happens in the future regarding the Common External Tariff is very much dependent on the on-going negotiations within the World Trade Organisation (WTO), formerly the General Agreement on Tariffs and Trade (GATT), which will generate a further lowering of duty rates world-wide.

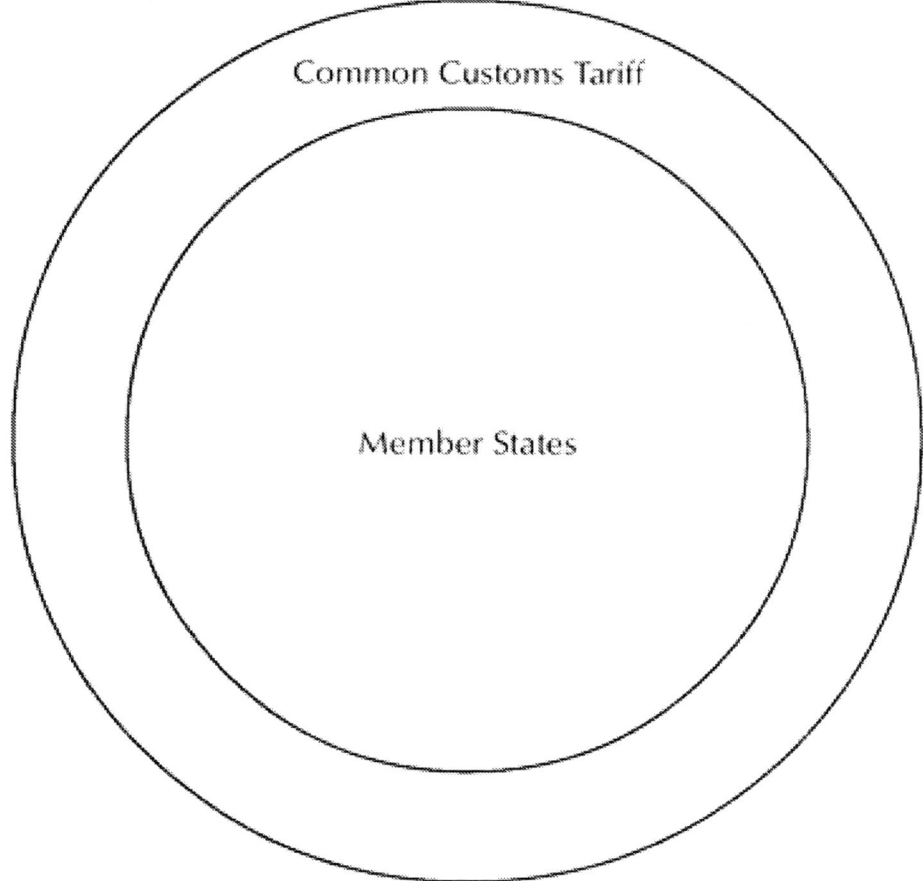

Fig. 6.3 - EU tariff status post-1992

The scenario of a 'Fortress Europe' in which the EU raise barriers against non-member goods is almost certain to be consigned to history.

Which country?

In terms of basic Customs procedures it is clearly vital for the UK trader to distinguish between EU and non-EU customers and suppliers.

The current member states of the EU (in the date order in which they joined) are:

- France
- Germany
- Italy
- Belgium
- Luxemburg
- Netherlands
- United Kingdom
- Ireland
- Denmark
- Greece
- Spain
- Portugal
- Austria
- Sweden
- Finland
- Czech Republic
- Cyprus
- Estonia
- Hungary
- Latvia
- Lithuania
- Malta
- Poland
- Slovakia
- Slovenia

Also, Switzerland, Norway, Iceland and Liechtenstein are members of the European Economic Area which is basically a waiting room for membership of the EU.

It is also planned that Bulgaria and Romania will join in 2007 and the EU is committed to continuing negotiations with Turkey.

The consequences of EU expansion are examined in more detail in section 9.2.

The complex picture of EU preferential trade agreements with non-member states is examined in more detail later, but for now we can make an important distinction between three categories of trading partners, they are either:

EU MEMBER STATES	eg Germany, Belgium etc.
EEA MEMBER STATES	eg Norway, Iceland
NON-MEMBERS	eg Japan, USA. etc.

The following diagram (Figure 6.4) shows the procedures which would apply to each element of control (export, transit and import) for each category of overseas country.

The terms used above will all be explained as we proceed to examine these procedures, beginning, quite logically, with the export of an international consignment.

Export procedures

The first point that should be made is that, since 1January 1993, trade between the UK and other member states of the EU should not be referred to as export or import. In terms of trade statistics we are dealing with DISPATCHES and ARRIVALS, and in terms of VAT, SUPPLIES and ACQUISITIONS.

For the sake of simplicity we will continue to use the words Export and Import when describing general procedures, and the technically correct descriptions when referring to specific VAT or Trade Statistics applications for EU trade.

Perhaps the best way to examine current Customs procedures for export clearance is to engage in a brief history lesson. Since the early 1980s there has been a continuous development of Customs procedures, all of which have genuinely served to simplify the administrative burdens on traders (honestly).

Let us take, as an example, a consignment of washing machines from the UK to, say, Italy, by road, in the mid 1980s. The exporter, or their agent, would have had to complete and present a full export declaration to UK Customs, primarily for statistical purposes. This would have probably been a C273 form or, if the goods were subject to specific export controls, then one of a range of 'shipping bills' such as a C63A, or a C1334, or a C1172, or a GW 60, etc. In addition a transit document, such as a T1 or T2, would be needed to move the goods through the countries of transit ie France, and in addition to that an Italian import declaration would have been lodged by the importer, or their agent, at the post of destination.

There were three distinct and separate Customs declarations, all containing basically the same information, and all operating in what was, supposedly, a Common Market. If the goods were moving the other way the

Fig. 6.4 - Controls applying to category of trading partner

	EXPORT	TRANSIT	IMPORT
UK → EU	INTRASTAT		INTRASTAT
UK → EEA	SAD	SAD	SAD
UK → Rest of World	SAD	TIR or TIF	????

situation would have been the same; an Italian export declaration, plus a T form, plus a UK import declaration (C10 or C11 or C1).

The next major development was the totally logical introduction of a single document which combined the three distinct areas of Customs controls, export, transit and import.

Known as the Single Administrative Document (SAD this was introduced on 1January 1988 and is known as the C88 in the UK The important point is that the SAD was not just introduced in the UK but in a total of eighteen European countries (the 12 member state of the EU at the time plus 6 ex-EFTA / EEA countries). It actually replaced something like 150 separate Customs documents throughout Europe, including every one mentioned for our Italian job.

The final, and most recent development, was on 1 January 1993 when, amongst a number of other Single Market initiatives, the INTRASTAT procedures were introduced which replaced the use of the SAD for intra-EU trade, but did not affect its use for EU trade with the EFTA countries. Therefore the SAD is now no longer relevant to trade within the EU.

We now have a situation, which is illustrated above, in which the INTRASTAT procedure operates alongside the SAD, their use being dependent n the country of destination.

Intrastat

The collection of trade statistics on intra-EU trade is now accomplished via three levels of declaration by exporters, depending on their level of business

1. All VAT registered traders must complete normal VAT returns which, on the current VAT 100 form, require information on total sales to EU customers and acquisitions from EU suppliers, in boxes 8 (Ex Works out) and 9 (Delivered in).
2. Those organisations which are conducting EU business of less than a specified annual threshold (£233,000 in 2003) need only supply a EC SALES LISTING (ESL) usually on a quarterly basis, on form VAT 101 (or annual for very small traders) listing their EU business specifying individual VAT numbers for customers and/or suppliers.
3. All traders above these levels must, in addition to the ESLs, also supply Supplementary Statistical Declarations (SSD) on a monthly basis within 10 working days of the end of the month.

It is not necessary to declare:

- Temporary exports
- Packing
- Samples
- Exhibition goods

Whilst these might appear to be very complex arrangements the fact is that for smaller traders (some 150,000 of them) the requirements are actually easier than they were, in that they no longer have to make individual SAD declarations for each consignment. For the larger companies (approx. 30,000) then the situation is no worse, it is simply a different form of statistical declaration.

Submission of declarations

The introduction of INTRASTAT has not changed the option that the trader has to use an agent to make declarations on theIr behalf, and many have continued to do so. One of the potential problems is that, because the information is presented in an aggregated format, the use of a number of different agents can make the compilation of information more difficult. Perhaps it means that the use of a single agent/forwarder does have advantages.

There is, however, no reason why traders cannot make the ESLs and SSDs on their own behalf.

The second point to make is that the Customs are keen to encourage traders and agents to provide information in other than paper format.

Intrastat form can be submitted:

- Via the Internet - where data is submitted on an on-line form or CSV file;
- Electronic Data Interchange (EDI) - data in the EDIFACT standard is transmitted by various methods.

   There is also an on-line facility for amending previously submitted data. This facility is available to all Intrastat users, agents submitting on behalf of Intrastat traders and larger branches of companies submitting data independently of their head office.

   The system is accessed by *username and password* - username provided when registered - via the Customs website. There are two methods of completion, an *on-line* electronic form for typing the data and an *off-line* option using a Comma Separated Variable (CSV) file format.
- For Traders there is also a browse facility for viewing previously submitted data.

For further assistance on the Intrastat e-form contact the EDI helpdesk, e-mail helpdesk.edcs@hmce.gov.uk or telephone 01702 367248.

VAT and the single market

It will be clear from the above that the collection of intra-EU trade statistics is now closely linked to the VAT regime which operates throughout the EU. The current situation is that UK sales to member states are still covered by a zero-rated invoice and subject to proof of export if required. In addition the buyer's VAT number must appear on the invoice.

Thus, what is known as the 'destination principle' still applies, in that EU VAT will be collected at the time of the acquisition (import) in the buyer's country. The only change here is that from 1 January 1993, for UK acquisitions from EU suppliers, we have reverted to the Postponed Accounting System (PAS) which allows importers to account for VAT on the 'Tax Due' side of their VAT returns. The requirement to pay, or defer, VAT on non-EU supplies remains.

The single administrative document (SAD)

As we have seen the SAD (C88) was introduced on 1 January 1988 and replaced almost 150 Customs documents within both the EU and ex-EFTA countries, combining the requirement for export, transit and import declarations into one document used by 18 western European nations

Since 1 January 1993 and the introduction of the Intrastat procedures, the SAD has become irrelevant to EU trade, but it is still extremely important for trade with non-EU members. These can be divided into the ex-EFTA countries and the rest, because the Ex-EFTA adopted the SAD on 1 January 1988 and have continued its use despite the EU moving over to INTRASTAT on 1 January 1993. Thus the SAD still operates as a full 8-page document for trade between the EU and Switzerland, Norway, Iceland and Liechtenstein. As we will see later, for trade outside of these countries only elements of the SAD will be relevant.

The combination of functions within the SAD can be simply expressed as:

• PAGES 2 & 3	EXPORT
• PAGES 1,4,5,& 7	TRANSIT
• PAGES 6 & 8	IMPORT

As an example, a consignment from the UK to Norway could be export declared, pass through posts of transit and be import declared at destination by just one completed SAD. By the same token an import from, say, Iceland, could complete all Customs controls with one SAD.

In practice, the so-called 'split use option' is more commonly used. This allows the distinct elements of the SAD to be separated so that the export declarations can be made separately from the transit documents and the import declarations. The separation of the import declaration from export and transit is very common, as the importer often lodges the import entry prior to the arrival of the goods.

New Export System (NES)

NES was launched at the Port of Dover in March 2002 – it was implemented at all UK maritime ports on 28 October 2002, with airports going "live" between then and mid 2003. It governs all non-EU exports and imports.

NES replaced the current export system and, although C88 paper declarations will still be accepted for full pre-entries, these documents will have to be keyed into CHIEF by Customs' own staff before the goods can be permitted to progress for shipment.

NES is available to all exporters and freight forwarders, irrespective of their volumes and through-puts, and Customs has encouraged them to take full advantage of the new system.

The CHIEF system

CHIEF (Customs Handling of Import and Export Freight), was originally responsible for controlling and recording all of the UK's international trade import movements, whether by land, sea or air. It links Customs offices around the country to ports, airports, inland facilities and several thousand businesses. It now handles all export declarations as well.

The changes

☒	No paper declarations.
☑	Electronic pre-entries replace the paper SAD (C88).
☒	The Simplified Clearance Procedure (SCP) and Customs Registered Numbers (CRNs) withdrawn.
☑	The Simplified Declaration Procedure (SDP) introduced which relies upon an initial electronic Pre-Shipment Advice (PSA) providing minimum information, followed by an electronic Supplementary Declaration within 14 days of export.
☒	Local Export Control (LEC) withdrawn.
☑	LEC replaced by Local Clearance Procedure (LCP).
☒	A new procedure for processing export goods inland at Designated Export Places (DEPs).

Under the New Export System declarations can be made via a number of electronic routes including:

- Community System Providers (CSPs)
- Internet e-mail with EDIFACT attachments
- X400 e-mail and EDIFACT attachments
- Completion of a web form online.

Technical requirements

The NES CHIEF Technical Interface Specification (TIS) can be downloaded from the Customs website, as, indeed, can details of the Community System Providers, and software suppliers. Just log on to www.hmce.gov.uk and follow the links to the New Export System.

The choice of routes:

1.   If you do not handle a large amount of export declarations then you may wish to use the web form. It is a relatively inexpensive route to CHIEF with very basic functionality.
2.   There are a number of low-user packages available from software suppliers which utilise browser and web form technology. You may wish to consider this as an option.
3.   The CSP and e-mail routes will be popular with freight forwarders. Both these routes require export processing software and, naturally enough, there are costs associated with this. So, you should budget for them. How much you will need to spend will depend on your own individual circumstances.

Export licensing control

The Export of Goods (Control) Order, issued regularly by the Department of Trade and available from HMSO, contains Schedule 1 which is a lengthy list of goods which require an export licence before they will be allowed out of the UK. This is commonly referred to as the Prohibition List and, whilst detailed reference is necessary, in practice it is possible to identify certain types of goods which are likely to attract such controls.

* Goods of Strategic Value (to our enemies?)
  This includes military equipment, ships, aircraft, weapons, navigation systems, etc.
* Goods of Technological Value
  This includes computer hardware, specialist testing and measuring equipment, etc.
* Goods of Cultural Value
  This includes antiques, works of art, the family china, London Bridge, etc.

It is very important to appreciate that a large part of these controls cover what is known as 'Dual Use' regulations. That is, even if the goods are intended for entirely civil and peaceful purposes, if they *could* be used in a manner which would attract control, then they are deemed to attract control.

Information can be obtained from the Export Control Organisation of the Department of Trade & Industry (DTI) and the granting of licenses will be dependent on the proposed country of destination. The license must be presented to Customs to support the export pre-entry. For goods subject to Common Agricultural Policy controls there is an equivalent licensing regime operated by the Intervention Board for Agricultural Produce and DEFRA and other government departments eg Environment may have specialised input.

Exports from bonded warehouses

All imports into the UK enter into bond. This describes premises which are operated under a bond, or guarantee, to Customs. Should the warehouse keepers allow goods to be cleared from the bond without the approval of Customs, given via an ' Out of Charge' message, then the guarantee safeguards Customs revenues. However, it is unusual for goods to be exported out of bond. Those which are taken out of bond are subject to EXCISE duty if they are consumed domestically. Excise, or Revenue Duty, is payable on certain imports, and has been for more than 400 years. The goods which are subject to this very specific charge include :

ALCOHOL	Spirits, beer, wine and even toiletries
TOBACCO	Cigarettes, cigars, smoking tobacco
MINERAL OILS	Petrol, diesel, lubricants

These goods attract excise on import into the UK and UK produced goods are subject to excise charges if consumed domestically but if exported are excise free. Thus whisky, for example, is excisable if consumed in the UK but free from excise if exported. The Customs are therefore very concerned to ensure that any goods for which excise has not been paid do leave the country. This is particularly important as excise represents 25% of central government revenue in the UK, (VAT actually represents 37 pe cent) and the UK has the third highest excise rates in the EU, second only to Denmark which is second only to Sweden.

Whilst on this subject we should note that since 1993 the movement of excisable goods between bonded warehouses has been supplemented by the addition of a new type of approved trader known as Registered Excise Dealers and Shippers (REDS) who will be approved to receive excisable goods from other member states of the EU. A freight forwarder, acting for a number of importers, may be a REDS.

Processing relief

Inward processing relief (IPR)

If goods are imported from outside the EU and subsequently re-exported then it is possible to obtain relief from the duty payable at import. The duty may be avoided by suspension at the time of import, in which case all the goods must be re-exported, usually within 6 months. Alternatively, the duty is paid and a drawback of duty is claimed for whichever goods are subsequently re-exported. It should be emphasised that the expression re-export applies only to goods which are destined for a non-EU country; that is, they must leave the EU. This procedure applies where the re-export is simply a repacked version of the import or, more importantly, where the re-export is the result of processing of the import. Complex manufacturing processes can be approved for relief as long as it can be proved that the imported commodities are genuinely re-exported. As an example, the import of printed textiles from the Far East and subsequent re-export of garments to the USA could qualify for relief.

Outward processing relief (OPR)

This describes the equivalent procedure where goods are exported, out of the EU, for processing and subsequent re-import. Again subject to prior approval, the Customs will allow relief on the value of the goods before the process and charge only for the 'added value' of the processing. Therefore, this procedure also applies to repair or replacement situations where no duty at all is payable, if the work done is free of charge to the importer.

There is a further procedure known as Returned Goods Relief where duty and VAT may be avoided for goods returned in the same state as at export, which often applies to defective goods.

Finally it is perfectly feasible to combine these two procedures. For example goods could be imported and processed under IPR and re-exported and re-imported under OPR. Discussions with your local Customs collection are essential to investigate the possibilities.

Transit systems

Having covered the procedural requirements related to UK exports/dispatches it is logical for us now to proceed to the next stage of the international movement which may involve the goods passing through Customs posts of transit on the way to their final destination. The words 'may involve' are used advisedly as not all international consignments will pass through posts of transit.

In the case of a sea or air movement then the goods will not actually transit any Customs territory during the journey. The goods on the vessel or aircraft will export clear out of a port of departure and import clear into a port of destination. They may call at other ports on route but they will not enter a country at one point and pass through to leave at another point, which is the essence of a true transit.

It is perfectly feasible for goods to be transferred from one ship or aircraft to another at a port part way through the journey, but this is actually *a transhipment*, not a transit. This transhipment will be done under Customs control, invariably through bonded warehouses, and the goods will not be imported and re-exported as long as they stay within the bonded premises. The ultimate example of this type of transhipment is the use of Freeports in which case the goods could even be processed before the re-loading .

Therefore true transit, in which the goods enter a country at one point and leave at another, applies only to international road and rail transits.

Another look at Figure 6.4 above will reveal that the distinction between EU, EEA and non-EU/EEA trade, which makes such a difference to the methods of export clearance used, is just as important when we consider transit procedures. The element of that diagram which is relevant to us now is reproduced in Figure 6.5.

Figure 6.5 - Transit procedures by destination

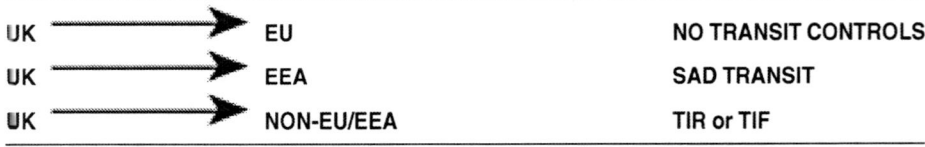

UK → EU	NO TRANSIT CONTROLS
UK → EEA	SAD TRANSIT
UK → NON-EU/EEA	TIR or TIF

Why transit controls?

First, a brief reprise on why transit systems should exist in the first place. The example we used earlier was a road consignment travelling from the UK to Italy and crossing France en route. The historical problem which the French Customs would have had is that they are allowing goods into their territory which may be subject to duty, tax, excise and levy, as well as other restrictions such as quota or licensing controls. The promise of the driver that the goods are not stopping in France is hardly likely to give the French Customs the security they need in order to allow the goods in free from such controls.

To add to the problem they would also consider the vehicle to be of value, sometimes more than the goods, and even the fuel in the tanks. The solution for the Customs authorities, all of them, not just France, was to insist on

Duty Deposits being lodged to cover the potential Customs revenues. Such deposits were refundable as long as the haulier could prove that the goods subsequently left the country.

The second major problem was the fact that, in order to asses the level of deposit necessary, the Customs would invariably examine the goods in order to determine their tariff classification and therefore the level of charges and controls appropriate. This would clearly be very time consuming on a journey involving a number of posts of transit and greatly increased the possibility of damage, and even pilferage, during the journey.

The growth in international road freight since the Second World War served to highlight the need for a solution to the dual problems of:

• Duty deposits
• Examination

and the solution was TIR.

Transport Internationaux Routiers (TIR)

The familiar white and blue plates that can be seen on many heavy goods vehicles represent the title of an international convention, established by the Economic Commission for Europe, which has been ratified by a very large number of Customs authorities throughout the world. It was ratified in the UK in 1959 and includes the USA, Japan and most of the Middle East and Eastern Europe. So how does TIR solve the problems.

Duty deposits

A TIR CARNET must be issued by an approved authority and accompany the goods throughout the journey. First a brief word about these documents called ' Carnets'. There are a number of different forms of Carnets used in international trade including ATA Carnets and Carnet de Passage en Douane (both covered in the next chapter) and even Carnets for the Paris Metro. The word simply describes a booklet of vouchers (or volets). In the case of TIR the Carnet is issued in the UK by either the Freight Transport Association (FTA) or the Road Haulage Association (RHA) on behalf of the International Road Transport Union.

Duty deposits are avoided by the provision of a guarantee by the carrier to the issuing authority, usually countersigned by a bank or insurance company. The carrier must undertake to abide by all TIR regulations. In simple terms this guarantee acts as a duty deposit, lodged in the country of departure, and replaces the need for such deposits at each post of transit. The Customs authorities in transit accept Volets from the Carnet, on entry into and exit from their Customs territories, rather than a duty deposit.

Carnets are available as 14 or 20 page documents, dependent on the number of transit posts involved.

Vehicle examination

The regular, and very time consuming, examination of vehicles and goods at posts of transit is avoided by the requirement for TIR vehicles to be approved. The approval, in the UK, is given, following inspection of the vehicle, by the Department of Transport (Vehicle Inspectorate) who act on behalf of Customs. This takes the form of a GV60 approval certificate and is issued on the basis that:

• the vehicle can be sealed so that it is not possible to add or remove goods without breaking the seal(s), and
• there are no concealed areas.

The purpose of the approval is to enable Customs, at the point of departure, to seal the goods in the vehicle with one or more seals. The Customs of transit then need to examine the seal(s) only and, as long as they are intact, will waive their right to examine the goods.

Approved vehicles carrying a TIR Carnet are able to pass through any number of Customs posts of transit without the need for examination or the payment of duty deposits.

TIR TABAC Carnets

On 1 September 1993 a new form of TIR Carnet was introduced, specifically to cover the high value movements of tobacco and alcohol. The problem in this case is that if goods are illegally diverted en-route then the Customs revenues lost are much greater than usual because such goods are subject to significant Excise duties. The specific problem was the disappearance of such goods as they transit into some Eastern European markets. The new Carnets require higher guarantee levels which reflect the greater risk and greater values.

So TIR was the first solution to Customs Transit problems and remains extremely important now. It should also be noted that the equivalent system exists for the movement of rail wagons and is known as TIF (Transport International par Chemin de Fer) and operates in the same way as TIR.

Whilst TIR is still very important to UK exporters it is important to note that it has no relevance to EU trade for which no transit controls exist.

EU transit

From 1973 to the end of 1992 goods were moved within the EU, with either a T1 or a T2 Transit form. However, as we have seen earlier, 1 January 1988 saw the introduction of the Single Administrative Document (SAD). Not only did the SAD become the basic export declaration for all of those countries, but it also replaced the T Forms. In fact pages 1, 4, 5 and 7 of the SAD became the new Transit Form, retaining the concept of T1 and T2 status, but with a clearly different format.

The New Computerised Transit System (NCTS)

January 2003 saw the introduction of a European wide system, based upon electronic declaration and processing, designed to provide better management and control of Community and Common Transit. It involves all EU Member States and a number of EEA and accession countries (22 countries in all).

The National Administration of each country will develop its own NCTS structure, according to centrally defined architecture, which will be connected, through a central domain in Brussels, to all the other countries. The NCTS will link some 3000 European customs offices and eventually replace the existing paper based system. The aim is that all traders will eventually input all transit declarations, and any other necessary messages, such as arrival of the goods, to the NCTS, electronically.

The UK, in common with several other participating countries, will use the Minimum Common Core (MCC) software developed by the EU Commission, which provides all of the basic data capture and messaging functionality necessary for effective connection to the European network.

A phased introduction of the NCTS in the UK commenced in January 2003. More information can be found on the Customs website www.hmce.gov.uk

Summary

It will be obvious that the development of the 'Four Freedoms' within a Single Market, the absence of transit controls within the EU, the simplification of procedures and the ongoing use of electronic declarations have all led to a severely reduced role for Customs in the day to day control of movements.

The closing of many internal Customs posts within the EU actually led to the European Commission sponsoring the St. Matthew project which is designed to re-train redundant Customs officers.

Why St. Matthew? Well he is the patron saint of revenue collectors.

More seriously, for many of the changes to work there has had to be a major change in the attitude of Customs towards goods entering their territories. Traditionally there has always been an assumption that goods, and people, are NOT in free circulation unless they can prove differently. The mandatory check on documents such as T Forms, and passports, has been necessary to provide the proof that the goods and people are not subject to specific controls.

One might, quite properly, regard this as an assumption of guilt until innocence is proved. The very important change in the philosophy of Customs is that they now work on entirely the opposite assumption that goods are *"regarded as community goods in the absence of anything to the contrary"*.

Whilst estimates vary there is no doubt that major savings are already being made in avoiding the frontier delays which affected the majority of freight movements throughout the EU. We should not forget, however, that none of these developments have reduced the power of Customs authorities to stop and examine people and goods, but only changed the regular and mandatory checks which previously affected all movements.

Customs would also say, with much evidence, that they are now using the resources they have in a much more efficient manner. By targeting deliberate evasions of controls, based on intelligence and internal system audits, they are becoming far more effective in the control of, for example, illegal drugs whilst not interfering with the vast majority of legal movements of goods and people.

6.2

Import procedures and documents

This second chapter in our coverage of Customs controls examines the final area of specific controls, that of import procedures. What we should always remember is that one company's export is another company's import, and all UK exporters should have a good knowledge of the controls which goods could attract at destination. We are therefore approaching the issue of Customs Import Procedures from the point of view of the UK exporter, rather than the UK importer. In reality the distinction is almost irrelevant to the modern international trader.

What we will also try to do is to identify the opportunities which may be available to UK exporters to minimise the costs and effects of Customs controls by prudent management of information and procedures. There are many opportunities missed by UK exporters because of the short-sighted perception that import clearance is the buyer's problem.

However it is worth just a few words regarding UK/EU import procedures if only to complete the picture we have built up in looking at export and transit procedures.

EU imports

Goods which enter the UK from another member state actually require no immediate import declaration. Just as Intrastat procedures collect export statistics using the VAT returns, EC Sales Listing (ESL) and Supplementary Statistical Declaration (SSD), the import statistics ie arrivals, are collected in exactly the same way. In addition the VAT which is due on such imports is now subject to the Postponed Accounting System (PAS) which actually operated in the early 1980s, which means it is simply accounted for on the 'Tax due' side of the trader's VAT return.

For imports from non-EU members the import element of the SAD (pages 6 & 8) serves as the import declaration for all E.U. members. Such entries may be made by the importing company, periodically for large traders, but the great majority are made by Clearing Agents on behalf of the importers. In such cases it is probable that the declaration is made using Direct Trader Input (DTI) procedures. This describes the process which allows declarations to be made direct from the agent's computer to the Customs computers, the printed paper version of which will be a 'Plain Paper SAD', that is an import SAD with all the necessary information but no printed layout. In these cases the requirement for payment of VAT on import has not changed, although it is very likely that such payment is deferred until the 15th of the following month.

Whilst it is difficult, or even impossible, to cover every country's import procedures outside of the EU, what we can do is to identify and explain the type and nature of import controls generally practised throughout the world. Outside of the EU there is very little, if any, standardisation of import declarations, but whichever particular document is required it will always fulfil the same basic purpose and apply the same range of controls.

Import controls

It is possible to break all import controls into two broad categories; they are either Tariff or Non-Tariff barriers. The word tariff describes the product classification system which is the beginning of all countries' import controls and which is examined later in this chapter. These controls would include:

Tariff Controls	DUTY
	TAX
	EXCISE
	LEVY
	LICENSING
	QUOTA
and often	TECHNICAL STANDARDS
	HEALTH & SAFETY STANDARDS
	(where imposed by Customs authorities)
Non-Tariff Controls	OTHER STANDARDS REQUIREMENTS
	CULTURAL BARRIERS
	NATIONAL BUYING HABITS ETC.

Duty

Duties are used as a specific fiscal control and applied selectively at a variety of levels by different countries. We already know that intra-EU trade is duty free and, as we will see later in this chapter, there are many situations where the origin of the goods may mean that they are not subject to duty.

Such duties are usually *ad valorem*, that is they are charged as a percentage of the (usually CIF) value of the goods. One of the great successes of the WTO (World Trade Organisation - formerly known as the General Agreement on Tariffs & Trade - GATT) negotiations over the years is that the average worldwide duty rate which 24% in the 1950s is now under 4% in the new millennium. However this does not preclude countries applying much higher rates on certain commodities, particularly when attempting to protect local manufacturers.

Tax

Within the EU it is Value Added Tax (VAT), or its equivalent in each member state, which is the standard fiscal charge on all sales, As we have seen, in the UK, it is either accounted for on EU imports or deferred (to the 15th of the following month) for imports from outside the EU. Rates within the EU currently range from 15% (ignoring the exempt / zero rates) to 38% for certain luxury items. Other countries may impose similar charges on imports in the form of Purchase Tax or Turnover Tax.

Excise

Sometimes referred to as Revenue Duty which accurately describes its purpose in that, rather than acting as a pure control, excise is designed to collect government revenue. Chapter 6.1 examined the export controls relevant to excisable goods, chiefly alcohol, tobacco and mineral fuels, which are designed to ensure that excise is collected on such goods which are consumed domestically, ie in the UK Clearly such excise will be applied to imports of these goods into the UK and, of course, on entry into most overseas countries. These charges can be very high - they certainly are in the UK - and are often specific duties in that they are expressed as a charge for a particular quantity or volume rather than as an *ad valorem* charge. For example, the excise on spirits imported into the UK is expressed as Euros per hectolitre (100 litres). As these charges represent some 25% of total UK government revenues it will be clear that the Customs prioritise their collection.

Levy

Levies are a specialised charge which, within the EU, generally affects only agricultural products and items processed from them. Thus basic commodities like sugar and starch will attract levies as may some foodstuffs. This is not necessarily a charge that would be encountered in many overseas markets.

Licensing

In previous sections of this handbook we have looked at both export and import licensing. Many overseas countries, particularly developing and under-developed countries, use specific import licensing to control every consignment. The existence of the required licence must be certain before any shipments are made as the goods will not be import cleared without the appropriate licence.

Quota

This describes a quantitative restrictions which may be imposed on certain goods, usually to protect local manufacturers. The Quota may be a quantity which is allowed in free from duty, subsequent imports being allowed but at the full rate of duty, or it may be that licences are issued only for that quantity and once used, no further imports will be allowed over the specified time period (usually 12 months).

Standards

Exporters will inevitably encounter an enormous range of different technical requirements across the world. The reason these may act as a barrier is that the exporter may actually not be able to comply with the standard or the certification requirements for that standard. Secondly, the cost of compliance, in terms of product modification, testing and certification, may make the cost of the product uncompetitive in the overseas market.

The above represent the range of common import controls which the UK exporter may come across. We could also legitimately include Pre-Shipment Inspection (covered in Chapter 5.2) and the use of Exchange Control as more indirect import controls, and we have to accept that in some overseas countries there have developed what might be termed 'unofficial' controls which can introduce significant compliance costs. It is an unfortunate fact but, in some countries, paying the right person can still be the only import procedure that matters.

In order to decide which controls are to be applied to each consignment, and at what level, there are three vital pieces of information which Customs authorities need:

- DESCRIPTION
- ORIGIN
- VALUE

and whilst particular requirements differ from one country to another there is invariably an import declaration accompanied by supporting documents. One of the most important supporting documents is one which is always prepared by the exporter, that is the export invoice. This may also be accompanied by other statements, especially as to origin and value, all designed to provide the above elements of information to the Customs.

The export invoice

The UK exporter is faced with producing a wide variety of different invoices, involving a range of third party procedures, dependent on the country of destination. Because the export invoice is of such importance to the overseas Customs authorities, it is they who insist on a particular format. The exporter could bill the buyer with almost any document from a standard commercial invoice to the back of an envelope, the more technical invoice requirements are purely the result of import Customs requirements.

Export invoices fall into 5 distinct types:

1. Commercial Invoice
2. Commercial Invoice with a Declaration
3. Commercial Invoice requiring third party Verification
   ○ Certified
   ○ Legalised
4. Consular Invoice
5. Specific Customs Invoice

Commercial invoice

The simplest situation is one where the importing country has no special requirements at all and the exporter uses the company's standard commercial invoice, just as for a home sale. The only difference will be the fact that the invoice is zero-rated for VAT.

Commercial invoice with declaration

It is quite common for countries to require a specific declaration to be typed on the invoice. The wording differs from country to country, and is often in the language of the importing country, but invariably declares the origin of the goods and that the prices are correct export prices. A typical declaration is reproduced in Figure 6.6

As we shall see later the import Customs are concerned that the origin and prices are legitimate. The exact wording of such declarations is available from a variety of reference sources, most notably, Croner's Reference Book for Exporters.

Certified invoices

The above declarations sometimes require a third party to validate them and the most common requirement is for a UK Chamber of Commerce to certify a set of invoices. They will stamp the documents with their own certification stamp, an example of which is reproduced in Figure 6.7. In theory they are certifying that the invoice and declaration are correct, but in practice they certify that the signatory of the invoice is one authorised by the company to make such declarations on behalf of the company. Exporting companies lodge the signatures of approved signatories with the Chambers for this purpose.

Legalised invoices

In some cases, in particular the Middle East, there is a requirement for a further stage of third party verification. The certified invoices are required to be *legalised* by the commercial section of the embassy of the importing country in the UK Again it is often a rubber stamp or sometimes a more complex verification. The procedure is that the exporter arranges certification at the Chamber of Commerce and then presents the document set to the appropriate embassy, in London, for legalisation. In the case of the 20 plus Arab League countries, all of which require legalisation, a streamlined procedure exists in which the local certifying Chamber sends the documents to the Arab British Chamber of Commerce (ABCC) who make the presentations to the individual embassies. This reduces the time taken for the operation to an average of 5 to 7 days.

It is not only the time delay that exporters must consider but also that charges are made for certification and legalisation. As an example, a set of documents certified and legalised through the ABCC will cost between £40 and £60.

In the case of Arab documents it may also be necessary to append a further declaration to the invoice certifying that the goods are not of Israeli origin or contain any Israeli materials.

Consular invoices

Consular invoices are particularly common in Central and Latin American countries. They require their own, unique, consular invoice form to be completed and returned to the Consulate for *Consularisation*. The format of such invoices varies enormously and they are often in the language of the country of destination. The Consulates, which are actually commercial sections of the embassies situated in regional centres, will check the whole set of documents before what might be a very elaborate consularising process. Quite apart from the time delay, it is possible that the Consular Fees could be quite high, sometimes even a percentage of the invoice value; so it is important that exporters have a good idea of the costs right from the quotation stage.

It is perfectly acceptable, and in fact might be seen as best practice, to show Consular fees as a separate item on the original pro-forma invoice quotation, along with the freight and insurance charges.

The requirements detailed above for Certified, Legalised or Consularised invoices can be seen as an attempt, by the importing country, to impose some controls in the exporter's country. The logic being that if documents are not appropriately verified then the import should not take place. Coincidently, they also raise revenue for the overseas country's commercial sections in the UK.

Specific customs invoice

These invoice forms are particularly related to ex-Commonwealth countries and are hangovers from the obsolete Commonwealth Preference System which, as we will see later, has been replaced by broader E.U. agreements. There are a lot less of these invoices in existence than at one time, many countries having gone over to a commercial invoice with a declaration. Where they still apply the exporter must complete the appropriate invoice form for the country of destination, which are available from specialist printers. They are often in the form of Certificates of Value & Origin (CV/O) and may bear reference to Current Domestic Values (CDV) to control dumping of goods. It is not uncommon that the exporter also produces a commercial invoice as a bill to the buyer.

Whatever the form of export invoice required they will all contain basically the same range of information:

- Seller and Purchaser (not always be the same as the exporter and importer);
- Goods description, quantity and value;
- Trade Terms (eg FCA, FOB, CIP, CIF etc.);
- Terms and Methods of Payment;
- Ancillary Costs (eg Freight and Insurance);
- Shipment details (points of departure and destination);
- Packing Specification: number and kind of packages, individual contents, sizes (in cms.), weights (Net and Gross in Kgs.) marks and numbers.

This latter information may be included on the face of the invoice but it is just as likely that it is attached to the invoice as a separate Packing Specification. Sometimes referred to as a Packing List or Packing Note the packing specification is basically treated as an extension of the invoice.

We have now established that the country of destination will directly effect the type and format of export invoice used and that it represents an essential element of the buyer's import clearance declaration. As we noted earlier, the three vital pieces of information which the Customs authorities at destination need to apply import controls are:

- DESCRIPTION
- ORIGIN
- VALUE

Description

This is the starting point for all Customs controls as the goods must first of all be very specifically identified in order to decide what particular controls apply to them. Customs authorities throughout the world are also wary about using words to identify commodities as there is clearly a language problem and also words can be vague and misleading. Therefore, the means used by Customs to identify goods depends on the use of number classification systems, or *nomenclatures,* which translate vague words into the hard data of numbers which mean the same throughout the world. It should also be noted that exporters have a duty to declare their exports for statistical purposes based on accurate tariff numbers.

Such classification systems form the basis of Customs Tariffs and it would not be beyond the bounds of possibility that every nation state in the world were to develop its own unique nomenclature. Thankfully, this is not the case and in fact there is a marked degree of harmonisation of classification systems across the globe. A potted history of the development of standardised classifications would start with:

The Brussels Tariff Nomenclature (BTN)

As the result of widespread discussions following the Second World War progress was made on the development of a standard product classification system. Not only was this seen as valuable in removing ambiguities in identification of goods from one country to another but it also greatly facilitated the collection of meaningful international trade statistics. The classification was produced by the Customs Cooperation Council, in 1957, as a 4 digit nomenclature which was promoted as a standard throughout the world. In fact almost 150 countries used the BTN as the basis of their tariff. For developing countries the BTN gave sufficient level of identification but for the developed nations it was quite common for the 4 digit code to be extended to give a higher level of sophistication to the classification. As we will see later, the longer the number the greater the specificity of the identification.

The BTN was partially redrafted IN 1965 and renamed the *Customs Cooperation Council Nomenclature (CCCN)* but remained a 4 digit code until the introduction of:

The Harmonized Commodity Description and Coding System (HS)

The HS represented a wholesale update of the CCCN and is a 6 digit classification which has again been adopted by the majority of trading nations. The reason for the update was the fact that the BTN had been drawn up in the 1950s and it had become quite clear that it was no longer relevant to the needs of Customs in the 1980s. If one considers the range of goods which were traded in the 1980s which actually did not exist in the 1950s it is quite clear that the original 9000 or so numbers needed to be expanded to the current 25,000 plus.

As an example, a company dealing in highly sophisticated optical fibres for computer applications was forced to classify the goods as Chapter 70 'glass... others', in the updated tariff such commodities are far more accurately identified in Chapter 90 as optical fibres. The predominance of 'others' as a safety net classification, for goods not specifically described in the old tariff, has been much reduced in the HS based tariffs. Also some trading nations, notably the USA, who have operated unique tariffs in the past have now incorporated the HS and therefore facilitated the further harmonisation of tariff classifications.

The current situation, as far as the UK is concerned, is that we operate the EC Combined Nomenclature, which is based on the HS and came into force on 1.1.88 as the E.U. Integrated Tariff (TARIC) and provides for 8 digit harmonisation within the E.U. and EFTA.

The typical structure of a tariff number for goods can be broken down into :

The 6 digit HS base is likely to be the same in most countries in the world and is extended by a further 2 digits common to all E.U. members. The 7th. digit identifies the rate of duty applicable, which should be standard throughout the EU, and the 8th. is the level of statistical collection of intra-EC trade figures (Intrastat). For all UK exports and imports from other EC members then the 8 digit code is sufficient, for imports from non-EC members then the full 11 digit classification is necessary to identify the appropriate EC import controls on such goods. In specialised cases, such as agricultural produce, wine and where anti-dumping duties are concerned, it is necessary to add a further 4 digits.

Finding a tariff number

We have established that the UK exporter has a duty to identify goods, with the correct tariff number, to the UK Customs for statistical purposes. Also the information supplied, for example on export invoices, could usefully identify the correct tariff number for the import Customs. In fact many

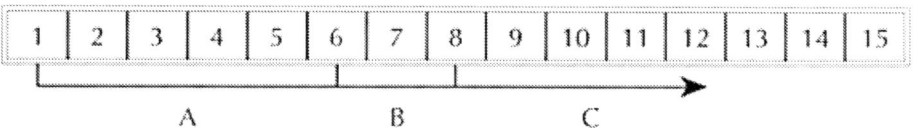

| 1 | 2 | 3 | 4 | 5 | 6 | 7 | 8 | 9 | 10 | 11 | 12 | 13 | 14 | 15 |

A   B   C

A - Harmonized Commodity Coding System (HS)
B - Intrastat
C - Community TARIC for third-country imports

overseas buyers may request that a particular description and tariff classification are included on the invoice.

It would be quite time consuming to start with the first line of the appropriate tariff and work through over 25,000 lines until you reach one that seems right, and, of course there is a more logical way. It may be that there is an alphabetical index which can immediately indicate the relevant part of the tariff. If not, then the logical process starts with finding the appropriate chapter. The HS is made up of 97 chapters listed from the most basic of commodities and gradually working through categories of products which become more and more sophisticated in terms of the amount of processing and technical enhancements.

Thus a very broad breakdown would look like:

Chapter 1	Live Animals
Chapters 2 - 25	Agricultural Produce
Chapters 26 - 38	Chemicals
Chapters 39 - 49	Articles of Plastic, Leather, Wood, Paper etc.
Chapters 50 - 63	Textiles
Chapters 64 - 84	Articles of Clothing, Ceramics, Glass, Iron, Copper etc.
Chapters 85 -97	Machinery, Locomotives, Aircraft, Ships, Furniture etc.

Once the correct chapter has been found it is then a matter of finding the appropriate sub-heading which identifies the goods more specifically and then the correct sub-sub-heading. As the classification number gets longer the identification of the goods becomes more and more exact.

Examples

A Riding Horse

01	Live Animals
0101	Horses, Asses, Mules and Hinnies (male horse / female donkey, before you ask)
010119	Horses (Not for breeding) (HS Level)
01011990	Horses (Not for slaughter)

Thus 01011990 would describe a horse not for breeding and not for slaughter. Admittedly not a 'horse for riding' but there isn't much else you could do with a horse, is there ?

X-ray tubes

90	Medical and Surgical
9022	Apparatus based on the use of X-rays
90223000	X-ray tubes

It will be clear that the UK exporter would need detailed advice from the overseas buyer to assess the most appropriate tariff classification.

What is meant by 'most appropriate'? The fact is that not only are tariff classifications highly complex, but also it may be that an exporter could legitimately describe goods in a variety of ways. Should this be the case it is potentially beneficial to consider carefully the description and tariff number quoted to importing Customs. However, it must be made very clear that it is vital that the correct and most accurate tariff number is declared as mis-declaration is an extremely serious offence and the penalties can prove very expensive to all parties.

Thus it may be perfectly acceptable to describe parts for the diesel engines of tractors as either 'Agricultural equipment and parts thereof' or 'Diesel engines and parts thereof'. Even if the overseas Customs reject the latter description in favour of the former, it is unlikely that penalties would be imposed for mis-declaration (although there are never any guarantees). As an example of a clear mis-declaration, describing children's buckets and spades for the beach as 'Agricultural equipment' is not a description that could very easily be justified.

It is also advisable that brand names or proprietary names of products are avoided as they will not be used as part of a tariff description. Likewise it is possible to describe goods on the basis of the materials of which they are made but it is the application to which the products are put which is often more important. Describing computer hardware as 'Plastic components' would clearly be unacceptable.

So exporters should take advice from their buyers and at least consider if there is scope for a legitimate choice of product descriptions used for particular overseas markets. It should be said, however, that Customs & Excise would adopt the view that the tariff allows only one valid classification for any commodity.

Origin

Once overseas Customs have accepted the tariff classification, or re-classified the goods themselves, then the tariff will indicate the range of controls, such as duty, tax, licence and quota, which apply to each particular commodity. In the case of the EU tariff the controls are actually integrated into the body of the classification (known as the Schedule). Such controls may be selectively applicable depending on the origin of the goods. This is because the EC has agreed a wide range of free and preferential trade agreements with other trading nations. These can be broken down into:

FREE TRADE	SWITZERLAND (LIECHTENSTEIN) , NORWAY, ICELAND ISRAEL, WEST BANK & GAZA, N. CYPRUS, FAEROE ISLANDS, YUGOSLAV REPUBLICS, ROMANIA, BULGARIA, MACEDONIA, MEXICO, S. AFRICA, CHILE .... ALGERIA, MOROCCO AND TUNISIA EGYPT, JORDAN, LEBANON AND SYRIA
PREFERENTIAL TRADE (reduced or zero)	AFRICAN, CARIBBEAN & PACIFIC (ACP) OVERSEAS COUNTRIES & TERRITORIES (OCT) GENERALISED SYSTEM OF PREFERENCES (GSP)
EU ASSOCIATION	TURKEY (ATR1)

The Free Trade agreements above are all bi-lateral, that is they give EU goods free entry into the overseas market as well as vice-versa. The Preferential agreements, which allow for free or reduced duty, are sometimes applicable to EU imports only and not necessarily EU exports to those countries.

Thus it may well be that the duty, and perhaps other controls, that commodities attract can be avoided by their originating in particular countries of supply. All such trade agreements are based on very precise Rules of Origin.

If goods are genuinely wholly produced in a particular country then proof of origin is not normally a problem, however where goods are processed in some way it can become more difficult. The principle used by most Customs authorities is that of *Sufficient Transformation*. In simple terms the Customs will require a breakdown of the component elements of a product and require a sufficient proportion of the value (in the EU a minimum of 60%) of the finished product to be originating, that is wholly produced in that country.

Rules of origin are invariably very complex because the Customs are attempting to control what is known as *Deflection* of *Trade*. This describes the shipping of goods via a third country to establish an erroneous origin; for example Japanese DVD Players, shipped into Malta, where they are relabelled and repacked and shipped into the EU as Maltese origin and therefore duty free. Clearly, repacking is never 'sufficient transformation' and such a process would be a serious offence.

Certificates of origin (C of O)

We have already established that the export invoice is sometimes accompanied by other supporting documents. In the cases where a declaration of origin on the invoice is insufficient then a variety of other documents may be appropriate dependant on the country of destination and, in some cases, the goods. These are:

1. European EU C of O

   Issued by Chambers of Commerce they can be certified by the Chamber, along with the invoices, or may be self-certified by the exporter.
2. Arab British Chamber of Commerce C of O

   as above but specific to Arab league trade and certified and legalised along with the invoices.
3. Certificates of Value & Origin

   Described earlier in this chapter as a form of export invoice. The origin declaration is incorporated in the invoice. May apply to ACP, OCT or GSP countries.
4. Status and Movement Certificates

   In the previous chapter we identified the function of the Transit element of the SAD in terms of moving through Customs posts of transit. You may recall that since 1 January 1993 this has applied only to goods destined for ex-EFTA countries. In such cases the T2 status of goods is also certified by the transit document.

In addition, for all those free trade countries mentioned above, a specialised, so-called, Movement Certificate is appropriate. This is the EUR 1 which is a four page document requiring authentication by UK Customs (see Application Form Figure 6.9). Such authentication may require the provision of proof of origin to the Customs authorities. For consignments below €6000 (typically) in value (previously covered by the EUR 2), or where the exporter was previously allowed to issue EUR 1s which had been pre-authenticated by Customs, then the Movement Certificate is replaced by an invoice declaration.

Trade with Turkey is quite a specialised area as Turkey is an Associate member of the EU. Exports to Turkey are covered by a particular form of Movement certificate, the ATR 1.

Whilst the major consequence of origin is the potential avoidance of Customs duties it should also be noted that origin will also be relevant to the application of other controls such as quotas and to the collection of accurate trade statistics. It may even be the case that financial aid has been linked with purchases from particular countries.

Value

Once Customs have decided on the description and the correct origin of the goods then it may be the case that ad valorem charges are applicable. In such a case the invoice value, often referred to as the Transaction Value, serves as the base for the calculation of charges. In the cases where the charge is specific to a particular quantity it is still the invoice which supplies the relevant information. In a number of countries, a statement of value is required, in addition to the invoice, for anything but low value consignments.

Just as with Description and Origin, the Customs procedures are designed to avoid any manipulation of the value of consignments which could cause anything but an 'equitable market value' to be quoted. The potential manipulation is, of course, an under-valuation of the goods in order to minimise the duties and taxes payable on such value. The importer may, for example have already paid in advance or be arranging transfers of funds for the elements of value not invoiced. Invoice valuations may be rejected by Customs in which case they have other methods of arriving at a value that is acceptable to them. Within the EC there are in fact 5 other methods of valuation if the invoice value is not acceptable.

It may seem rather silly but there can also be cases where values on invoices are actually over-estimated. The offence here is usually an infringement of that country's exchange control regulations, that is, the buyer is moving hard currency out of the country. This may be held illegally in bank accounts outside the country.

The information given throughout this chapter leads us to the inevitable conclusion that sensible exporters should take a direct interest in the controls which their goods attract at destination, and how the document set prepared here affects the application of such controls. The three vital pieces of information, description, origin and value are probably the pieces of information most manipulated in international trade. The reputable exporter should be wary of the consequences of cooperation in obvious mis-declarations; whilst direct action may only be taken against the importer, the long term consequences to their trade in that market may be unacceptable. It may also be the case that this leads to export mis-declarations for which the chances of being the target of more direct action are obviously greater.

Customs management

Having examined the whole range of Customs controls from export, through transit to import, the first point to bear in mind is that compliance with Customs requirements is mandatory and, for no other reason than that non-compliance can be expensive, it is important that exporters are aware of those procedures which affect their exports.

Remember, ignorance is never an excuse. However if we start from the premise that compliance is essential this does not preclude opportunities for good management to reduce the impact of Customs controls on a company's international trade.

An analogy, which may not appear at first to be directly relevant, is that of a case which was heard at the European Court of Justice some years ago. The company concerned had been fined a very large amount of money for unlawful claims of agricultural subsidies and its appeal was being heard. The peculiarities of the Court's procedure require that all the legal arguments are prepared in writing prior to the brief verbal hearings. In this case their argument was in three parts:

1. We committed no offence and should not be fined at all.
2. We did commit the offences but the fine should be reduced.
3. Can we have time to pay (please)?

The fact that all three arguments were presented in one go seemed totally logical to the advocates concerned.

So how is this relevant to the way exporters approach Customs procedures? It is simply that the same logic applies. You should:

• Avoid controls and charges completely.
• Minimise the costs, and consequences, of those that cannot be avoided.
• Take as long as possible to comply or pay.

AVOIDANCE

First, a very important point. Evasion of Customs controls is illegal, avoidance is good management. There is a growing number of 'Tax Avoidance' consultants, but no 'Tax Evasion' consultants. Of the procedures we have examined in the last three chapters several do provide opportunities.

Description	A selective and informed choice of product description could reduce charges and avoid quota restrictions
Origin	Correct statements of origin, properly documented, can again avoid all charges.
Inward Processing Relief	If imported goods are re-exported relief or drawback of duty can be arranged. (see Customs Notice 221)
Returned Goods	Goods exported and subsequently returned within 3 years, in basically the same state, can avoid duty and tax (see Customs Notice 235).

Temporary Exports

Certain types of goods which are temporarily exported can avoid all Customs controls and charges by the use of an *ATA Carnet*. We have seen that a Carnet is simply a book of vouchers. In the case of the ATA Carnet ('Temporary Admission .... Admission Temporaire) which is issued by Chambers of Commerce three categories of goods are covered:-

• Exhibition goods
• Samples
• Professional equipment

all of which will enter one or more countries only to leave at a later date. As long as all the goods which enter actually leave, the vouchers of the ATA Carnet replace all other Customs procedures.

It should be emphasised that this does preclude the sale of exhibition goods or samples in the overseas market. Also, if samples are genuinely of no commercial value, then they are not subject to Customs controls anyway and the ATA would be irrelevant.

Remember, it is Customs who decide what is of commercial value and what is not. Professional equipment can be a very wide definition including tools, measuring equipment, props, costumes, sound and lighting systems, instruments, display and demonstration equipment etc.etc.

Up to the end of 1992 the EC used an equivalent document called the E.U. Carnet, but since the removal of internal frontiers on 1 January 1993 this document has become obsolete. By definition the ATA is also of no relevance to EU movements.

Freezones

A number of ports and depots throughout the world have been designated, by their government authorities, as Freezones. They are areas in which goods are exempt from Customs controls. In the UK they are:

- Belfast Airport
- Birmingham
- Cardiff
- Southampton
- Prestwick Airport
- Liverpool

and there are many more throughout the world. They typically receive goods as imports and allow a wide range of handling, and selective processing , without any Customs interference until the goods leave the freezone area. If goods are re-exported they actually attract no customs controls whatsoever.

Minimise

If we cannot actually avoid controls and charges then we should look to at least reduce them to a minimum.

Valuation

It is important that the genuine transaction value is evidenced by the invoice but it may also be the case that certain monetary amounts can legitimately be excluded. This does differ from one country to another but it may be that items such as on-carriage (the transport costs from port of entry to final destination), turnover taxes, commissions, royalties and documentation fees can, and should be, excluded from the valuation.

Outward processing relief

Where goods are exported and re-imported following processing, the re-imports attract relief of part of the duty. The procedure must be agreed prior to the original export.

Take time

Whatever charges and controls are unavoidable it makes sense to take as much time as is allowed before compliance or payment.

Warehousing

Many countries, including the whole of the EU, allow imported goods to remain in a Customs warehouse, in which case they do not become subject to Customs controls. In the EU, goods can be left up to 2 years in the warehouse, but the handling allowed is severely limited in that the goods can be checked and re-packed but no real processing will be allowed. The goods do not have to comply with controls or pay duties and tax until they leave the warehouse.

Deferment

Both duty and tax can be deferred in many countries so that it is paid some time after the time of import. In the UK approved traders and agents can supply guarantees which defer the payment of duty until the 15th of the following month. Tax, such as VAT, can be deferred in the same way, or, for EC imports, can be accounted for on the VAT returns.

Conclusion

The last two chapters have covered what might appear to be a bewildering array of customs procedures and controls. There is, however, a logic to the current situation facing UK exporters and there is little doubt that an appreciation of the developments, particularly since taking up our membership of the EU in 1973, will lead to easier compliance with mandatory procedures and a greater awareness of the possibilities for cost saving which can be provided by a broader knowledge and better understanding of Customs requirements.

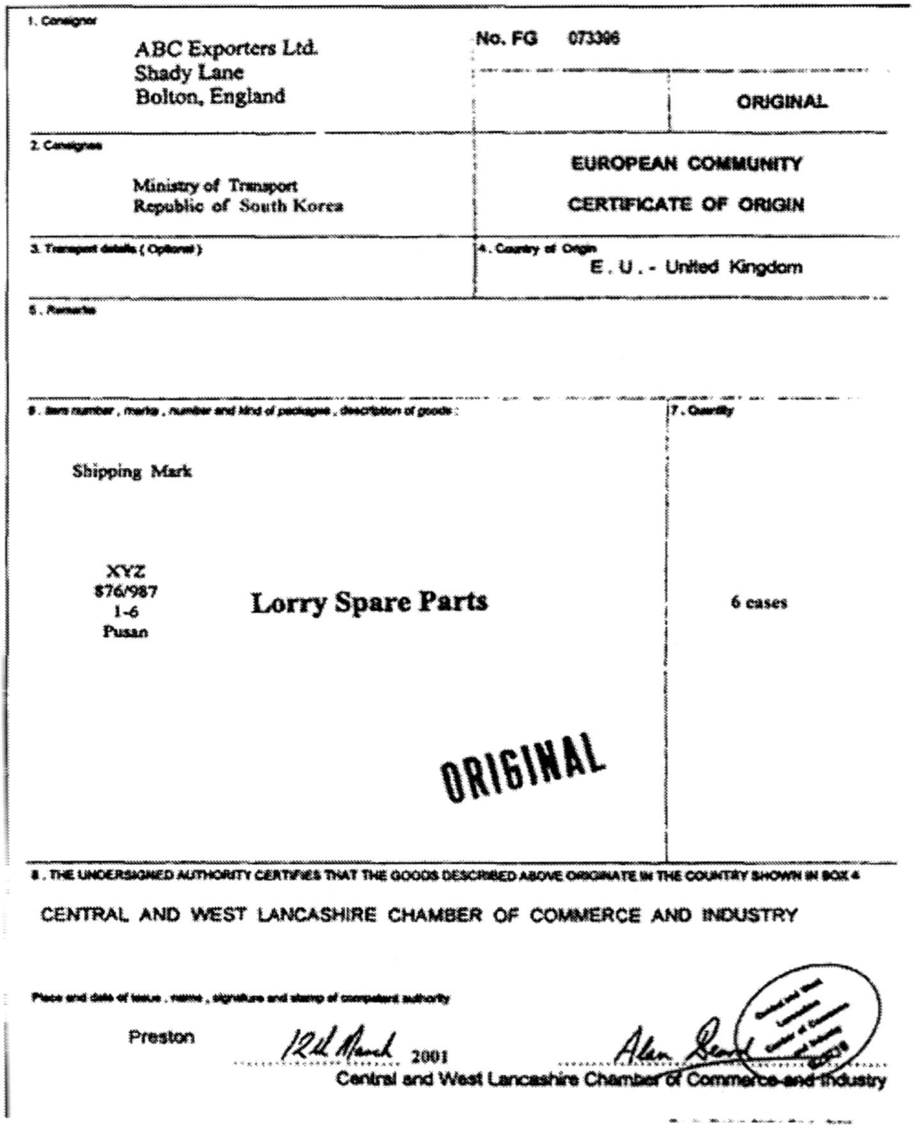

1. Consignor		No. FG 073396	
ABC Exporters Ltd. Shady Lane Bolton, England			ORIGINAL
2. Consignee		EUROPEAN COMMUNITY	
Ministry of Transport Republic of South Korea		CERTIFICATE OF ORIGIN	
3. Transport details (Optional)		4. Country of Origin E . U . - United Kingdom	
5 . Remarks			

6. Item number , marks , number and kind of packages , description of goods :	7. Quantity
Shipping Mark XYZ 876/987 1-6 Pusan **Lorry Spare Parts** ORIGINAL	6 cases

8 . THE UNDERSIGNED AUTHORITY CERTIFIES THAT THE GOODS DESCRIBED ABOVE ORIGINATE IN THE COUNTRY SHOWN IN BOX 4

CENTRAL AND WEST LANCASHIRE CHAMBER OF COMMERCE AND INDUSTRY

Place and date of issue , name , signature and stamp of competent authority

Preston   12th March 2001

Central and West Lancashire Chamber of Commerce and Industry

Fig. 6.2.1 - Example ot certified invoice

Consignor ⟨المرسل⟩ [1]		CERTIFICATE OF ORIGIN
		G/ 331255
		Consignor's ref [4]
Consignee ⟨المرسل اليه⟩ [2]		شهــادة منشــأ
		CERTIFICATE OF ORIGIN
		تشهد السلطة الموقعة بأن البضائع الوارد بيانها أدناه
		The undersigned authority certifies that the goods shown below
		originated in ⟨منشأها⟩ [5]
Method of Transport ⟨طريقة النقل⟩ [3]		غــرفــة الـتـجـارة الـعـربـيـة الـبـريـطـانـيـة
		ARAB-BRITISH CHAMBER OF COMMERCE

Marks and Numbers ⟨الأرقام والعلامات⟩	Quantity and Kind of Packages ⟨كمية ونوع الطرود⟩	Description of Goods ⟨مواصفات البضاعة⟩	Weight (gross & net) ⟨الوزن القائم والصافى⟩ [6]

غــرفــة الـتـجـارة الـعـربـيـة الـبـريـطـانـيـة

ARAB-BRITISH CHAMMBER OF COMMERCE

مكان وتاريخ الاصدار Place and Date of Issue	Issuing Authority	سلطة الاصدار

Fig. 6.2.1 - Example of legalized invoice

APPLICATION FOR MOVEMENT CERTIFICATE

EUR1 No.

1 Exporter (Name, full address, country)

2 Application for a certificate to be used in preferential trade between

THE EUROPEAN ECONOMIC COMMUNITY

and

(Insert appropriate countries or groups of countries or territories)

3 Consignee (Name, full address, country) (Optional)

4 Country, group of countries or territory in which the products are considered as originating

EEC

5 Country, group of countries or territory of destination

6 Transport details (Optional)

7 Remarks

8 Item number: marks & numbers | Number and kind of packages (1): description of goods

9 Gross weight (kg) or other measure (litres, cu. m., etc.)

10 Invoices (Optional)

(1) If goods are not packed, indicate number of articles or state "in bulk" as appropriate

11 CUSTOMS ENDORSEMENT

Declaration certified

Export document (2)

Form ________ No. ____

Customs office ________

Issuing country or territory

UNITED KINGDOM

Date

Stamp

(2) Complete only where the regulations of the exporting country or territory require

12 DECLARATION BY THE EXPORTER

I, the undersigned, declare that the goods described above meet the conditions required for the issue of this certificate

(Place and date)

Fig. 6.2.1 - Application for Movement Certificate (EUR1)

Part 7

Risk Management

7.1

Cargo (marine) insurance

The exporter faces a great many risks in conducting business internationally, quite apart from the fact that the buyers may not be particularly keen to buy their goods. Even assuming that we have an established market for our products and services there still exist many potential practical problems in ensuring that such business actually leads to the receipt of sufficient revenues. We can identify three major risks which must be addressed by the typical exporter.

Physical risk

Goods moving internationally face a very real risk of physical loss or damage. This may simply be damage caused to the goods in handling and transit, possibly due to inadequate packing or bad handling, or loss due to accidental diversion or deliberate pilferage or theft. It is clear that the risks are generally far greater for export consignments than for domestic movements due to the length of international journeys, the range of transport modes involved, the increased handling and the great variety of conditions encountered.

A typical breakdown of the causes of loss or damage on an international journey would look something like:

* Poor handling and stowage	44 %
* Physical damage on/in conveyance	33 %
* Theft and pilferage	22 %
* General Average	1 % (see later)

It is possible for the exporter to arrange insurance cover for all of these risks.

Credit risk

Even if the goods arrive complete and undamaged the problems do not stop there because there is the risk that the buyer will not actually pay for the goods. This may be perfectly legitimate in that there is a contractual dispute between buyer and seller; after all, the exporter may have shipped total rubbish to the importer. However we must accept that non-payment may be the result of a dishonourable intention of the buyer. This takes many forms from non-acceptance of the goods, through taking over the goods and deliberately delaying payment, to simply not paying for the goods.

It is possible for the exporter to arrange insurance cover for such risks.

Cargo (marine) insurance

Many forms of insurance cover exist throughout the world but there is little doubt that Marine Insurance is one of the oldest. In the UK, the first rationalisation of the marine insurance market was devised by an Elizabethan Act of Parliament in 1601, to be followed by the development of the Corporation of Lloyd's which allowed, and still allows, underwriters to offer insurance cover. Until quite recently the language of marine insurance continued to use the flowery phrases of Elizabethan English, but modernisation in the 1980s has supplied us with more efficient, but some might say, a lot less interesting policies.

The principle of 'averaging' is at the heart of marine insurance and is perfectly described by a phrase taken from the original Elizabethan Act: 'so that... it cometh to pass that... the loss lighteth rather easily upon many than heavily upon few, and rather upon them that adventure not than those that do adventure.'

Wonderful stuff, and a very precise description of the fact that if only one or two people carried all the risks of, for example, a sea voyage then they might be less inclined to adventure. In fact, a the Act goes on to say, it was an encouragement to trade internationally because the risks were shared by a large number of people: '...whereby all merchants, especially the younger sort, are allured to venture more willingly and more freely.'

The underwriters of such risks were actually so called as they signed their name under the risk, stated on 'the slip', along with other underwriters who also took part of the risk. To this day Lloyd's underwriters accepts risks on behalf of their 'syndicates' and company underwriters accept risks on behalf of their companies.

It should be noted that modern international trade now involves modes of transport other than sea freight and it is probably more appropriate to use the expression 'Cargo Insurance' which covers road, rail and airfreight movements, as well as the common combinations of transport modes now used.

General Average

This is one of the oldest principles of cargo insurance and still has relevance today. It covers the situation where: ' there is extraordinary sacrifice or expenditure, intentionally and reasonably incurred, for the purpose of preserving the imperilled property involved in the common maritime adventure.'

This will include situations where goods are jettisoned to save the ship, or are damaged by water used to extinguish a fire, or the vessel is diverted to a port of refuge, and many other situations where loss of certain goods preserves the rest of the cargo and the conveyance. The basic principle is that all the parties involved, including the vessel owners, contribute to the loss. General Average is declared and an Average Adjuster will, eventually, calculate the amount of the claim. It is often necessary for the cargo owners to sign a General Average Bond and for the insurers to provide a General Average Guarantee in order to obtain possession of the goods from the carrier. As all standard policies cover General Average claims, the cost of the claim will be met by the insurers.

To insure or not to insure

An exporter can choose not to insure the goods against loss or damage in transit and simply carry the risk. However, this poses a number of problems:

1. The terms of sale agreed between seller and buyer may impose a requirement on the seller to arrange for cargo insurance. This would apply to terms such as CIF, CIP. In such cases the seller must arrange adequate insurance and prove it with documentation.
2. In the event of loss or damage it may be that action is possible against the carriers in charge of the goods at the time. The carriers have limitations on their liability and it requires some expertise to sustain successful claims. One of the advantages of a cargo insurance policy is that the exporter does not have to carry out actions against liable carriers.

The situation in practice is that the vast majority of exporters arrange for insurance cover against the physical risk of loss or damage to the goods in transit. So how do they arrange this?

Specific (Voyage) policy

It is perfectly feasible for an exporter with an international consignment for shipment to approach an insurance company, invariably through an insurance broker, and request that an insurance policy be drawn up for that particular consignment.

This is often referred to as a Voyage policy as it covers only that specific shipment. Purely out of historical interest, the traditional Lloyd's voyage policy is reproduced in Figure 7.1.1 It should be noted that the Lloyd's policy, the SG (Ship or Goods) form in use from 1779, became obsolete in 1983 with the introduction of the modern language Marine All Risks Policy (MAR) of which Figure 7.1.2 is the standard form.

It may be difficult to make out the fine print of the SG form but an examination would reveal that the cover offered is somewhat antiquated as in *'men of war, fire, enemies, pirates, rovers, thieves, jettisons, letters of mart and countermart, surprisals, takings at sea, arrests, restraints, and detainments of all kings, princes , and people etc. etc.'*

Whilst pirates do still attack cargo vessels it will be clear that modern trade requires cover which is a little more sophisticated. Incidentally a letter of mart permits piracy on certain foreign vessel, and was granted, for example, to Francis Drake by Elizabeth I, the letter of countermart saying, 'you have to stop now'.

For many years this basic Lloyd's policy was extended by the addition of clauses produced by the Institute of London Underwriters, known as the Institute Cargo Clauses, which were basically 'All Risks', 'With Average' (WA) covering specified partial loss, and 'Free from Particular Average' (FPA) excluding part losses. War Clauses and Strikes, Riots and Civil Commotions Clauses (SRCC) were often added as well as a number of quite specialised clauses covering particular situations or types of goods.

The update in 1983 saw the SG form replaced by a very simple MAR (see Figure 7.2) policy the cover being expressed in the new clauses which are now (A), (B) or (C), plus War Clauses and Strikes Clauses. In simple terms, Cargo Clauses (A) are the equivalent of 'All Risks', (B) covers less than (A) and (C) covers less than (B), with a corresponding decrease in the insurance premiums. There is also an Institute Cargo Clauses (Air) which are the equivalent of the (A) clauses but obviously for air movements. A detailed examination of the clauses provided by the insurance underwriters or brokers would clearly be of use to the exporter, but a brief comparison of the clauses is shown in Figure 7.1.3 below.

Later in this chapter we will look at what might be seen as more important: that is, what risks are excluded from these policies.

Today therefore, an exporter approaching an insurer for a Voyage policy would now receive a MAR policy with attached clauses and pay the appropriate premiums.

This is a perfectly feasible operation for the exporter making, perhaps, one or two consignments a month but it would clearly be very time consuming to approach an insurer for potentially hundreds, or even thousands, of shipments which the average exporter will be making. There has to be a better way and of course there is.

Open policy

The most common situation is that exporters use a broker to approach insurance companies and agree the raising of a policy which is drawn up to cover many shipments and not just one. This may be a 'Floating Policy' which is raised for a particular value and which is gradually reduced by the value of each shipment until it is used up and requires renewal.

This type of policy is less common than it used to be, particularly because the exporter is often require the payment of an average premium in advance. By far the most common form of policy is properly referred to as the 'Permanently Open Policy', so called because it will be drawn up for a period

(No.   )

No Policy or other Contract dated on or after 1st Jan., 1996, will be recognised by the Committee of Lloyd's as entitling the holder to the benefit of the Funds and/or Guarantees lodged by the Underwriters of the Policy or Contract as security for their liabilities unless it bears at foot the Seal of Lloyd's Policy Signing Office.

Be it known that

Reckitt and Watson Ltd.

as well in   their   own name as for and in the name and names of all and every other person or persons to whom the same doth, may, or shall appertain, in part or in all, doth make assurance and cause themselves and them, and every of them, to be insured, lost or not lost, at and from

Warehouse Hackney via London to Warehouse Belo Horizonte via Rio de Janeiro

Upon any kind of goods and merchandise, and also upon the body, tackle, apparel, ordnance, munition, artillery, boat, and other furniture, of and in the good ship or vessel called the Rail and/or Conveyance

and S.S. Ionian sailing 1st May, 19xx.

£ 559.00

£559.00 on 5 cases electric drills.
With average in accordance with the terms and conditions
of the Institute Cargo Clauses (W.A.) including
Warehouse to Warehouse.

25p %

Dated in London, the   2nd April, 19xx.   R. Shepheard

(In the event of loss or damage which may result in a claim under this Insurance, immediate notice should be given to the Lloyd's Agent at the port or place where the loss or damage is discovered in order that he may examine the goods and issue a survey report.)

LLOYD'S POLICY SIGNING OFFICE.

Fig. 7.1.1 - The Lloyd's Voyage Policy (example)

of time, subject to renewal, and will allow any number of shipments over that period. The expression often used is that the policy is 'always open irrespective of declarations'. The wording of such a policy, designed to cover every shipment by that particular exporter, might be:

Per:	Any Conveyances or held covered at a premium to be arranged for Air &/or Parcel Post.
Voyage:	World / World
	Via any route and including transhipment
On:	Electrical Materials &/or other materials.

Such a policy could hardly be more open, covering the shipment of any materials, from anywhere to anywhere, by any route, and by any means of transport. It will usually contain a schedule of premium rates which will depend on the country of destination and the level of cover, with the Institute Cargo Clauses detailing the actual cover. These open policies are sometimes referred to as 'Declaration Policies' because the exporter is making shipments which the insurers know nothing about until they are declared to them, which they must be periodically. But first, the exporter has a problem with the document set.

Under the contracts we mentioned earlier in which the exporter is responsible for arranging, and paying for, cargo insurance there is a clear need to include, in the set of documents, some documentary proof that the

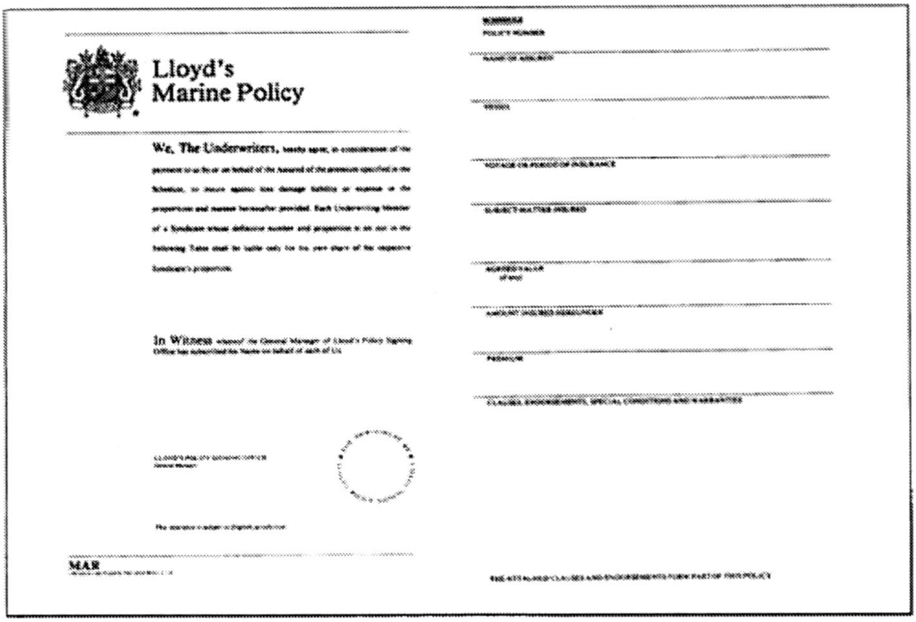

Fig. 7.1.2 - Marine All Risks Policy

Figure 7.1.3 - Comparison of (A), (B) and (C)clauses

	(A)	(B)	(C)
LOSS OR DAMAGE REASONABLY ATTRIBUTABLE TO			
Accidental damage, theft, malicious damage	✗	✗	✓
Fire or explosion	✗	✗	✗
Vessel stranded, grounded, sunk or capsized	✗	✗	✗
Collision with any external object except water	✗	✗	✗
Discharge of cargo at a port of distress	✗	✗	✗
Earthquake, volcanic eruption or lightning	✗	✗	✓
Theft	✗	✓	✓
LOSS OR DAMAGE CAUSED BY:			
General Average sacrifice	✗	✗	✗
Jettison	✗	✗	✗
Washing overboard	✗	✗	✓
Entry of sea water	✗	✗	✓
Total loss of any package overboard or dropped whilst loading or unloading	✗	✗	✓

contractual obligation to arrange insurance cover has been performed. The problem is that the exporter only has one Open Policy and it is not practical to send that to buyers as part of the document set. It is probably buried in the Company Secretary's safe anyway. The solution is that the exporter will produce an 'Insurance Certificate' for each individual shipment.

Such Certificates will be completed by the exporter on blank forms or templates supplied by the insurers, which have been pre-signed by the underwriter. An example is reproduced in Figure 7.1.4 and it will be clear that they contain only very basic information regarding the shipment. Thus the production of documentary evidence of the cargo insurance is accomplished by the relatively simple completion of an Insurance Certificate, and this is invariably acceptable.

The only situation in which an Insurance Certificate would not be acceptable is where a Letter of Credit insists on an Insurance Policy. In such a case the bank would reject a Certificate as being inferior to a Policy and the exporter would have to obtain a Voyage Policy from the insurers or ,of course, have the Letter of Credit changed.

Finally the exporter has to declare to the insurance company details of all the shipments made in order for them to calculate and invoice for the insurance premiums. This is done periodically, usually monthly, either on paper declaration forms supplied by the insurers, or by providing copies of the Certificates produced over that period. It is increasingly common for such information to be supplied on computer tape or disk or even transmitted direct into the insurance company's computers as electronic messages.

Principles of insurance

It is important that exporters have a basic understanding of some of the underpinning principles of insurance generally, and particularly their practical implications to cargo insurance.

Insurable interest

This expression was actually used in chapter 4 with reference to one of the functions of trade terms such as FOB, FCA, CIP etc. in that they identified a point in the journey where the risk of loss or damage to the goods transferred from the seller to the buyer. Technically there is an actual transfer of the 'insurable interest' in the goods.

The principal of insurable interest is a vital one to all forms of insurance. In order to take out a policy the policy holder must have an insurable interest in the insured matter. In the case of cargo insurance this means that they must 'benefit from the safe arrival of the goods or be prejudiced by their loss'.

CERTIFICATE OF INSURANCE

Exporter	CERTIFICATE NO. ZINT
	Exporter's reference
	Forwarder's reference

Consignee

CONDITIONS OF INSURANCE

☐ Institute Cargo Clauses (A)

☐ Institute Cargo Clauses (B)

☐ Institute Cargo Clauses (C)

☐ Institute Cargo Clauses (Air) (Excluding sendings by Post)

Selling agent

Further subject to Institute War Clauses and Institute Strikes Clauses (Cargo) (Air Cargo)

Institute Classification Clause

Other UK transport details

Institute Radioactive Contamination Exclusion Clause

Other Special Conditions (see reverse)

| Vessel | Port of loading |
| Port of discharge | Final destination | Insured value | Premium |

| Shipping marks, container numbers | Number and kind of packages, description of goods | Gross Weight | Cube (m³) |

PROCEDURE IN EVENT OF CLAIM

1 It is the duty of the Assured and their agents to take such measures as may be reasonable for the purpose of averting or minimising a loss and to ensure that all rights against Carriers Bailees or other third parties are properly preserved and exercised

2 Follow the procedures stated overleaf.

3 Apply immediately for survey of damaged goods to the Agent stated below or if none stated to the nearest Institute of London Underwriters or Lloyds Agent or to Zurich International Head Office as shown on reverse

This is to certify that Zurich International has insured the above mentioned goods for the voyage and value stated on behalf of

Under Policy No

Claims Payable at

By

This Certificate is not valid unless counter-signed

This Certificate requires endorsement by the Assured

Signatory's company

Name of signatory

For Zurich International (UK) Limited

Desmond W White, Managing Director

ZURICH INTERNATIONAL UK

Dated

Signed

Figure 7.1.4 Certificate of insurance

Without such a principal it would be possible for any individual to take out a insurance policy on any eventuality they could think of. For example a policy could be raised which paid out if an English football player broke a leg during a game. If this policy were taken out by the Football Association then they would clearly have an insurable interest, but if it were possible for any individual to take out such a policy then it would simply be another form of gambling, that is a bet of premiums which pays out if a player actually does break a leg. Insurance is not intended to be a form of gambling and therefore the policy holder has to prove this 'vested interest'.

It is also necessary to prove insurable interest in order to make a claim against a policy and this can pose a problem if the claim is actually made by a non-policy holder. This situation can arise in contracts subject to CIP or CIF conditions. As explained in chapter 4 these terms mean that the seller is responsible for arranging the insurance and, as we have seen above, this will invariably done under an Open Policy in the seller's name. However the 'insurable interest' transfers either at ship's rail, port of shipment for CIF contracts or when the first carrier takes over the goods under CIP. Thus, the responsibility for loss or damage to the goods transfers to the buyer at the port or depot in the UK even though the seller has insured rights through to the final destination.

It is possible for the buyer to make a claim on the seller's open policy because of two clauses:

Exchange risk

Even if we are able to deliver goods in good condition to the buyer and the satisfied buyer pays us on time it is still possible for the unwary exporter to lose money. In the event that the exporter is invoicing in a foreign currency it is possible that the pounds sterling funds eventually received, following exchange of the foreign currency revenues, are less than was anticipated because of fluctuations in the relevant exchange rates.

It is not possible for the exporter to arrange insurance cover for such risks. It is however possible to manage the contingency for such risks.

Claims Payable Abroad (CPA)

The insurers will accept a claim either at the overseas destination, usually through the nearest Lloyd's or Company's agent, or here where the policy was issued. All they require is that the claim is properly documented and, as the original documents can only be in one place, there is no possibility of dual claims. Thus it is perfectly possible for the buyer to pay the seller the full CIF or CIP value and use the documents to make the insurance claim for the insured value.

Just what claims documents are required we will examine later but we still have the problem of the buyer establishing an insurable interest in order to make the claim. This is solved by: Policy Proof of Interest (PPI)

In simple terms this means that possession of the policy is sufficient to prove insurable interest. In reality it is the insurance certificate, and supporting claims documents, which provide such proof. Such certificates would be endorsed on the reverse side to make such a transfer possible, in the same way that Bill of Lading may be endorsed to transfer title in the goods.

Indemnity

Most insurance is based on the fact that the insurers promise to indemnify the insured; that is, they promise to put them back into the situation they were in before the loss. It is obviously not a principle of life insurance.

In practice, the indemnity on cargo insurance policies is expressed as an amount of money, the insured value of the goods. Whilst it is possible that the insurers could replace lost or damaged goods with exact equivalents it is clearly impractical, and therefore cargo insurance is invariably based on Valued Policies.

The Marine Insurance Act 1906 specifies that the insured value of the goods must be the ' prime cost plus all expenses incidental to shipping plus charges of insurance', in practice the typical insured value is CIF or CIP + 10%.

The additional 10% is there to represent the buyer's potential profit. After all, the seller's profit is in the ex-works price and if the goods had arrived then the buyer would presumably have made a profit on top of the CIF/CIP price they have agreed to pay. The insurance company is in fact indemnifying both parties.

This seem even more logical when you consider the situation in which the buyer is making the claim. They claim the full CIF/CIP price that they have paid the seller plus a percentage to cover their lost profits. In this respect it is perfectly acceptable to the insurers to insure goods for CIF + 20% or CIF + 30% because the premiums are also calculated on the insured values.

It is possible to agree an 'Excess' on the value in which case the exporter will always bear a percentage of the loss, and have no claim if the loss is below the excess amount. Alternatively a 'Franchise' amount might be agreed in which case a loss below the amount would preclude a claim, as with the excess, but losses above the amount specified would be met in full; that is, the exporter would not carry any part of the loss so long as it exceeded the franchise percentage.

Uberrimae fidei (utmost good faith)

Once again, this is a principle which applies to all forms of insurance. The insurers are almost totally dependent on the insured to disclose any relevant information regarding the insured risks. Thus a person taking out a life insurance policy who failed to disclose a serious medical problem would find that the policy could be 'voided' by the insurers. There is an important application of *Uberrimae fidei* to the type of Open (Declaration) policies commonly used for cargo insurance.

Imagine the situation in which an exporter makes a shipment by road to Germany at the beginning of June and it arrives intact during the second week of June. At the end of June the seller must declare all the month's shipments to the insurance company in order for them to calculate the premiums. However, the safe arrival of the German consignment could persuade the seller not to declare the shipment because, after all, the insurance was not actually required for that consignment.

This would be a clear and serious breach of good faith and, if deliberate, would almost certainly lead to the policy being voided, that is, cancelled by the insurers. It is obviously inequitable for the insured to avoid paying premiums on goods which they already know have arrived safely. Goods are declared 'safe or not safe, lost or not lost'.

Good faith works both ways. Imagine the situation in which the goods are actually written off due to a road accident on their way to Germany. The insurance company's good faith is that they accept the claim, at the end of June, even though the loss occurred before declaration, ie before they knew of the consignment.

Subrogation

In the event that loss or damage occurs due to an insured risk then a claim will be made on the insurance company. If we assume that the claim is successful then the insured will regard the matter as closed. However, if nothing else happens we have a carrier, who may well be liable for the loss or damage, who has apparently avoided any liability.

It is the principle of subrogation which avoids this outcome, in that it allows the insurance company to take action against liable carriers in the name of the insured. The exporter, or importer, must maintain any rights of action against carriers, by avoiding giving clean receipts and advising loss or damage as soon as is possible, ideally within 3 days, but these rights are subrogated to the insurance company once the claim has been paid.

It is very fair to the insured in that the claim must be paid first. The insurance company cannot make a claim on the carrier and only pay the insured if the action against the carrier is successful. The insured will have a valid claim irrespective of the carrier's liability. Also, in the unlikely event that the insurers actually receive more in their claim on the carrier than they have paid to the insured, then the insured receives the difference.

The whole issue becomes somewhat more complicated because the carriers will often have taken out insurance to cover their liability to the owners of the goods. This is known as a Goods in Transit (GIT) policy and valid claims will be met by the carrier's insurance company. What this means is that claims against carriers are often made by insurance companies and that disputes may well be settled between the two insurance companies involved.

Contingency (seller's interest) insurance

Many exporters find that there are situations where they are making export shipments for which the buyer is responsible for cargo insurance. The most obvious cases would be CPT or CFR shipments, although the same situation applies to FCA and FOB sales. In some markets CPT/CFR shipments are very common as the importer's country have a requirement that cargo insurance is taken out with one of their national insurance companies, rather than a foreign company in the seller's country. This is particularly common in African markets.

The risk here is that loss or damage can occur and the buyer refuses to take up the goods or documents, it may even be that the buyer has not actually insured the goods. If the buyer attempts to avoid liability, and legal action is often pointless, it can lead to a substantial loss to the exporter. Seller's Interest insurance, sometimes called Contingency insurance, covers the contingency that the buyer is responsible for insurance, loss or damage occurs, and the buyer has failed to insure. In such a case, and for a relatively small premium, the seller would be able to make a claim. It is often important that the existence of such cover is not revealed to the buyer.

Proximate Cause

It is perfectly reasonable for insurance companies to prefer that claims are made for loss or damage due to risks which are actually covered by the policy. In fact many claims fail simply because the cause of the loss is not an insured risk. Just what the insured is not covered for is listed below, but first the principle of 'Proximate Cause' need to be explained.

When a loss occurs it is often the result of not one clear event but of a series of events which, cumulatively, lead to a loss. What the insurers must do is establish the actual cause of the loss, what they describe as the 'active, efficient cause', that is the Proximate Cause.

As an example of this in action consider a situation in which a road vehicle is in collision during transit. If goods are damaged in the collision then there is a valid claim as collision is an obvious insured risk. However if the goods are not damaged but the vehicle is, and this results in a delay of the journey for repairs, and your Christmas cards arrive at the wholesalers on Boxing Day then there is no claim because delay is not an insured risk. It is therefore important to investigate the process of events leading to a loss, and thus establish the Proximate Cause, and then ensure that this is an insured risk.

Rather than list what risks are insured it is actually easier to identify those which are specifically excluded from the (A), (B) and (C) policies.

You are not insured for

Delay

As we have seen above, if any loss occurs because of the late arrival of the goods then there is no claim. It may be in this case that action is possible against the carrier, the transport conventions defining what would be considered unreasonable delay in delivery, but not against the insurers.

Wear and tear

The exporter has to plan for predictable factors which could lead to loss, perhaps of value, to the goods. Normal wear and tear is never covered by the policy and the exporter has to prepare for the possibility of, for example, a rough sea voyage. In fact the consequences of 'the ordinary action of the wind and waves', is not covered. It is, after all, no surprise that it gets a bit windy in the North Atlantic.

Inherent vice

This describes things which goods are apt to do and are therefore predictable. For example it is obvious that metal has a tendency to rust, particularly in damp conditions, and the exporter must take steps to avoid such damage, by priming or the use of silicone gels or shrink-wrap, rather than rely on the insurance policy. Similarly, cotton can rust, fishmeal ferment, concrete set and perishables go off, all of which must be managed by the exporter.

Ullage

This is almost a form of inherent vice but is specifically applied to liquids. In the context of cargo insurance it describes loss of liquid due to evaporation or 'ordinary leakage or loss in weight or volume' which is excluded from policies.

Wilful misconduct of the assured

This may be obvious but is extremely important in that the documentation supporting claims must prove that the claimant has acted prudently and that the loss is not the consequences of their direct actions or their negligence. A clear example would be to attempt to make a claim for damaged goods which included Bills of Lading which were claused 'inadequate packing'. Any claims where there is evidence of insufficient or unsuitable packing are likely to fail.

Claims documents

Assuming the claim is actually being made for the consequences of an insured risk, the second reason that claims may fail is that they are not correctly documented. The insurance companies do not require excessive documentation and ask for nothing that is not relevant to the claim. The documents typically requested would include:

1. Original policy or Certificate
   Bearing in mind that the Policy is Proof of Interest (ie Insurable Interest) this is essential. It also describes the subject matter, insured value and appropriate clauses.
2. Invoices and Packing Specifications.
   Needed to assess the percentage of a part loss and specifically where lost or damaged goods were packed.
3. Original Bill of Lading or other transport document.
   Proves the goods were in apparent good order and condition when shipped and evidences the contract of carriage should action be later taken against the carrier.
4. Survey Report or other evidence of loss or damage.
   An independent report of the nature and extent of the loss should ideally be produced by an approved agency eg Lloyd's Agent.
5. Landing Account/Weight Notes at destination.
   The carrier's or stowage broker's record of the out-turn of the goods at destination. Useful for identifying where damage took place in the container or on the vessel or haulage unit.
6. Any correspondence with the carrier / other parties.
   Obviously the insurers wish to maintain any legal rights against other parties and insist that the insured do not give them away.

Not an unreasonable set of documents to require and every one there for a specific, and understandable, purpose.

7.2

Credit insurance

Assuming the exporter is able to actually get the right goods, in perfect condition, to the right place at the right time the problems are not yet over because it may be that the buyer, for a variety of good and bad reasons, does not pay for them. The management of this credit risk is a task which occupies an increasing amount of the time and resources of the typical exporter as the credit risk in world markets increases.

There is little doubt that the credit risk faced by international traders is greater than it has ever been. In many markets, particularly third world countries, there is a probability of delay in payment and a distinct possibility of non-payment. In fact something like 75% of the countries in the world would be bankrupt if they were companies, in that their liabilities far exceed their assets.

This is the result of recurring world recessions in the last twenty years, which affect developed and developing countries alike, and, in particular, the increasing problem of third world debt, much of which is unsustainable ie interest payments cannot be made, let alone any repayment of capital amounts. Add to this the drop in the majority of basic commodity prices in world trade, increasing economic problems of the emerging second world of the ex-Communist countries and world trade has enormous financial problems.

It may be useful to briefly examine the origins of such widespread credit risk, particularly in developing countries. There is much which is taken for granted by traders in developed countries like the UK.

A UK company wishing to buy goods from an overseas supplier can invariably trade in pounds sterling. Even if the supplier does not wish to accept pounds sterling then they can easily be converted into US Dollars, or Euros by the importer or the exporter.

The situation is not the same, for example, for a Ghanaian trader. It is highly unlikely that any supplier would be prepared to accept Ghanaian currency, which is Cedis incidentally, as payment for goods, and the buyers Cedis cannot be converted into other, so called, hard currencies, being a non-convertible ' soft ' currency.

So how does a Ghanaian buy, and pay for, your goods as an exporter ? If they are lucky they are able to earn hard currencies from their own exports. Some countries would be underdeveloped if it were not for the good fortune they have in owning resources, invariably natural resources, which earn them hard currency. The Middle East is a perfect example of a group of countries which are rich because of natural resources. Some other developing countries, which at one time were able to export commodities at good market prices, have found that a downturn in world commodity prices has severely reduced their earnings.

Finally there are many countries which have no valuable resources, and in fact have trouble feeding themselves. In the latter two cases the only way that funds can be made available to pay for imports is to borrow, and third world debt is the core of the credit risk problem. We are now in a situation in which many overseas countries cannot even service their debts, by making interest payments, and where millions of US dollars worth of loans are being written off by western banks.

In such a situation the exporter has to be extremely careful in managing the risk of non-payment.

In Part 8 we will examine the range of alternative methods of payment available to the exporter which can provide varying degrees of security, from the most secure, cash in advance, to the least secure, open account. The security which the exporter enjoys is obviously improved further by a sensible approach to credit control, involving the proper use of credit information, credit limits for individual buyers and operative blacklists. All of this can be made much easier by the operation of a credit insurance policy.

The basic risks can be broken down into two categories:

Buyer Risk	Default, Dishonour
	Insolvency
	Failure to take up goods
Country Risk (Sovereign Risk)	Government action eg failure to transfer currency

and the exporter's assessment of risk must take into account both aspects.

Credit risk insurance is provided by a number of specialist organisations, of which the most important are:

Gerling N.C.M. Credit Insurance Ltd.

Gerling N.C.M. Credit Insurance Ltd. was formerly a part of the UK government's Export Credits Guarantee Department (ECGD), now privatised, it covers about 25% of UK exports. Since its privatisation in 1991 the basic policy has not changed and is typically a Comprehensive Short Term Policy covering credit periods of up to two years.

Cover is available for both buyer and sovereign risk subject to the seller operating within either written credit limits from the insurers or discretionary limits which can be calculated from the companies trading experience. The limits are obviously affected by the method of payment in use. Generally Gerling N.C.M. would require a fair spread of an exporter's business but are prepared to negotiate premiums for selective contracts, which could include pre-shipment, as well as post-shipment cover. They insist that the seller bear a percentage of the loss, providing payment cover themselves of between 80 per and 90 pr cent. The purpose of the exporter's exposure is to maintain some interest from the seller in recovery of the debt. As with contingency cargo insurance, the existence of a credit insurance policy should not be revealed to the buyer.

Export Credits Guarantee Department

ECGD remains a UK government department concerned only with contracts with credit periods over 2 years and generally with project finance. This includes a range of pre-shipment and supplier credit arrangements which relate to the sometimes complex payment schemes associated with overseas projects.

Private underwriters

There an increasing number of companies offering international credit insurance who can supply almost any form of cover subject to the agreement of appropriate premiums. They include:

- Lloyd's Underwriters
- Euler Trade Indemnity
- Hermes (Germany)
- Coface (France)
- Cobac (Belgium)
- Siac (Italy)

Generally credit insurance policies operate in a similar way to the Open Cargo Insurance policies examined in Chapter 7.1, although each insurer will make their own particular administrative arrangements. Typically premiums will be negotiated in advance, in some cases being averaged over all customers and markets, and it may be that a fixed fee or advance payment of a percentage of premiums is required.

Insurance and the exporter

The typical exporter will operate both Cargo and Credit insurance policies and therefore conduct business in the knowledge that such security exists in the event that things go wrong which are, of course, outside of their control. However it is very important to understand that:

1. The security operates only in the situation where the exporter is not at fault. We established earlier that, pretty obviously, there is no cover where the loss is due to the misconduct of the exporter, but the situation may not always be clear cut. For example there may be a situation in which the sellers consider that they have fulfilled all contractual obligations, but the buyer disagrees. A typical example would be a dispute regarding the quality of goods supplied. In such a case there is not necessarily clear misconduct on the seller's part but, nevertheless, the insurance companies will not entertain a claim until the contractual dispute is settled. If, however, the sellers can prove to the satisfaction of the insurers that the buyer's complaint is simply an excuse for delay or dishonour, a not uncommon scenario, and that they have fulfilled the contract, then a claim will be accepted. The moral is that exporters do need to maintain a high quality of administration, and the documentation evidencing it, to ensure that they can prove performance of all their contractual obligations.

2. The insurers expect the insured to minimise not only the possibilities of loss but also the consequences of losses when they happen. An example of this, mentioned earlier, is the fact that claims on carriers for loss or damage should be made as soon as possible, and certainly within 3 working days. The basic and very important principle is that the insured must act as 'a prudent man uninsured'. With apologies for the single gender (this is a quote from Lloyd's underwriters in the 1600s) the phrase does concisely describe the expectations of the insurers. The policy is not a safety net for a lack of concern on the seller's behalf, and all insured parties must conduct their business as if an insurance policy does not exist.

7.3

Exchange risk management

It is becoming increasingly common for UK exporters to do business with overseas buyers in currencies other than Pounds Sterling. The currencies used would invariably be the 'hard' convertible currencies of developed countries, in particular the US Dollar and the Euro.

In the cases where the UK exporter chooses to deal in pounds sterling with overseas customers, there is a clear possibility of risk for the buyer in that the cost of the pounds sterling that they need to pay, in terms of the amount of their own currency needed to purchase pounds, may well increase due to fluctuations in the relative values of the two currencies. In modern commerce the exchange rates of currencies are subject, sometimes, to surprisingly large movements.

Having regard to the importance of the Balance of Payments to the value of a country's currency relative to others, there is a perfect logic to the economic theory which describes the corrective mechanism controlling such fluctuations. To use the UK as an example, if the pound weakens against other currencies, ie becomes worth less in that it takes more pounds to buy the same amount of foreign currency, then UK exports become cheaper to foreign buyers. Consequently, UK exports increase, the Balance of Payments deficit is reduced and the pound strengthens. The converse situation is that a strengthening pound makes exports more expensive to foreign buyers and the consequent reduction in exports leads to a weakening pound. The theory is wonderful until one considers the fact that many UK exporters, especially the bigger ones, choose to invoice in other currencies and the model above operates in reverse. For example the exporter receiving US dollars, with a weakening Pound, actually benefits from the change.

Movements in exchange rates are broadly subject to supply and demand within the market for currencies. This is affected by the demand for trading currency ie an increase in American exports can lead to an increased demand for US$, but also by the differences in interest rates from one country, and one currency, relative to another. The higher the interest rate available on the money market to foreign depositors, the more that currency will be demanded.

It is the long term expectation that the pound will weaken against other hard currencies, plus the need to provide a risk free package deal to the buyer, which has led to a marked increase in foreign currency invoicing by UK exporters over the last twenty years.

The simple risk faced by the UK exporter is that the calculated export price, based predominantly on pounds sterling costs, which is then converted to a foreign currency price at the current exchange rate, has to be calculated some time in advance of the eventual receipt of those funds and the pounds. Sterling revenues may well be less than was planned when the export sale was agreed.

Assuming that the decision is taken to invoice some overseas buyers in their own currencies then the exporter has a number of options in relation to managing the risk.

Do nothing

Not a very dynamic approach but, nevertheless, one that could be justified. It may simply be the case that the exporter is prepared to accept whatever the exchange rate happens to be when the foreign currency payment is actually received. The rate on that day, which is known as the 'Spot Rate', may actually favour the seller, if the pound has weakened against that currency. It also has the advantage of simplicity, which makes it very attractive to many traders.

However, the opposite situation could apply, as has been the case in the early 2000s, and there is a clear risk that the seller could lose substantial revenues, possibly even sustain losses, should the exchange rate have moved against them. This is a particular problem where the amounts involved are large and the profit margins are small. Therefore, the average exporter looks for ways in which to minimise or remove the risk.

Currency accounts

The most obvious way to remove the exchange risk is not to exchange at all. That is, the seller simply keeps the foreign currency in foreign currency accounts. The absence of exchange control regulations within the UK means that the UK exporter can maintain accounts, in any currencies, in the UK In many cases it will also be possible to hold foreign currencies in accounts overseas.

The typical regular exporter in the UK would maintain multi-currency accounts in pounds sterling, euros and US dollars. Apart from the fact that any exchange risk is eliminated, it may also be the case that the interest earned on such accounts, which would depend on the type of account, could be superior to interest rates paid on sterling accounts. It may even be possible to borrow foreign currencies at beneficial rates.

However, the main benefits of currency accounts apply to the situation in which a company is selling and buying in foreign currency. The ideal situation would be where the receipts and payments actually balanced each other out, but there are still great benefits even when there is no balance, with any shortfall being made up by borrowing currency and any surplus being held in interest-bearing accounts. Also, there is often the option to take advantage of movements in spot rates by exchanging currency where there is a revenue benefit.

Forward exchange contract

It is possible to approach a bank and be given a rate for selling (your receipts) or buying (your payments) foreign currency at a future time. What this does is to guarantee an exchange rate to the trader, at the time when prices are being calculated, and allows them to rely on that rate irrespective of the actual spot rate at the time of the exchange. The banks will quote Forward Rates for anything from 1 month to 5 years, but the standard periods are 3, 6 and 12 months.

The rates they offer differ depend on whether the bank is buying or selling the currency and will be expressed as a 'premium' for currencies that are strengthening, which is deducted from the spot rate, or 'discount' for weakening currencies, which is added to the spot rate.

Some basic rules for the calculation of a forward exchange transaction are:

- *You are the bank*
  That is to say that all rates are quoted and calculated from the point of view of the bank.
- *Banks buy high and sell low*
  Again this is logical from the bank's point of view.
- *Add a discount*
  Which represents a currency which is weakening ie its value is falling against the contract currency.
- *Deduct a premium*
  Which represents a currency which is strengthening ie its value is rising against the contract currency.

The great advantage of Forward Exchange contracts is the fact that the exporter knows exactly what rate will be used when the currency is eventually received and converted. However there are potential problems in that the contract must be met even if the payment has not been received from the overseas buyer. Late payment would entail the exporter having to purchase the correct amount of US dollars, at the spot rate, in order to meet the forward contract, and then having to convert the eventual dollar payment, again at spot. It also means that the exporter cannot gain an advantage if the actual spot rate is better than the forward rate.

In the cases where the exporter has some doubt about the exact time payment would be received, it is possible to negotiate an 'Option Forward'. This would establish a rate which could be taken up over a period of time, eg 1 - 3 months, and therefore give an element of flexibility to the timing of the exchange.

However, this does not give the exporter the option to take up the forward rate or not; the forward exchange contract MUST be honoured at some time during the period allowed. Also the bank will attempt to quote a rate which will be the best for them over that time period.

An example

Option Forward Exchange Contract

We contract to sell 100,000 Euros (€) to the bank in exchange for Pounds Sterling. The Euros to be available sometime between the beginning of Month 1 and the end of Month 3:

Spot Rate	1.41 – 1.44
1 Month Forward	1.49 – 1.54
3 Months Forward	1.57 – 1.63
Remember ...	YOU ARE THE BANK
	THE BANK BUYS HIGH AND SELLS LOW

and will take the most favourable rate to itself for the period of the option - it will take the lowest selling rate and the highest buying rate thus:

Option rate (1 to 3 months) 1.49 – 1.63

The Euros are sold to the bank which converts them at the buying rate of 1.63 to the pound. The exporter thus receives £61,349.69 (less bank charges).

N.B. The figures above are for demonstration purposes only and have been simplified for clarity. They do not relate to actual spot or forward rates which would normally be defined to four decimal places and would not exhibit such large ranges in value.

Currency option

In this case the exporter does have the option to take up the forward rate or to ignore it and convert at spot if that is more favourable. There will still be a fixed forward rate, known as the 'strike rate', and either a stated date or a time period for that forward rate to be taken up. In return for the option to take the forward rate or ignore it the exporter (or importer, of course) will pay an 'up front' premium, the amount of which is dependent on the 'strike' rate agreed and the time period.

Contrary to popular belief the forward rates used in the above contracts are not the bank's guess at what the rates will be in the future, but are simply a spot rate adjusted to take into account the differences in the interest rates for the two currencies and effectively compensates the party who has held the currency with the lower interest rate for the period of the contract.

Summary

We started Part 7 by examining the range of risks faced by an exporter and have attempted to identify the ways in which the typical exporter deals with such risks as:

Physical loss / damage	Cargo Insurance Policy
Non-payment	Credit Insurance Policy
Loss on exchange	Currency Accounts
	or Forward Exchange Contracts

However none of the solutions mentioned above are compulsory. Traders have a perfect right to choose not to insure against these risks and may have good reasons not to. If, for example, the costs of the premiums on a credit insurance policy exceed the claims then it could actually be more cost-effective not to insure. This should also be coupled with the fact that the better the level of professionalism displayed by the trader, notably in terms of shipping the goods, credit control and payment collection, then the less important becomes the 'safety net' of the insurance policy.

Part 8

Export Finance

8.1

Business finance

Legal entities

The person or people running a business may organize it in one of three basic ways, all different both from the legal and tax points of view:

- as a sole trader,
- as a partnership,
- as an incorporated company.

Sole trader

The sole trader is a one-person business, in many cases the individual who started the business. It is easy to set up as there are no legal formalities, except for the registration of any business name to be used. This means that they are the most common form of enterprise in the UK.

The sole trader will have to provide the capital for the business – from their own resources or a loan from the bank or from various forms of Government funding for small firms.

Advantages:

- easy to establish with minimal capital required;
- all the profits of the business (after expenses and taxation) go to the owner;
- as the owner work for themselves it is a good incentive to run it efficiently;
- no decisions have to be shared nor do the profits.

Disadvantages:

- all debts of the business are the owners' responsibility the owner has 'unlimited liability';
- there may be tax disadvantages;
- if the owner becomes ill the business is at risk;
- it can be difficult to raise extra capital for expansion.

Partnerships

The original Partnership Act of 1890 defines a partnership as 'the relation which subsists between persons carrying on a business in common with a view of profit'. This simply means a partnership is made up of members who are in business and whose aim is to make profits.

Partnerships are generally allowed to have between 2 and 20 members – although there are exceptions. Banks, which are formed as partnerships, cannot have more than 10 partners. Accountancy firms and solicitors are usually partnerships; they can have more than 20 partners. Partnerships can be set up without a contract, but a written agreement is preferable in order to solve any disagreements which may arise.

All the partners are equally responsible for the debts of the partnership; they therefore have unlimited liability.

Advantages:

- easy and cheap to set up – usually more capital is at the disposal of the partners;
- the partners can pool their knowledge, experience and resources;
- no legal formalities are required to set up a partnership, but an agreement is highly desirable;
- in case of illness there exists a better chance of continuity;
- profits -after-tax - are divided amongst the partners, as agreed in any Partnership Agreement.

Disadvantages:

- unlimited liability which means that the partners may be personally liable for any business debts;
- there is always the risk of relationships breaking down between partners actions of one partner are binding on the others;
- when one partner dies there may be problems because the family of the deceased person may choose to take out their capital from the business. In this case the partnership may have to be wound up or dissolved.

Incorporated companies

An incorporated company is one which now has its own legal personality. This 'legal person or identity' has implications for the way companies keep their accounts and for the terminology used. Because a company is a 'distinct legal person' it can own things, it can buy and sell in its own right and it can owe money. It can sue and it can also be sued, taken to court, and even fined by the court if found liable. It must be set up and run in accordance with the Companies Acts.

The financial accounts of a business are the accounts of the company; they are **not** the accounts of the owners (ie the shareholders) of the company who are legally, quite distinct. This is why the Capital of the company, comprising money invested by the shareholders, is shown as a liability in the balance sheet ie the company owes the money to the shareholders.

The owners of the company are the so called 'members' or shareholders, who have a role to appoint the directors of the company. The shareholders have no liability for the debts of the company beyond payment in full at the face value of the shares they hold. Control is usually organised on the basis of one vote per one share. The profits earned by the company may be retained by the company or distributed to the shareholders as dividends.

Advantages:

- a company is a separate legal entity – it is distinct from the people who run it;
- limited liability means that the owners are not responsible for the debts of the company except in cases of fraud or personal guarantees;
- losses can be carried forward and offset against profits in good years;
- in the eyes of the public a company may be seen as more reputable;
- ownership is transferable;
- certain tax advantages may exist.

Disadvantages:

- closer regulation by law;
- more complicated accounts than other forms of business organisation;
- more expensive to set up.

There are three basic types of incorporated companies:

(a) private limited company,
(b) public limited company, or
(c) quoted public limited company.

Private limited companies

Those companies with 'Limited' (Ltd.) after their name. They may not offer shares to 'the public at large' and share transfers between members are restricted. The shares can only be sold privately (thus *private* limited company) and with the agreement of the other shareholders.

Private limited companies only have to publish their accounts in a summarised form; thus they are able to retain some privacy. The accounts have to be available if the public asks for them.

Public limited companies

Denoted by 'PLC' after their name, the company may offer its shares to the public. Individual shareholders may sell them without restriction, but it must have a minimum share capital of £50,000. PLCs are the largest type of company in the private sector.

The shareholders have the right to attend, vote and speak at the company's Annual General Meeting (AGM) and to elect the Board of Directors and the Chairman.

Quoted public companies

The shares of most public companies are traded ('quoted') on the Stock Exchanges. The price at which such shares are bought and sold is quite distinct from the nominal or 'par' value of such shares. The price represents the market's expectation of future dividends or increases or decreases in the market price of the shares.

All private limited or public limited companies have to be registered with the registrar of companies (all such documents are recorded and available for inspection at Companies House - Cardiff and Leeds. Electronic copies of company documents may also be procured from Companies House). Such documents will include the Memorandum of Association, the Articles of Association, a Statutory Declaration and a Certificate of Incorporation.

The Memorandum of Association contains amongst other details, the amount of shares which the company has the authority to issue to investors (the authorised capital). The proportion of the capital that has been taken up by the public and subscribed for is called the 'issued capital'.

Sources of funding

The main sources of business finance are:

- Retained profit
- Short term finance – usually from banks in the form of loans or overdraft facilities
- Long term capital market – the trading of stocks and shares takes place within Stock Exchanges

A significant source of funds for businesses is retained profit. After paying a proportion for Corporation Tax and a proportion to shareholders as dividends, the remainder is designated as retained profit. Profits retained in the business are shown in the balance sheet as reserves.

Businesses can also raise finance from external sources but, naturally, this always involves a cost. Besides banks, where a business can raise finance in the form of an overdraft, a secured loan, or a mortgage, finance can also be raised from other financial institutions or the general public.

There are two ways of doing that:

1. Issue shares ie invite the general public or financial institutions to become shareholders
2. Issue debentures or some other form of debt instrument ie borrow from the general public or financial institutions.

Equity or share capital

A combination of share capital, long term loan capital and short term facilities (eg an overdraft from a bank) is the most common arrangement.

Ideally, a significant proportion of the company's finance will be provided by ordinary shareholders as this is permanent capital invested in the company which will not normally be paid back.

Ordinary shares

Ordinary shareholders have a share in any profits that have been made that year after tax has been deducted and interest on any loans paid. If the directors agree, the shareholders are paid a share in the profit in the form of a dividend. A dividend is simply the sum of money payable to a shareholder.

Preference shares

These shares have a fixed rate of dividend, expressed as a percentage of nominal value, which is paid before the dividends of an ordinary shareholder. Preference shareholders do not have a right to a vote.

Cumulative preference shares

A company may not earn enough one year to be able to pay a fixed rate of dividend on its preference shares. With a cumulative preference share any shortfall is carried forward to the next year.

Debt or loan capital

Debenture or secured loan stock

Debentures are the written acknowledgements of debt, and are documents given to people or institutions who lend money to companies. The document will inform the lender:

- when they can expect to be repaid,
- how much in interest they can expect to receive

Debenture holders do NOT:

- own the company;
- have a vote;
- have a say in running the business.

However, they do have:

- a right to receive their interest every year or half yearly;
- a right to sell their debentures on the market.

and their interest is paid out before anything is paid to the holders of preference and ordinary shares.

The security usually come in the form of a floating charge over the assets of the business which gives the holders of the debenture the right to appoint an administrative receiver in the event of default. The advantage, from the borrower's point of view, is that the rate of interest is usually significantly lower on a debenture than on an overdraft.

Unsecured loan stock

Unsecured loan stock is also a tradable debt instrument but is similar to preference shares, although it ranks above preferences shares in a liquidation. Loan stock is used commonly in structuring venture capital deals and in situations in which loans to larger companies are syndicated among a number of banks.

Convertible loan stock gives holders the right to convert the whole or a part of their stock into ordinary shares at predetermined dates and prices.

Working capital

The funds needed to finance the business can be divided between fixed capital and working capital.

Fixed capital is that which has been used to buy fixed assets such as machinery and buildings, which cannot be converted quickly into ready cash.

Working capital is the difference between the current assets and current liabilities of the business ie the funds which are left after all debts are paid and are therefore available to run the business by paying salaries, suppliers etc. It can also be called 'the circulating capital' of the business because of the way some of the resources of the business circulate around through the various types of current assets.

- Fixed assets
  Assets which the firm buys which are not for processing or resale eg plant, equipment, buildings, vehicles etc. They are in most cases subject to depreciation.
- Current assets
  These are the things which belong to the business just like fixed assets but they are not permanent - stock, work in progress, debtors and cash.
- Current liabilities
  These are the amounts which a business owes eg overdraft, trade creditors, etc.

Stock

Can be made up of raw materials, work in progress and finished goods. Excessive stock levels are an inefficient use of resources.

Debtors

Those who owe the company. A willingness to wait to be paid ie giving L/C in the form of termed payments, may give a marketing advantage and, in exporting, may be a significant factor.

Trade creditors

Those whom the company owes in the course of its business. The longer we can take to pay the longer we can use that cash for other, profitable purposes. But – when a company hits a cash crisis it is often at that point when suppliers decide, perhaps unexpectedly, to start legal proceedings.

Short-term investments

These are easily realisable investments. However the percentage return on that type of investment will be lower than other less flexible investments.

Overdrafts

It is attractive and profitable to run a business using the bank's money – but there are limits on the facility the bank will allow and they can always withdraw or reduce such a facility. The bank's security is a legal floating charge over all the assets of the business.

Exports and working capital

An exporter needs to watch working capital even more closely for two reasons:

1. The time involved in shipping goods to distant customers (and for remittances to get back into the exporter's bank) means that the 'debtors' figure is likely to be larger for the equivalent volume of UK business.
2. Large 'debtors' figure may stay large because of increased bad debts and the difficulty of chasing delayed payments in overseas markets.

The solution to this problem are those techniques called 'trade finance' or in the case of an exporter 'export trade finance'.
They include:

- Negotiating or discounting Bills of Exchange.
- Documentary Letters of Credit (L/Cs).
- Forfaiting.
- Factoring.
- International L/C unions.
- Facilities provided by Export L/C Agencies (eg the Export L/Cs Guarantee Department)

Financial reporting

Accountants follow agreed principles when recording the transactions of a business. This enables the management and others to monitor the progress of the business through examination of a variety of sources of data
These sources of data are:

- The Balance Sheet
- Profit and Loss Account (P&L account) and other related relevant documents
- Management information (management reports) which includes more frequent reports than the Balance Sheet and the P&L account.

The balance sheet

A Balance Sheet shows what the company owns and what it owes at any one moment in time.
A simple (horizontal) structure would be:

Sources of Finance	Fixed Assets
Current Liabilities	Current Assets
TOTAL	TOTAL

A balance sheet always balances because everything the company owns must have been paid for by money acquired from elsewhere; from shareholders or banks or the sale of current assets such as stock etc.

It is now more usual to use a vertical layout as in Figure 8.1.1

Fig. 8.1.1 - Vertical balance sheet layout

Sources of Finance	TOTAL
Fixed Assets plus	
Working Capital (ie current assets minus current liabilities)	TOTAL

Profit and loss account

It would be quite possible to add together all the expenses of a business incurred during an accounting period, deduct the total from the sales revenue for the same period and arrive at the profit figure. That would not tell us very much, so the profit calculation is broken down into these steps:

- Cost of manufacture – this is the total expense involved in purchase and manufacturing of goods for sale;
- Gross Profit – this is the profit earned by the business by trading (the trading account);
- Net Profit – from the gross profit we can deduct all the incidental expenses of running the business to calculate the "net profit".

Figure 8.1.2 illustrates a simple layout:

Fig. 8.1..2 - Profit and los account layout

Opening Stock	Sales revenue
plus	
Purchasesl	
minus Closing Stock	
Cost of Goods Sold	Gross (Trading) Profit
minus	
Expenses	Net Profit

Management information (reports)

Sales orders

An 'orders received', or a weekly or monthly sales summary report. 'Year-to-date' and budget comparison figures are commonly included.

Cash flow forecast

Shows the value and timing of revenue and expenditure for a period. The relationship between cash flowing in and out of a company is particularly important to small companies.

L/C status

A report showing the payments record of existing customers and highlighting delays in payments as part of a L/C control system

Outstanding orders

This report will assist sales administration when handling enquiries from customers. More importantly variations in the size of the 'order book' will give early warning of future dangers. A decrease in orders indicates a decrease in cash receipts in several month's time; an increase suggests a factory overload and delayed dispatches arising fairly quickly.

Sales analysis

A regular monthly or more frequent sales analysis will alert management to changes in market conditions or sales performance. Investigations can be made and corrective action taken before damage is done to the commercial prospects of the business.

Stock levels

A good stock control system will incorporate sales orders received to show both 'allocated stock' and 'free stock'.

Dispatches

'Year-to-date' totals and budget variances give strategic guidance to management. Comparison with promises shown in previous 'despatch schedules' highlight immediate problems within the company.

Debtors' ledger

Ledger entries will indicate who has bought what, how frequently and the promptness of payment.

Aged debtors' report

This analysis will rate customers according to the age of outstanding, unpaid bills, and by reference to individual allowed L/C limits.

Business costs

Costs can be divided into two categories:

- Costs which are either direct or indirect
- Costs which are either variable or fixed

Direct costs and indirect costs (overheads)

Direct costs are those costs directly attributable to an individual cost unit such as a manufactured unit or a production run, eg materials, labour.

All other costs which are not directly related (to a cost unit) are called 'indirects' or 'overheads', eg light and heat, rent and rates etc.

Variable and fixed costs

Variable costs are all those which increase or decrease if more or less of a cost unit (product or service) is produced. The essential point here is that the term 'variable cost' is applied only to those costs that must vary if the production volume changes. A typical example would be the cost of components purchased for assembly. In the simplest cases variable costs vary in direct proportion to the volume of products or service. If the volume doubles or halves so does the cost.

All other costs which are not variable are 'fixed', that is they do not change as volume changes. eg salaries (as opposed to wages per hour), rent, advertising expenditure etc. Such costs are sometimes referred to as 'sunk costs' in that the business must pay them irrespective of the level of business.

Unfortunately, not all costs fall into these categories so neatly.

Direct, fixed costs

The depreciation charge on a machine that has been purchased to produce only one specific product and no other. The depreciation charge is direct to that cost unit (the product) but is fixed. It could remain the same whether a lot or a little is produced.

Variable overhead

The factory's electricity bill. If the factory shut for a week the consumption would be zero; if the factory went on to double shift the consumption would double. Clearly the electricity cost is a variable one. But since electricity is used by all the activities of the factory, for all the products, the cost is an indirect or overhead cost.

Budgets

A budget is a tool for management control. The quality of any budget is only demonstrated when management can use it to control the business in such a way that it successfully achieves its objectives.

A budget is a set of inter-related business plans for an organisation, exhibiting quantified and feasible plans of action and forecasts of results, together with the premises or beliefs on which those plans are based.

There are at least four ways in which a properly prepared budget will help management to run the business:

Strategy

The preparation of a budget will enable managers to see if the company's strategy makes sense. It allows examination of the practical details of that strategy and the assumptions (mainly about markets) on which that strategy is based.

The numbers

By quantifying the various forecasts, management can see if the business is likely to achieve its objectives, in the light of assumptions about the business environment.

The risks

By highlighting potential problems or areas of risk the management can estimate the sensitivity of forecast profits to errors in the basic assumptions on which the budget is built.

Monitoring

By providing performance targets management are able to monitor progress and they can concentrate on those aspects of the business where the 'actuals' have diverged from the budget figures.

Does it matter?

Where 'actuals' diverge from the budget managers need to decide whether they are:

- small enough to be ignored;
- the natural effect of other changes which are already being attended to;
- suggesting that some of the basic budget assumptions may be wrong;
- of unknown significance until the budget figures have been re-worked.

In the case of significant variances from the planned figures a well-prepared budget will give a good, practical, guide to the correct remedial action. In some cases the necessary counter measures may be simple and obvious; in other cases the whole company strategy may have to be re-thought.

Five rules of budgeting

1. A budget is not a licence to spend money, but part of the process of delegating responsibility.
2. When preparing a budget or any other type of business plan, always start with the sales forecast.
3. Implementing the budget involves:
    o motivation, so everyone is working to the same objectives
    o communication, so people can talk to each other about it
    o monitoring or 'how are we doing so far?'
4. The actual figures will always be different from the budgeted ones; it is the size of the variance which matters.
5. Budgeting is a continuous, rolling process, so it is always 'monitor, revise, monitor' and so on.

Absorption costing and marginal costing

Absorption costing

An absorption cost is the total cost divided by the number of units produced. If we want to know the cost of a product or batch there is no problem with the direct costs. We simply take all those costs directly attributable to that product or batch and add them up. It is the indirect costs which are the problem.

If these can be 'apportioned' in some way to each cost unit then the total costs attributed to all the cost units together will equal the actual total costs of the business. This process of spreading the indirect or overhead cost over the range of cost units is what absorption costing does.

The problem with absorption costing

When those indirect costs are apportioned to each cost unit the calculations must include some *assumption* about volumes of production and sales. The more we expect to produce of a product the more thinly those overheads can be spread - the lower the calculated cost for the product.

If these assumptions about volumes turn out to be wrong, the cost figures will be wrong ie overheads will be over or under-absorbed.

Also, an arbitrary allocation of indirect costs over a number of different products or production departments can directly affect their apparent profitability.

Marginal costing

A marginal cost is the cost of producing one extra unit and will therefore be made up of variable costs. It is not about absorbing overheads. It only considers the variable costs associated with a product.

A marginally costed product can be sold at a marginal price, which will be lower than a full absorption price. A product which looks to recover only its variable (direct) costs will make no contribution to the fixed (indirect) costs of the business.

This is, unfortunately, a method sometimes used to lower the prices of excess capacity goods dumped in overseas markets and should not be part of any long term export strategy.

Contribution

Because we can measure very accurately the direct costs of a single unit and because of the problems associated with the allocation of indirect costs to that unit; contribution is often used as a more accurate measure of a unit's profitability.

Contribution is revenue minus direct costs and is therefore an accurate figure. The assumption is that, subject to an appropriate allocation of indirect cost, the unit which generates the greatest contribution will also generate the greatest profit.

It is called contribution because it 'contributes to the indirect costs and thereafter to profit'. In other words contribution is indirect costs plus profit.

8.2

International payment methods

As the majority of companies trading internationally are profit-making, or are at least attempting to be profit-making, it is fairly obvious that the receipt of payment is essential to that purpose. It is clearly the responsibility of the exporter to operate in a way which maximises, and ideally guarantees, the possibility of payment being received in full and on time.

This primarily relates to the choices made regarding the terms and methods of payment used for particular countries and customers. Also, as will become obvious as we examine these methods, the whole export order process needs to be carried out correctly in order to ensure collection of payment. In particular the documentary procedures, and the quality of documents they produce, are very often the deciding factor as to whether the money is paid or not.

To clarify the distinction made above:

- TERMS of payment are the time allowed for payment to be made ie the L/C period allowed. This is usually expressed as sight payment, where no L/C period is allowed or in blocks of 30 days eg 60, 90, 180 days etc., following a date specified in the contract which could be from sight of documents, or from date of shipment or from the invoice date.
- METHOD of payment is the means by which the money will be paid and the exporter has a range of choices which offer varying degrees of security.

Figure 8.2.1 ranks the basic methods of payment from the least secure to the most secure.

The trader obviously has to make a choice as to the appropriate terms and method of payment right at the beginning of the process when the quotation is first made and this choice will be affected by a variety of factors:

The market

Certain methods of payment are clearly more common in particular markets than are others, so the exporter invariably has a 'rule of thumb' as to the usual method for a particular market. In this context it is no surprise that for high risk markets, for example West Africa, then Cash in Advance is not uncommon and Letters of Credit (L/Cs) are very common. On the other hand a developed market like Germany exhibits a preponderance of Open Account contracts.

Companies like Standard & Poor's and Moody's can provide long term ratings of countries and also large corporations like banks. For the typical exporter shorter term ratings are obtainable from Dun & Bradstreet and other specialised agencies.

The buyer

Irrespective of the traditional and accepted method of payment in a particular country, the seller's perception of the buyer risk, or lack of it, can override any 'rule of thumb'.

Criteria which would affect this decision include:

- Previous Experience
- Trade References – from other companies with which they are trading
- Bank Report – may not give much detail
- L/C Report – more detail but more expensive
- Agents Report – may look to present a better picture than is accurate
- L/C Risk Insurers – see chapter 7

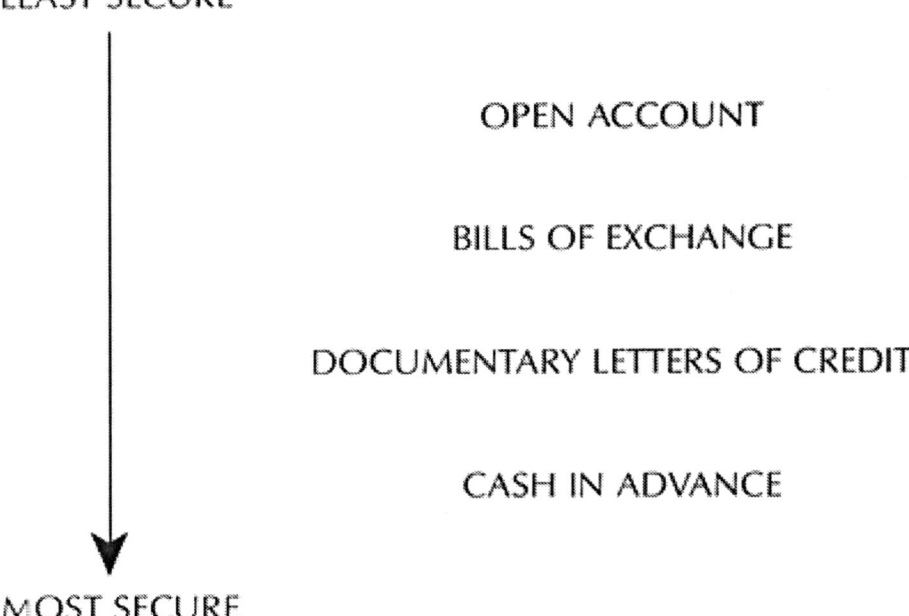

LEAST SECURE

OPEN ACCOUNT

BILLS OF EXCHANGE

DOCUMENTARY LETTERS OF CREDIT

CASH IN ADVANCE

MOST SECURE

Fig. 8.2.1 - Payment methods ranked according to security

The competition

This does overlap with the two factors mentioned above in that the typical method of payment adopted in a market is clearly the one most likely to be offered by the competition in that market. It could be the case that the competition faced by a particular exporter is prepared to use terms and methods of payment as a marketing tool. That is, they are prepared to agree longer L/C periods or less secure, and often cheaper, methods of payment in order to secure business.

Any decision regarding the terms and method used must be based on the application of all the above factors and underpinned by a very clear understanding of the operation of the various methods, the risks involved and the ways in which good management can minimise those risks.

Cash in advance/with order

First, the most secure method of payment for the exporter, if you can get it. It is because of exporter's perceptions of an increased credit risk in world trade, and the fact that they do not regard L/C as an absolute guarantee, that there has been a clear increase in the incidence of advance payments.

It is increasingly the case that overseas buyers in certain high risk countries also accept it as the normal method of payment subject, of course, to their exchange controls. In this context many African markets are regularly paying in advance . In the case of large projects, it is not unusual for a percentage of the payment to be made in advance, the balance often being paid in instalments.

The money can be transferred just as for an open account payment, the only difference being that the transfer takes place before shipment (or even before manufacture) against a pro-forma invoice (see chapter 4) rather than a final invoice.

Open account

The least secure method of payment and therefore only used regularly in low risk markets. It is thus quite common in Western Europe and the USA The seller will send the goods and all the documents direct to the buyer and trust them to pay on the agreed date.

It is important that it is made absolutely clear:

When payment is due

This may be on receipt of documents or goods, which would invariably be sent direct to the buyer or after a L/C period of typically 30, 60, or 90 days after a specified date eg date of invoice.

Where the payment is going

An export invoice should specify:

- Full company name
- Full business address
- Name of bank
- Name of account holder
- Bank branch address
- Account number
- Sort Code
- SWIFT code (see below)

How the payments will be made

Cash

Because of the problems associated with money laundering in world trade ie illegally earned money being used to buy goods for legitimate sale, it is advisable that cash is refused for anything other than small amounts from individuals.

Buyer's cheque

Apart from the chance of the cheque 'bouncing', the real problem is that the cheque will have to be returned to the buyer's country to be cleared and this can often take anything from one to six weeks.

Banker's draft

In effect, a cheque drawn by one bank on another is more secure than the buyer's cheque and will clear in the seller's country. The time delay in the draft being raised and posted to the seller followed by clearance still occurs.

International transfer

An international transfer represents the fastest way of making payment and results in the exporter receiving cleared funds direct into its bank account. In fact, there are three ways in which transfers can be made:

- Mail Transfer
- Cable / Telex Transfer (often known as TT or Telegraphic Transfer)
- SWIFT (Society for World-wide Interbank Financial Telecommunications)

The latter method is the fastest. It is an automated inter-bank system similar to BACS in the UK and offers a secure and rapid method of financial transfers between international departments of banks. In some cases, like Western Europe, SWIFT may be used automatically.

It is very much in the seller's interest to minimise the delay between the buyer paying and the funds being cleared and available .The delay is sometimes referred to as ' Float Time' and banks make a lot of money out of 'float'.

Documentary collections

The use of Bills of Exchange, sometimes called drafts, introduces a new documentary requirement for the exporter in that the Bill of Exchange will be drawn up by them in addition to the other shipping documents. The security which bills of Exchange offer is based on the fact that the procedures involve the banks in arranging for collection of payment from the buyer on behalf of the seller.

The exporter, having agreed such a method of payment with the buyer, will draw up a Bill of Exchange which will form part of the document set which will be sent to their bank in the UK who will send the documents to a bank in the buyer's country, often the buyer's bank, who will negotiate payment. The procedure is illustrated in the flowchart Figure 8.2.2.

The layouts of Bills of Exchange do vary but a traditional blank Bill is shown in Figure 8.2.3.

However, this document format could be seen as rather old fashioned and it is not necessary to use a particular printed form. A much simpler layout, as shown in Figure 8.2.4 would be just as acceptable.

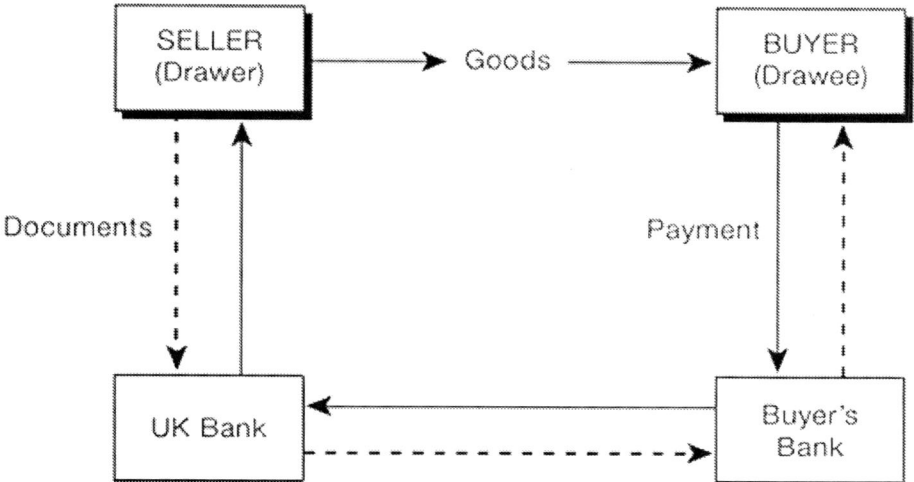

Fig. 8.2.2- Processing the Bill of Exchange in export trade

The reason why a Bill should contain the words 'First of exchange second unpaid' is that it is common for two, or even three, Bills to be drawn up. This is based on the same, rather antiquated logic, of having two or three Bills of Lading (see chapter 5) designed to ensure that at least one arrives successfully at destination. The second Bill will contain the words ' second of exchange first unpaid'.

Once the exporter has drawn up the Bill/s of Exchange and assembled the full set of shipping documents, they are then sent to their bank along with the appropriate completed letter of instruction. The major banks use their

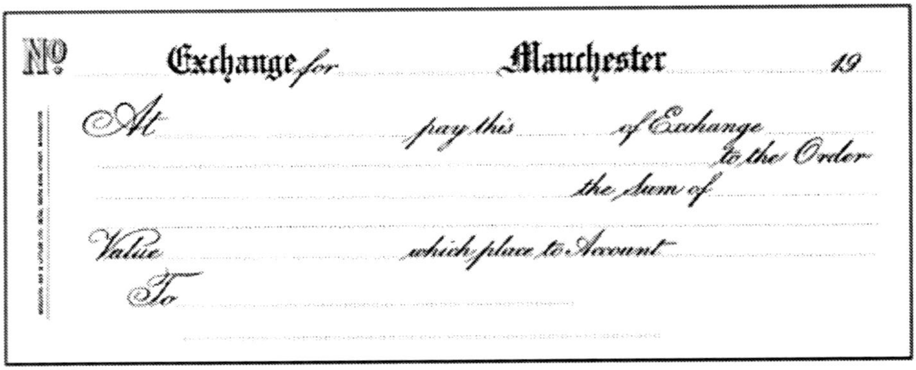

Fig. 8.2.3 - Traditional blank Bill of Exchange

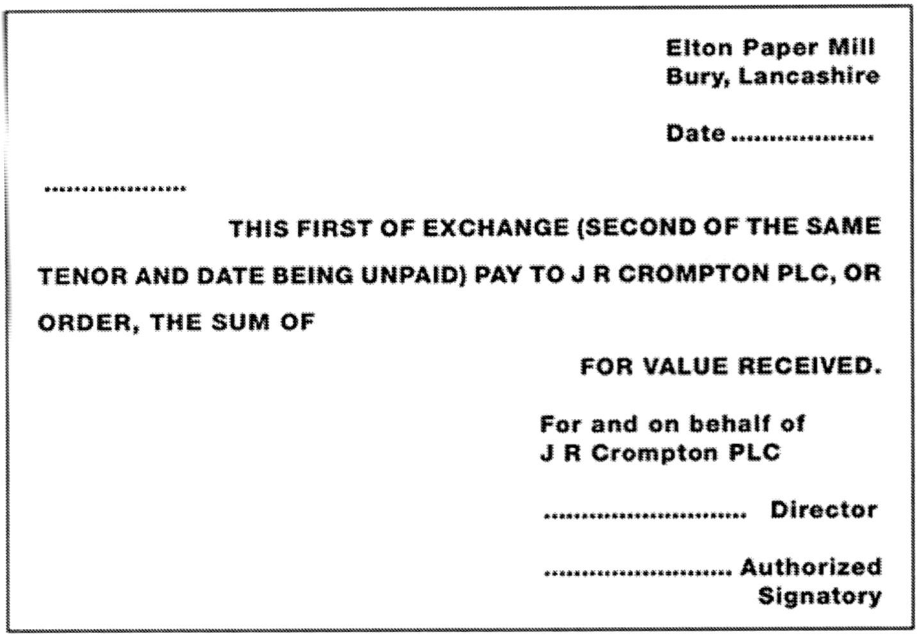

Elton Paper Mill
Bury, Lancashire

Date ....

THIS FIRST OF EXCHANGE (SECOND OF THE SAME TENOR AND DATE BEING UNPAID) PAY TO J R CROMPTON PLC, OR ORDER, THE SUM OF

FOR VALUE RECEIVED.

For and on behalf of
J R Crompton PLC

.... Director

.... Authorized
Signatory

Figure 8.2.4 - Typical blank Bill of Exchange

own versions of instruction forms most of which are presented in the form of tick boxes and they will include clear reference to the procedures followed not only by the UK bank but also the overseas bank.

The documents will be dispatched either to the UK bank's correspondent or the buyer's bank, who will make the collection.

The point is that a Bill of Exchange is defined in terms of the information it contains rather than the way it is laid out. The following definition, from the English Bill of Exchange Act 1882, is supposedly the finest legal definition in the English language :"...an unconditional order in writing, addressed by one person (the drawer) to another (the drawee), signed by the person giving it, requiring the person to whom it is addressed to pay on demand, or at a fixed or determinable future time a sum certain in money to, or to the order of, a specified person or to bearer (the payee)."

The expressions in brackets are the titles the banks would use to identify the parties. The exporter is the Drawer in that they actually draw up the Bill of Exchange and the importer is invariable the person to whom it is addressed and therefore the Drawee . The Drawee is the Payer or Acceptor of the Bill and the money will be paid, at the specified time, to the Payee, which is usually the exporter but could be another party or even the Bearer, ie the person holding the Bill, to claim the funds.

Bills are either drawn up at Sight (Figure 8.2.5) or at a number of days after sight or another determinable future time.

In the case where the amount is payable at sight, ie no L/C period will be allowed, the overseas bank will require the buyer to pay the due amount at sight of the documents. The reason this provides security for the seller is that the bank will not release the documents to the buyer unless payment is made. This is referred to as Documents Against Payment (D/P) and the

---

No. *120*

Exchange for £12,560 . . . . 200—

AT SIGHT . . . . *of this* FIRST BILL *of Exchange*

(SECOND . . . . *of the same tenor and date being unpaid) pay to the*

order of OURSELVES . . . . *the sum of*

TWELVE THOUSAND FIVE HUNDRED AND SIXTY POUNDS ONLY

FOR AND ON BEHALF OF

To ADAM STEVENS LTD   RICK O'SHAE LTD
NEW YORK USA   Director

Fig. 8.2.5 - Typical blank Sight Draft

buyer will not be ale to take possession of the goods without first paying for the documents, particularly if a Bill of Lading is part of the document set.

A typical 90 day Bill is shown in Figure 8.2.6.

Where the exporter has agreed to allow a L/C period, for example 90 days, then the Bill is referred to as a Termed Bill or Usance Bill. The latter description denotes the fact that the buyer has a period of use of the goods before having to pay. The L/C term allowed in the Bill can run from the date of shipment (as evidenced by the transport document), the date of the Bill or even the date of invoice.

In the case of a Termed Bill the overseas bank will not collect payment in return for the documents but will instead release the documents against Acceptance of the Bill. This usually requires only a signature, of the Drawee, and often a company stamp. The L/C term of the Bill is known as the Tenor and when this expires ie 60 days later, the Bill is said to have Matured and will be represented for payment. This procedure is described as 'Documents Against Acceptance (D/A)'.

It is important to appreciate that in the case where documents have been released against Acceptance there will be no automatic payment transfer when the Bill matures. The buyer must still make the payment and it is perfectly possible for dishonour to take place.

In the cases where there is non-payment of a Sight Bill, or non-acceptance of a Termed Bill, or non-payment of an accepted Bill on maturity, it is important in many markets that a Protest is made. Whilst this procedure does not apply in every country overseas there are many in which the lack of a protest will lead to a loss of all legal rights against the buyer.

As any protest must be made the next working day (in practice 3 days grace are allowed) then it is important that the banks are instructed in

---

No. *156*

Exchange for £18,240 200–

AT 90 DAYS . . . . *after* DATE . . . . . of this FIRST BILL *of Exchange*

(SECOND . . . . *of the same tenor and date being unpaid) pay to the*

order of OURSELVES . . . . *.the sum of*

EIGHTEEN THOUSAND TWO HUNDRED AND FORTY POUNDS ONLY

FOR AND ON BEHALF OF

To FERNANDO BROS. LTD   IVOR BIGGEN LTD
CARACAS, VENEZUELA   *Director*

Figure 8.2.6 - Typical Termed or Usance Draft

advance. Even in the cases where the exporter has little desire to take legal action then the protest can be sufficient to prompt payment from a buyer who is simply 'playing for time'. Also lists of protested Bills are published in the financial press or bank gazettes of some countries and buyers will usually wish to avoid this. Finally most L/C insurance companies will require protest to be made as part of their policy requirements. Figure 8.2.7 reproduces an example of a protest which was actually made in Nigeria. Only the names have been changed to protect the guilty.

The above procedures describe what are known as Documentary Collections in that the bank handles the set of shipping documents as well as the Bill of Exchange. It is possible to arrange for what are known as Clean Collections in which the documents are sent direct to the buyer, rather than to the bank, the Bill of Exchange being handled by the banks in the normal way. This is only used where there is a large element of trust between seller and buyer and the Bill is simply a convenient way to collect and transfer the payment.

It is even possible to simply instruct an overseas bank to release the documents against payment without including a Bill of Exchange. This is known as Cash Against Documents but does not provide the security of a Sight Draft and operates according to local practice rather than a set of rules.

In this respect the advantage of both Clean and Documentary Collections is that the banks handling such collections invariably operate under the same set of procedural rules. These are known as the Uniform Rules for Collections and are a publication of the International Chamber of Commerce, (ICC Publication No. 322) available from your local Chamber of Commerce.

Avalised Bills of Exchange

As we have seen, a Termed Bill accepted by the Drawee is not a guarantee of payment on maturity, but it is possible to arrange for the accepted Bill to be avalised by the buyer's bank. This must be arranged in advance and involves the bank adding their 'Pour Aval' endorsement , or guarantee. to the accepted Bill. In such a case the exporter has a bank's promise to pay rather than the buyer's. This is not as secure as a Letter of L/C in that the buyer must accept the Bill of Exchange first, but it does have the great advantage of producing an accepted Bill which can be discounted.

This describes the process whereby it is possible to receive a discounted amount of the Bill value at the time of acceptance rather than wait for it to mature. The 'Pour Aval' on the Bill means that a number of agencies will be prepared to advance funds, in particular there are financial institutions who specialise in what is known as 'Forfaiting' who will advance funds at good rates. Such Forfaiters will also become involved in long term forfaits of high value Bills over long periods of time.

By This Public Instrument

Be it known and made manifest that on the......22nd...... day of ....JUNE......

in the year......ONE THOUSAND NINE HUNDRED & SEVENTY NINE...... I Frank Odunayo

Akinrele, Notary Public, duly authorised, admitted and sworn, practising in Lagos, Nigeria,

West Africa do hereby certify that on this the............22nd............ day of............JUNE......

IN THE YEAR OF OUR LORD ONE THOUSAND NINE HUNDRED & SEVENTY NINE

at the request of.........ARAB BANK NIGERIA LIMITED   (BALOGUN SQUARE)......

of the Colony of Lagos, Nigeria, Bankers and holders of the original Bill of Exchange a

true copy of which is on the other side written, I, Frank Odunayo Akinrele of the said

Colony, Notary Public, duly authorised, admitted and sworn, did cause the said Bill of

Exchange to be taken to No....26 Kingomdy STREET, LAGOS NIGERIA............ and to

be produced and exhibited to....XYZ ELECTRICAL STORES LIMITED......

on whom it was drawn, at No....26 Kongodwy Street, LAGOS NIGERIA......

......and cause to be demanded

payment thereof,......Then J. Smith (Jr.) Brother for and on behalf of ...

XYZ Electrical Stores Limited,   Said:- "My Director is not in office

but he will be informed to take necessary arrangement for payment."

......

and so, I am unable to obtain payment of the said Bill of Exchange.

Whereupon, I, the said Notary, at the request aforesaid, did cause protest to be
made and by these presents do solemnly protest against the drawers of the said Bill of
Exchange and all other parties thereto, and all others concerned for Exchange, re-exchange,
and all costs, damages, charges and interest present and future for want of payment of the
said Bill of Exchange.

Thus done and protested at Lagos in the presence of:-

Adeyeye
T.A.O. ADEYEYE
130. Broad Street
Lagos Nigeria

Dated the......22nd......day of......JUNE IN THE YEAR OUR LORD......
ONE THOUSAND NINE HUNDRED AND SEVENTY NINE......

Which I Attest,

Public, Nigeria.

Figure 8.2.7- Protest for non-payment (example)

Documentary Letter of Credit (L/C)

Most exporters will feel that a promise from a bank to pay is an improvement on a promise from the buyer and we have seen above that the addition of a bank's Pour Aval on an accepted Bill of Exchange gives distinct advantages. The ultimate form of bank guarantee used in international trade is that of the Letter of L/C which, in simple terms, is a letter from a bank promising to pay an amount of money.

However the typical operation involves the use of Documentary Letters of L/C which promise to pay only if the documents stated on the L/C are provided by the exporter. In this respect they are very much conditional guarantees of payment.

The procedure, which begins with the seller and buyer agreeing payment by Letter of L/C, requires the buyer to arrange for the L/C to be opened by their bank at the time the order is placed. From the exporter's point of view the Letter of L/C would need to be received before the order was accepted and checks on its acceptability would take place right at the beginning of the order process.

The buyer will instruct their bank, known as the Opening or Issuing bank, to raise the L/C and agree with them the specific documentary requirements. The L/C will then be passed to the exporter, known as the Beneficiary, through the Issuing bank's correspondent bank in the exporter's country. If this bank happens to be the exporter's bank then it is pure coincidence and it may be the case that a transcribed, retyped, version of the original L/C is what the exporter will eventually see.

The UK bank may simply pass the L/C to the exporter, in which case they are the Advising Bank and the exporter has the Issuing bank's promise to pay subject to the provision of the required documents. It may be that the UK bank adds its confirmation to the L/C ie its own promise to pay, and will be referred to as the Confirming Bank. As we will see later the UK exporter may feel that the Confirmation of a UK bank is an improvement on the Issuing banks promise.

Once the L/C is received by the exporter it is important that it is checked immediately to ensure that the documentary requirements, and the time periods allowed, are acceptable. If amendments are required it is advisable to request them immediately from the Issuing bank, through the Advising or Confirming bank.

This procedure is shown graphically in Fig. 8.2.8.

Assuming that the L/C is acceptable to the exporter they will then proceed with the manufacture, packing and shipping of the goods in order to produce a set of shipping documents in compliance with the L/C. These documents will be presented to the UK bank who will check that they comply with the L/C requirements and, assuming they find no discrepancies, they will pay the exporter.

Unfortunately the reality is not always quite so simple and in fact the statistics show that between 60- 80% of document sets presented to UK banks against L/Cs are rejected because of documentary discrepancies. They actually go wrong more often than they go right. To see why such problems are experienced it is necessary to look in more detail at the Letter of L/C process.

Documentary requirements

Figure 8.2.9 is an example of a typical letter of L/C. Whilst it is still possible to receive the original paper from the Opening Bank it is far more likely now the exporter will see a hard copy of the SWIFT transmitted L/C . This represents a standard format and fields.

The average L/C will require:

1. Drafts (Bills of Exchange) which are often drawn on the Issuing or the Confirming bank. That is to say, that the Drawee on such Bills will be a bank rather than the buyer.

    The Bills will reflect whether the L/C is payable at Sight or contains a L/C term as can be seen from figure 8.2.9 which requires a 90 day Bill

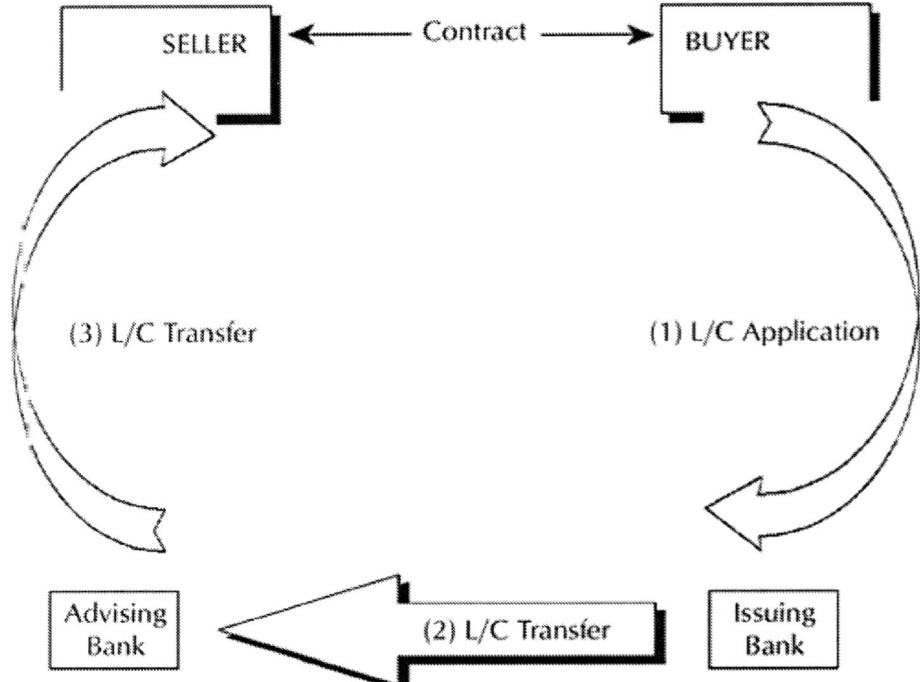

Fig. 8.2.8 - Processing a letter of credit

drawn on Shinhan Bank (42C and 42D) In both cases the Bill will contain a clause referring to the relevant letter of L/C.

Assuming that no documentary discrepancies are found the bank will pay against the Sight Draft or will accept the Termed Draft. These Bills are known as Bank Bills and such a Bill, drawn on and accepted by a UK Clearing bank would be ' Good Paper' in that a discount of the Bill would be very easy. The acceptance of, for example Barclays bank, of a Bill due to mature in 90 days would be seen as an absolute guarantee of payment on maturity. In fact Barclays would be happy to discount their own Accepted Bills.

2. Export Invoices will be required in a prescribed format (see chapter 5) and in sufficient numbers. Any required certifications and legalisations must be arranged and it may be that Certificates of Origin or other status documents are requested.

3. Insurance Policy or Certificate which will be necessary if the contract is one which requires the exporter to arrange for the cargo insurance ie CIF, CIP. Such cover must be for the risks and the amount specified.

4. Transport Documents which could be Bills of Lading, Air Waybills, Road or Rail Consignment notes (see chapter 5) or even Freight Forwarder's receipts.

The above represent the typical documentary requirements on a L/C but there could obviously be a number of additional documents depending on the specific consignment involved. These may include Packing Specifications, Consular Invoices, Inspection Certificates, Clean Reports of Findings, Standards Certificates, Black List Certificates, Phytosanitary Certificates, Veterinary Certificates, Halal Certificates etc.

The Letter of L/C will also impose other conditions on the exporter most noticeably the strict time limits imposed on shipment and document presentations, and will allow, or not allow, transhipment and part-shipment. Obviously there will be a fixed value which cannot be exceeded.

Fig. 8.2.9 - Example of unconfirmed letter of credit

Issuing bank		Shinhan Bank Seoul
Form of Doc. L/C	40A	Irrevocable
Doc. L/C Number	20	1234
Date of Issue	31 C	1/1/2003
Expiry	31 D	31/3/2003
Applicant	50	Korea Importing Company
		Changwon City
		Kyungsangnam - Do
		Korea
Beneficiary	59	Fog on the Tyne Exporting Co
		Newcastle
Amount	32 B	GBP 12,027.25
Available with/by	41 D	Any bank by negotiation
Drafts at	42 C	90 days after sight
Drawee	42 D	Shinhan Bank London
Partial shipments	43 P	Prohibited
Transhipment	43 T	Prohibited
Loading in charge	44 A	UK port
For transport to	44 B	Busan Port
Latest date of shipment	44C	10/3/2003
Description of goods	45A	1000 Units of Geordie widgets
		CIF
Documents required	46A	Signed commercial invoice packing list
		Full set clean on board ocean bills of lading made out to the order of Shinhan Bank Seoul marked freight prepaid, notify applicant
		Certificate of origin
		Original insurance policy endorsed in blank for the invoice value of the goods plus 10%, covering institute cargo clauses (all risks or 'A') including institute war clauses and institute strikes clauses
Additional conditions	47 A	All documents must be issued in the English language if they are not they may be disregarded.
		All presentations received by us with discrepancies will attract a fee of GBP25.00 per presentation.
		This charge, unless otherwise stated by us, will be for the account of the beneficiary.
Details of charges	71 B	Charges for beneficiary's account except opening bank's charges.
Presentation period	48	Within 21 days after date of shipment but prior to the expiry of the L/C.
Confirmation	49	Without.

Advise through	57 D	Bank of Scotland International
		Trade Services Princes House
		55 West Campbell Street Glasgow G2 6YJ
		SWIFT: BOFSGB2S

The problems arise when the exporter presents the documents, against the L/C, to the UK bank who will examine them to assess whether they comply with the L/C requirements. The banks operate on what is known as the 'Doctrine of Strict Compliance' which means that they insist that the documents comply exactly with the L/C requirements.

As illustrations of how far the banks will take the Doctrine of Strict Compliance the following are examples of typical bank rejections :

- ABC Engineering Ltd. are described as AVC Engineering Ltd. on the L/C. Despite the fact that they are obviously the beneficiaries of the L/C they would have to have the L/C amended or produce a letterhead with their name spelt wrongly.
- 20,000 RELLS of Insulating Tape are described on the L/C and the exporter uses the correct description of ROLLS on the invoice, which the bank, of course, reject. In their defence they would say that there may be a technical trade expression which distinguishes RELLS from ROLLS.
- A quantity of 5.000 Kgs. Industrial Laminate is described as 5,000 Kgs. on the invoice and the bank reject for an incorrect description. You will have noticed that there is a (,) instead of a (.) .

The above examples , which mostly relate to word descriptions, are the result of the detailed examination which the exporter's documents receive when presented , and there are many other reasons for rejection which are mentioned below.

The justification of such a level of compliance is that, if payment were made by the UK bank, they having found no discrepancies, then it is probable that the Issuing bank would find such discrepancies and therefore refuse to pay the Advising bank.

The situation is even worse for the UK Confirming bank who will pay the exporter without recourse and will not be able to recover any funds should the Issuing bank not pay.

The banks do not operate wilfully or independently in rejecting documents presented to them but apply a very strict set of rules which are known as the Uniform Customs & Practice for Documentary L/Cs. These rules are publication 500 of the International Chamber of Commerce and the current version has operated from 1.1.94 day-to-day practice (known as UCP 500). In early 2003 the ICC have also published e-UCP 500 which addresses the issues related to the use of electronic documents as opposed to hard copy.

The first solution for the exporter is to attempt to ensure that the letter of L/C is acceptable when it is received. A number of organisations, including the banks, will provide Letter of L/C checklists which can be useful for this purpose, and an abbreviated version would look like:

Is the L/C irrevocable?
Is it confirmed by an acceptable Bank?
Is your name and that of your customer complete and spelled correctly?
Do expiration and shipping dates give sufficient time to arrange shipment?
Is the L/C amount sufficient to cover the order value and the currency as
    agreed?
Is the description and quantity of goods correct?

Are partial shipments permitted?
Is transhipment permitted ?
Is shipment permitted from any place In the UK or only one named place?
Does the named destination you quoted agree with L/C?

Can you obtain properly executed documents to conform with L/C?
can you produce and submit the documents in the time allowed (if no fixed
    time is
specified you have 21 days from the date of shipment)
Is any specified agency required to issue any of these certificates?
Can you comply with insurance risks required and is a Policy or Certificate
    required ?

On presentation:

Have all the required documents been provided?
Is there sufficient data in the documents to show that they all relate to the
    same transaction?
Are the following points consistent throughout the documents and L/C

- Amount of L/C?
- Description of goods (quantity, weight, dimension)?
- Shipping marks and import licence number?

Are the documents signed, where required?
Have correct number of original and copies of documents been provided?

Bill of exchange checklist

Have you supplied the required number of bills?
Is the amount correct? ie in agreement with invoice amount (unless L/C
    specifies otherwise eg 90% of invoice amount.

Has it been manually signed and if signed 'for', 'pro' or 'per' a company, is the capacity of the signatory shown? (Not required if 'pp' or 'per pro' is used)

Is the tenor correct (at sight, at 120 days sight etc)?

Is the drawee correct (as stated in the L/C)?

Is the payee correct, and if you are the payee, have you fully endorsed the reverse

Bill of lading checklist

Has it been issued by a shipping company? (ie it must indicate the carrier on its face)

Is special authorisation included in the L/C if any of the following applies?

B/L is not 'clean' (marked to the effect that packaging and/or goods are defective).

B/L is either a:

- Charter Party B/L
- Forwarding Agent's B/L
- Received for Shipment B/L

Is Consignee's name and address correct?

Is Notify party's name and address correct?

Are ports of departure and destination correct? (ie same as the L/C)

Is it correctly marked ' Freight Paid', 'Freight Collect' etc?

If issued to order of shipper, is it suitably endorsed?

Are any alterations or notations suitably authenticated?

Have all originals been duly signed by the carrier or an agent.

If by an agent, is there an indication of the name and capacity of the party on whose behalf that agent is acting?

Have any non-negotiable copies been provided where required?

Has correct number of originals been provided (most L/Cs call for a full set).

Air transport document checklist

Is special authorisation included in the L/C if any of the following applies?

- Air Transport Document not 'clean'
- Air Transport Document is a Forwarding Agents Air Transport Document

Is Consignee's name and address correct?

Is Notify Party's name and address correct?

Are airports of departure and destination correct?

Are any alterations or notations suitably authenticated?

Is it correctly marked 'Freight Paid', 'Freight Collect' etc?
Is it stamped with carrier's stamp, showing flight number and departure date, if requested?
Is it the original for consignor?

Multimodal transport document checklist

Is Consignee's name and address correct?
Is Notify Party's name and address correct?
Is it correctly marked 'Freight Paid', 'Freight Collect' etc?
Are any alterations / notations suitably authenticated?
Has it been properly signed?

Commercial invoice checklist

Is the description of goods *exactly* as stated in the L/C?
Is price of goods exactly as stated in the L/C?
Is it correctly addressed (to the IMPORTER or other party specified in the L/C)?
Are the terms of shipment correct (FCA, CIP etc)?
Have separate charges for eg packing, Consular Fees, been included which are not specifically permitted by the L/C?
Do identifying marks and numbers agree with the L/C?
Does the L/C require that an Import Licence number be shown?
Is a special declaration or certification required?
If signed invoices are required, does a signature appear on all copies?
Have you supplied the correct number of invoice original and copies?

An understanding of the most common discrepancies which UK banks find in examining Documentary L/C presentations can be instructive in terms of the UK exporter avoiding common rejections. A current 'top ten ' would look like :

1. Late shipment
2. Documents not presented in time (within time allowed or 21 days)
3. Absence of documents requested in the L/C
4. Claused Bills of Lading/Carrier Receipts
5. No evidence of goods 'shipped on board '
6. Description of goods on invoice differs from that on the L/C
7. Documents inconsistent with each other
8. Insurance not effective from the date of shipment
9. Bill of exchange not drawn up in accordance with the L/C
10. Invoices or CofOs not certified as requested

It can be seen from the above that the bank not only check the documents against the L/C, but also against each other. This means that rejections can happen even when there is no specific breach of a letter of L/C requirement. An example of this would be a case where the shipping marks shown on the invoice differ from those on the Bill of Lading. The bank would reject the documents even though a specific shipping mark is not mentioned on the L/C at all.

In the event that documents are rejected by the bank then the exporter has a number of possible strategies:

1. The discrepancies can be corrected and the documents represented to the bank . (The 60-80% statistical rejection rate is on FIRST presentation and it is often possible to represent and obtain payment on second presentation). Another example of bank practice is illustrated by the fact that, if the original error/s are corrected and the documents represented to the bank, they may well accept that the original causes of rejection are now acceptable but could reject because the time limit for presentation of documents (time specified in the L/C or 21 days) has by then expired.

2. In the event that the errors cannot be corrected then the exporter must except that the security of the L/C has been lost. The bank may simply contact the buyers, via the Issuing bank, and inform them of the nature of the discrepancies. The buyers then have the right to accept or reject the documents as they see fit.

It may be that the documents themselves are dispatched to the Issuing bank 'for collection', which means that we have reverted to a Bill of Exchange to collect payment, or even that the documents are sent to the overseas bank for the buyer to inspect 'in trust'. In either case the buyer has the right to reject the documents and therefore reject the goods.

It is possible for the UK bank to pay ' with recourse ' and usually against a form of indemnity from the exporter, although this may only be available for certain discrepancies, such as late (stale) documents.

The fact that the goods are actually on the way to, or even arrived at, the destination merely adds to the problems of the exporter. To take this just a stage further, the situation in which goods have arrived at destination and the buyer has legitimately rejected the documents, is a very difficult one for the exporter. The worst consequence is that, if the goods are not cleared (into the importing country) or re-exported (returned to the exporting country) then they will eventually be auctioned off. The more congested the overseas port or depot is then the sooner this will happen. It could easily be only a matter of weeks rather than months. In such a case there is a clear hierarchy in terms of the distribution of the auction revenues.

Customs & Excise (you guessed it)
Demurrage charges (fines for delay)
Other warehousing & storage charges
Auctioneers fees
Any other receiving authority charges
Any outstanding carrier's charges
(and last and very definitely least)
The owners of the goods ie the exporter

A situation to be avoided at all costs... particularly when the person who picks up the goods at auction just happens to be the original buyer who rejected the documents in the first place.

So, the security of the Letter of L/C brings with it a clear responsibility for the exporter to produce a set of documents which comply exactly with the L/C and with each other. Should discrepancies occur it is almost guaranteed that the bank's checking system, which may involve 2 or 3 separate examinations, will find them and the security of the L/C is lost. The Documentary Letter of L/C is very much a Conditional guarantee of payment.

Types of Letters of L/C

Irrevocable

An irrevocable L/C cannot be cancelled or amended without the consent of all parties It is irrelevant if the buyers change there mind or even go out of business. The only thing that can invalidate the L/C is if the issuing bank go out of business, or a government moratorium means that trading must cease with a particular country.

Revocable

It is possible, but unusual, to trade with revocable L/Cs which, as the name suggests, can be cancelled or amended by either party. The obvious problem for the exporter being the possibility of the buyer simply cancelling the guarantee. The UCP 500 states that L/Cs will be regarded as irrevocable unless they state that they are revocable.

They are only used where the parties are closely related and as a means of efficient funds transfer, not as security of payment.

Confirmed

As mentioned above it may be in the exporter's interests to obtain the promise of a bank in their own country to pay, by adding their confirmation to the L/C, in addition to the issuing banks promise. Whether this is insisted upon or not should depend on an informed assessment of the reliability of the Issuing bank and not simply as a blanket request.

Transferable

In the cases where a 'middleman' operates between a manufacturer and an end-user it is possible for a L/C to be raised showing the agent as the beneficiary but also allowing the transfer of a percentage of the L/C to the manufacturer. The difference is the agents profit and the manufacturer must meet the conditions of the L/C to obtain their payment, just as the agent must.

In similar situations it may be that the first L/C, paying the agent, is used to raise a second L/C for a lesser amount, paying the manufacture, with identical documentary requirements. These are known as Back To Back L/Cs.

Revolving

Where a series of identical shipments are to be made it is possible to raise one L/C to cover all of them rather than a separate L/C for each shipment. They are known as revolving because after payment against a shipment the amount payable is reinstated for the next shipment.

Deferred Payment

These are becoming increasingly popular where a L/C term has been agreed but the parties wish to avoid raising a Bill of Exchange under the L/C. This will usually be because the Bills attract stamp duty in the issuing country. When correct documents are presented the bank do not 'accept' a Bill of Exchange but instead give a 'letter of undertaking' advising when the money will be paid.

Standby *L/Cs*

This type of L/C is unusual in that both parties hope it will never be used. They are used in two situations:

1. where the seller is trading on open account but requires some security of payment. They are raised by the buyer as a normal L/C but require the Issuing bank to make payment to the seller only on presentation of documents evidencing non-payment by the buyer within the open

account agreement. That is to say, as long as the buyer continues to pay on time under the open account the L/C will not be drawn on.

2. to replace Performance Bonds (see chapter 4) issued by the buyer and required under most tender procedures. They have the advantage over normal bonds of being regulated by the UCP 500 rules. They are well known in the USA and becoming increasingly common in many markets.

Summary

The Documentary Letter of L/C is an important and very common method of payment in international trade, primarily because of the security it offers to the exporter. However we must accept that the security of the bank guarantee inherent in the L/C is tempered by the documentary conditions imposed.

It is an unfortunate fact that the majority of presentations to UK banks are rejected on first presentation because of documentary discrepancies. It is vital that exporters not only establish systems which eliminate documentary errors but that they also understand the 'rules of the game'. The banks do not invent reasons for rejection, they genuinely play by the rules, and the rules are the Uniform Customs & Practice for Documentary L/Cs ICC Brochure No. 500 and Guide to Documentary L/C Operations (ICC No. 415). Copies are available from Chambers of Commerce or the ICC web site at www.iccbooks.com.

Factors

It is possible for exports to actually avoid the problems of collecting overseas debts by factoring them to specialist financial institutions. The factors will take over the invoices of the exporter and pay a percentage of their value.

This is calculated on the traders average credit period and level of bad debts, and is often paid at the end of an agreed period from the invoice dates. The exporter is therefore able to accurately predict receipts with all the cash flow advantages that entails.

It may be that these payment are made with or without recourse should the buyer not pay on time. The larger factors operating internationally are obviously very adapt at credit control and debt collection.

This will invariably cost more than if the exporter were to successfully collect their own debts and perhaps we do not wish to pass our debt collection procedures on to third parties who do not consider customer relations or the business implications. It does smack of 'passing the buck'.

Countertrade

Over the last twenty years there has been an enormous increase in countertrade throughout the world and the recent break up of the state-planned economies of Eastern Europe has only served to accelerate this development. Some estimates suggest that in anything up to 33 % of world trade, countertrade at least forms part of the negotiations, although final payment might actually be made in currency.

It is obvious that the severe hard currency shortages experienced by many developing countries lead to countertrade being seen as the only way in which international trade can occur in some situations.

The expression countertrade actually covers a variety of possible procedures which include:

Barter

The direct exchange of goods for goods. Overseas markets with excess commodities trade them for negotiated quantities of imported goods with no cash changing hands. It is not uncommon in Africa and Latin America, and is preferred by some oil-dependant economies. There are specialist consultants who will handle the disposal of the bartered products on behalf of the exporter.

Counterpurchase

As a condition of securing the export order the seller undertakes to purchase goods or services from that country. Two contracts are agreed, one sale and one purchase, and payments are made on negotiated cash or L/C terms. The counterpurchase contract can be anything from 10 % to 100 % (or even more) of the value of the export sale.

Buy-back

A form of barter in which the suppliers of capital equipment, such as manufacturing plant, agree to accept payment in the form of the output of the manufacturing unit. An important variation of this is practised by Ikea who establish factories, mostly in Eastern Europe based on Western European equipment, and buy-back the production. This has the distinct added advantage that the small to medium sized European manufacturers supply equipment direct to, say, Poland but receive payment from Ikea.

Offset

A condition of the export would be that materials and components which originate in the importing country are incorporated in the finished product which they eventually receive. This is particularly relevant to high technology products such as aircraft and defence systems and may even involve the exporter participating in the establishment of production units in the overseas market.

Evidence accounts

Traders with significant levels of business in certain markets may be required to arrange an equivalent amount of counterpurchased exports from that country. For example a multinational company with a local manufacturing subsidiary may be required to balance the import of materials and equipment with equivalent exports. The 'evidence account' attempts to record the balance of imports and exports over a period of time.

8.3

Forms of countertrade

Countertrade is an inherently *ad hoc* activity. The mechanics vary according to local regulations and requirements, the nature of the goods to be exported and the current priorities of the parties involved. The terms used to describe the main modes of trading vary, often interchangeably, fuelling confusion. The most common forms of countertrade, and the terms usually applied, are:

Counterpurchase

Concurrently with, and as a condition of, securing a sales order, the exporter undertakes to purchase goods and services from the country concerned. There are two parallel but separate contracts, one for the principal order - which is paid for on normal cash or credit terms - and another for the counterpurchase. The value of the counterpurchase undertaking. may vary in value between 10% and 100% (or even more) of the original export order. The agreement can vary from a general declaration of intent to a binding contract specifying the goods and services to be supplied, the markets in which they may be sold, the penalties for non-performance, and perhaps other matters. The goods offered may be quite unrelated to those exported, and the agreernent may involve parties unrelated to the sales contract. Counterpurchase was the most common mode of countertrade, particularly with eastern Europe and with a number of developing countries, notably Indonesia.

Barter

The direct exchange of goods for goods. The principal exports are paid for with goods (or services) supplied from the importing market. A single contract covers both flows and, in the simplest case, no cash is involved. In practice, supply of the principal exports is often held up until sufficient revenue has been earned from selling the bartered goods. Though less common than counterpurchase, barter has been sought by some African and Latin American countries with extensive currency restrictions, and by some oil-dependent countries.

Buy-back

A form of barter, in which suppliers of capital plant or equipment agree to repayment in the future output of the investment concerned. For example, exporters of equipment for a chemical works may be repaid with part of the resulting output from that work. Most common in connection with exports of process plant, mining equipment and similar orders, buyback arrangements tend to be much longer term and for much larger amounts than counterpurchase or simple barter deals.

Offset

A condition of exporting some products, especially those embodying advanced technology to some markets, is that the exporter incorporates into the final products specified materials, components or sub-assemblies, procured within the importing country. This has long been an established feature of trade in defence systems and aircraft, but is becoming more common in other sectors, especially where the importing country is seeking to develop its own industrial capabilities. A variant of offset arises in some large contracts, for which the importing country often demands that successful bidders establish local production and other forms of long-term industrial cooperation.

Switch trading

Imbalances in long-term bilateral trading agreements sometimes lead to the accumulation of uncleared credit surpluses in one or other country; for example at one time the UK had a large credit surplus with Poland. These surpluses can sometimes be tapped by third parties, so that UK exports to Brazil might be financed from the sale of Polish goods to the UK or elsewhere. Such transactions are known as 'switch' or 'swap' deals, because they typically involve switching the documentation (and destination) of goods on the high seas. Switch deals can be very complex, involving a chain of buyers, sellers and brokers in different markets.

Evidence accounts

Companies or traders with a significant level of continuing business in certain markets may be required to arrange counter purchased exports from those markets at least equivalent to their own imports with the country concerned. For example, a multinational firm with a local manufacturing subsidiary in a developing country may be required to ensure counter-purchased exports of equivalent value to their subsidiary's imports of materials and equipment. Since it is not practical to balance this kind of trade item by item, the firm may maintain an "evidence account", debiting its own imports and crediting the exports it has arranged over a period. The evidence account must be maintained more-or-less in balance year by year.

Part 9

New Horizons – looking ahead

9.1

ICT and export documentation

SITPRO

The most important organisation in the UK charged with developing systems for the electronic production of export documents is SITPRO Limited, formerly The Simpler Trade Procedures Board. Set up in 1970 as the UK's trade facilitation agency and reconstituted as a company limited by guarantee in April 2001, SITPRO is one of the Non-Departmental Public Bodies for which the Department of Trade and Industry has responsibility. It receives a grant-in-aid from the Department.

SITPRO is dedicated to encouraging and helping business trade more effectively and to simplify the international trading process. Its focus is the procedures and documentation associated with international trade.

SITPRO's mission is to use its unique status to improve the competitive position of UK traders by facilitating change through:

- identification and removal of barriers in the international trading process;
- identification and promotion of best trading practices;
- delivery of practical, value for money electronic commerce and associated trading solutions; and
- influencing future trade policies.

SITPRO offers a wide range of services, including advice, briefings, publications and checklists covering various international trading practices. It manages the UK aligned system of export documents and licenses the printers and software suppliers who sell the forms and export document software.

For further information contact:
SITPRO Ltd
Oxford House
8th Floor
76 Oxford Street
London W1D 1BS
Tel: 020 7467 7280
Fax: 020 7467 7295
Email: info@sitpro.org.uk

Electronic Data Interchange (EDI)

In simple terms EDI can be described as 'the transfer of structured data by agreed message standards from one computer system to another, by electronic means.'

In essence, EDI is a means of paperless trading and was a natural evolution from paper documents as data carriers, to computer and telecommunication systems as automatic carriers and processors of data. In traditional business processes, such as ordering and invoicing, paper documents contain structured information in various 'boxes'. In EDI this information is mapped into a structured electronic message. In operation EDI is the interchange of these agreed messages between trading partners to ensure speed and certainty and better business practice in the supply chain.

EDI allows the electronic transmission of a wide range of information between businesses which would otherwise be paper based. Since its introduction in the late seventies its use as a replacement for paper-based systems has increased dramatically. The concept involves defining a standard format for the transmission of data between two businesses, which allows the whole transaction process to be automated. Thus, the actual applications at each end (eg accounting software) need not be identical.

The difference between EDI and other types of E-Business is that while E-Business can be thought of as the exchange of electronic information in any format, EDI is done through a standardised format. This makes it especially useful for large volumes of repetitive documents such as purchase orders and order acknowledgments and, increasingly, standard documents used in international trade eg invoices, certificates of origin, transport documents, Customs declarations etc,

The American National Standards Institute (ANSI) has a group of EDI standards called 'X.12'. These standards can be customised for use within specific industries. ANSI X.12 is widely used in North America.

EDIFACT (Electronic Data Interchange for Administration, Commerce and Transport) is a more recent standard that is gradually becoming accepted, particularly in Europe.

Benefits

The use of EDI has brought substantial benefits and savings to companies that have implemented it. One of the principal reasons for using EDI is to eliminate the mountain of paper documents which is produced, moved, handled, corrected, transcribed and copied in normal business. Well designed and well structured EDI overcomes the disadvantages of paper documents as data carriers and provides a number of specific benefits:

- *Speed and certainty:* enables companies to concentrate on core trading activities and provides the ability to respond to customer's demands more accurately and confidently.
- *Operational:* reduced costs is one of the key benefits offered by EDI, covering areas such as paper and postage bills, and reduced stock holding costs. The elimination of manual data entry and manual filing systems is another major saving, as is the reduction in data entry errors, which have previously resulted in increased processing and administration costs.
- *Removal of inter-enterprise trade barriers:* international standards for product identification and EDI communications, removes communications barriers in key transactions in the trading cycle.
- *Strategic:* EDI can result in fundamental changes to an organisation that brings about long-term strategic benefits. One such benefit is a 'Faster Trading Cycle', where the speed and accuracy of ordering and invoicing systems are vital to main business operations. Another is 'Just-in-time' manufacturing practices, where companies produce minimal-sized batches of finished goods only when they are needed (ie responding to market pull). This has become more common, partly because of EDI, allowing companies to save on storage costs of both raw and manufactured stock.
- *Bargaining power:* in a highly competitive market EDI can be a powerful weapon in a company's corporate armoury. The ability to offer significant cuts in product delivery and data processing time is an important component of a company's corporate image and competitive edge.
- *Improved cashflow:* enables suppliers to send accurate and timely invoices. Vast improvements are possible in matching invoices with purchase orders for example, resulting in reduced errors or queries.
- *Security and error reduction:* this will include the elimination of errors in transcribing documents from one medium (paper) to another (computer) and a reduction in mismatching of orders.

Trends and developments

The main reason for using EDI is that it provides a standardised rigid format for exchanging data. However this is also a disadvantage in that it is relatively inflexible. Setting up ad-hoc relationships cannot normally be done as relationships and data formats have to be formally agreed before any transactions can take place.

Traditional EDI is now therefore under threat by newer technologies based on Extensible Markup Language (XML). XML is the world standard platform for electronic business transactions.

The key benefits of XML are:

- it can be read by both humans and computers;
- it facilitates the optimal structuring of data;

- it can be extended to accommodate future needs;
- it is free and/or inexpensive;
- it is widely available;
- it is easy to learn;
- it is supported by all major software vendors.

XML-based EDI allows the transfer of data between companies without the format of the data having to be rigidly pre-defined and therefore companies can carry out e-business with new trading partners much more easily. XML-based technology is well suited to use over the Internet, which has a much lower cost than the Value Added Networks of conventional EDI.

EDI continues to play an important role in business in traditional supply chain relationships between trading partners. Large organisations that have invested heavily in large and sophisticated EDI systems are unlikely to re-engineer their business processes overnight and re-invest in new systems in order to facilitate new technologies such as XML. EDI has been a trusted and successful data transfer mechanism for these organisations and will continue to be a major part of their operation for some time. However, this is not to say that these new technologies are to be ignored.

SITPRO has recognised that there is currently a myriad of standards available in XML and that what is needed is one single global standard for use across existing and future transfer mechanisms. To this end SITPRO has agreed to the adoption of the draft ebXML standards for transactions and relationships with SMEs following the completion of the initiative.

Another notable trend is the change of focus within the UN/EDIFACT Working Group. Traditionally the group has focused solely on the development and maintenance of the UN/EDIFACT standard and Directories. There has been a shift in thinking within the working group to incorporate the emerging trends and technologies surrounding the area of structured data transfer, such as business process modelling and XML.

The legacy of EDI remains an important part of the modern b2b arena. However, because of the rapid developments in technologies such as XML, the EDI community has taken the opportunity to reassess its priorities. The key point here is to utilise the vast knowledge and experience from years of work on EDI, especially in terms of naming and defining data, and harness this with the drive of the emerging communities to build a common understanding of business processes and data to be transferred across existing and future platforms.

WebElecTra

WebElecTra has been designed by SITPRO to help traders take advantage of e-commerce developments to help with the process of international trade. SITPRO has been working hard to take the essence of trading best practice and put it into a simple system which supports On-Line completion of the standard forms necessary for international trade.

From the last quarter of 2000, traders and freight forwarders have been able to log on to WebElecTra compliant web sites (which are listed on the SITPRO site at www.sitpro.org.uk) and complete trading documentation electronically.

SITPRO guarantees that WebElecTra branded systems will conform to the national and international documents which meet UN standards and which have been managed by SITPRO for the last 25 years. These documents included purchase orders, standard shipping notes, dangerous goods notes, export cargo shipping instructions, Customs C88s and many others, and are the correct Government sponsored version of the forms needed for International trade. SITPRO also guarantees that these forms will be kept up to date so that users will always have the certainty that they have the correct versions of the trading documents.

All WebElecTra branded web sites will also carry comprehensive help and validation eg assistance with completing the different parts of the forms, and validation of data entered. In addition, an advanced set of trading business rules is being built in so that the system will prompt the user for extra information or additional procedures when it detects that they are needed for particular goods, destinations etc.

WebElecTra will allow traders to send electronic messages to those freight forwarders, carriers, banks, customs and other government departments, which can accept them. These trading partners will only need to use a web browser to complete the transaction.

Where organisations in other countries will only accept paper documentation ElecTra also provides the solution. As an example, a prospective purchaser might see some of a trader's good for sale on the Internet. On clicking a button, they would be presented with a purchase order, which they would complete and send back to the trader through the WebElecTra server. The trader would then complete the acknowledgment of order (automatically partially completed from the purchaser's data) and send it back, and at the same time send an Export Cargo Shipping Instruction/ Standard Shipping Note etc. to the appropriate recipients. All common data would be automatically filled in. Customs declarations can be automatically posted from the data as well.

One of the key points of ElecTra and WebElecTra is the continued compatibility with the standard paper documents, and so at any state the trader can print out the documents (eg for filing, sending with the goods) and so effectively switch back to paper trading for those countries or authorities who insist on paper. The aim is to facilitate trade, not to compel users blindly to adopt electronic trading. However, as electronic business grows, ElecTra will support both Internet and Electronic Data Interchange requirements. ElecTra is here now, and here to stay, to support your trading requirements.

For further information email **webelectra@sitpro.org.uk**.

Bolero.net

International trade has traditionally been fraught with financial, logistic and time inefficiencies, costing world business hundreds of billions of dollars every year. Created by the world's logistics and banking communities, bolero.net is getting rid of these inefficiencies by moving world trade onto the Internet, allowing documents and data to be exchanged online between all parties in the trade chain.

bolero.net offers:

- **Global buy-in**
  Seven out of the world's top ten banks have now signed up to bolero.net, as well as major trading houses such as Mitsui and Marubeni; and carriers such as K Line, Cosco and Evergreen.
- **Open platform**
  Unlike "proprietary" developments that force businesses down one particular path, bolero.net is committed to providing a neutral, open system. This gives technology and consultancy service suppliers to the logistics, financial services and trading community a new market opportunity to build "bolero.net enabled" products and solutions, addressing specific trading needs or "bolero.net qualified" consultancy services, addressing specific implementation needs.
- **Certainty**
  A ground-breaking, globally patented legal infrastructure creates 'certainty'. Every member of the bolero.net community is properly vetted and bound by its structures.
- **Security**
  bolero.net matches and exceeds the comfort factor that businesses currently have when conducting trade transactions by paper. bolero.net's messaging system is operated by S.W.I.F.T, an organisation that sets the gold standard for operational integrity. bolero.net's services utilise the latest encryption technology, messages are validated and a rigorous registration procedure acts as the gatekeeper for prospective members of the bolero.net community.
- **Information exchange**
  $bolero_{xml}$ is a validated, global, cross-industry XML standards solution that allows all parties of a trade chain to seamlessly "talk" to each other by automating their information exchange.

boleroXML

The objective of boleroXML is to enable users of bolero.net to take full advantage of electronic commerce by providing a set of standard electronic documents that will facilitate interoperability amongst the members of the community.

The goal is to eliminate the need for bilateral data interchange agreements that describe the structure and contents of electronic data being exchanged between two parties. This will be achieved by providing a set of common standards that can be applied multilaterally. Interoperability is a term used to describe the ability of different computer systems to work together, facilitating business transactions across organizations.

Strategy

The boleroXML strategy is based on the notion that the existing data interchange standards fail to meet the above mentioned criteria. Standards are vital to the exchange of information among parties. When all parties consistently use the same terminology and framework, documents and data flow seamlessly.

SITPRO are taking the lead in enabling members of the bolero.net community to take full advantage of electronic commerce by developing a set of simplified electronic trade documents, known as boleroXML documents. The boleroXML documents are founded upon a common business model that is technology-independent.

To achieve this, the boleroXML focuses on following principles:

- A "single standards" approach is adopted in that only boleroXML standards are offered on the messaging service.
- boleroXML standards are based on a single common business model.
- boleroXML standards are developed independent of any syntax but implemented on the messaging service in the syntax which has the most long-term support at that time (currently XML).
- boleroXML standards are developed at the request of and in close consultation with the industries served by bolero. In the case of standards that are intended to be used across industries (eg, Commercial Invoice) SITPRO will ensure that one and the same document can be used by the various industries. In those cases where standards are industry specific, they will agree them with the relevant industry.
- boleroXML standards use 'best of breed' from existing EDI standards (eg, SWIFT, UN Location Codes, ISO Country Codes).

Methodology

The advent of business-to-business electronic commerce has presented members of the Bolero community and the trade community at large with a unique opportunity to revisit the original purpose of trade documents.

The methodology employed by bolero.net is to focus on the core business needs. The most widely used trade documents are analyzed and documented from a business perspective. The aim is to provide consistency across trade documents, eliminate redundancies and remove ambiguities.

Current BoleroXML documents include:

Commercial Documents

- Commercial Invoice
- Contract
- Credit Note
- Debit Note
- Freight Invoice
- Price Fix Letter
- Price Fix Rolling Letter
- Proforma Invoice
- Purchase Order
- Purchase Order Acceptance
- Purchase Order Cancellation
- Trade Confirmation

Transport Documents

- Advance Shipment Notice
- Air Waybill
- Arrival Notice
- Bill of Lading
- Booking Confirmation
- Cargo Analysis Voyage Report
- Cargo Movement Event Log
- Cargo Report Export
- Cargo Report Import
- Combined Transport Document
- Despatch Advice
- Destination Declaration
- Firm Booking Request
- Forwarders Cargo Receipt
- Forwarding Instructions
- House Air Waybill
- House Bill of Lading
- NVOCC Bill of Lading
- Packing List
- Provisional Booking Request
- Sea Waybill
- Shipping Instructions
- Statement of Facts

Certification of Goods Documents

- Certificate of Origin
- Certificate of Origin Application
- Certificate of Quality
- Certificate of Weight
- Certificate of Analysis

Insurance Documents

- Insurance Certificate
- Insurance Policy

Banking Documents

- Advice of a Third Bank's Documentary Credit
- Beneficiary's Documentary Credit Amendment Acceptance or Refusal
- Collecting Bank's Collection Instruction
- Collection Advice of Non Payment or Non Acceptance
- Collection Amendment Advice
- Collection Amendment Request
- Collection Status Advice
- Collection Status Request
- Credit Advice
- Debit Advice
- Documentary Credit
- Documentary Credit Acknowledgment
- Documentary Credit Advice
- Documentary Credit Advice of Discrepancy
- Documentary Credit Advice of Discrepancy Discharge
- Documentary Credit Advice of Discrepancy Refusal
- Documentary Credit Amendment
- Documentary Credit Amendment Advice
- Documentary Credit Amendment Request
- Documentary Credit Application
- Documentary Credit Copy
- Documentary Credit Notification
- Documentary Credit Reimbursement Authorisation
- Documentary Credit Reimbursement Claim
- Exporter's Collection Instruction
- Exporter's Documentary Credit Presentation Instruction
- Issuing Bank's Documentary Credit Presentation Instruction
- Notice of Completion
- Paying Bank's Documentary Credit Presentation Instruction
- Payment Instruction
- Presenting Bank's Collection Instruction
- Remitting Bank's Collection Instruction
- Standby Documentary Credit

Customs Documents
- Administrative Accompanying Document
- CFSP Clearance
- Entry Acceptance Advice
- Export Declaration
- Export License
- Import Declaration

Export documentation software

In addition to the developments described above there are a large number of commercial providers of software packages designed to produce all the documents that an international trader might require. In fact a search for 'export documentation software' with Yahoo for example actually produces 'about 516,000' results.

A selection of the main providers in the UK would include:

TradePoint Systems Ltd.

www.tradepointsys.co.uk
E-mail: info@tradepointsys.co.uk

TradePoint have been selling export documentation systems for 33 years. Their mid-range product Export Manager, developed on the IBM AS/400 (now the I-Series) is a genuine export management tool, with a user definable status module that enables user tasks and procedures as well as documentation to be user-defined down to customer level. Integration with most AS/400 major line of business solutions means that Export Manager is just another menu option within such systems.

The acquisition of PC SPEX has added versatility to the product range with links from most major ERP systems available. The ability to e-mail documents directly from SPEX enhances communications links with the user's trading partners and data output to major spreadsheet packages offers sophisticated analysis and reporting of export shipments. SPEX was originally developed by SITPRO as the *de facto* standard document system based on UN guidelines.

Derwent Systems Technology Limited

www.dstuk.com
Email: rsack@dstuk.com
TRADEX 2000 Export Windows 32 bit software allows the export department to easily and quickly prepare the entire range of SITPRO and Customs documents, removing the time-consuming process of typing individual documents. Tradex2000 can easily be integrated with main corporate systems. Users can also modify or create screens, print forms, calculations and data-bases using Tradex2000 'drag 'n drop' Windows design tools. There is no need to incur expensive programming costs. Changes can be done in a fraction of the time of conventionally programmed systems. Because Tradex is so flexible and easy to modify and extend, it is ideal for meeting the needs of business, now and in the future. As a single or multi-user system this is an easy to use, cost effective, efficient Windows solution.

Exportmaster Systems Limited

www.exportmaster.co.uk
Email: info@exportmaster.co.uk
Exportmaster has been a significant provider of software for exporters since 1985. It offers not only export documentation software but also a wide range of modules from which much more
comprehensive export sales, shipping and management systems can be built. It is generally integrated with corporate processing systems, but can be installed stand-alone where appropriate. Special features include calculation of export margins, quotations, maintenance of freight and shipping rates, distribution cost calculation, tracking, progress-chasing and straightforward facilities for users to design their own documents and reports. For traders, it offers product sourcing, purchasing and goods received facilities. Exportmaster is true 32-bit software for Windows PC and network platforms.

ExportPro Limited

Email: sales@export-pro.com
Web Site www.export-pro.com
ExportPro Limited supplies proven Windows networked software for manufacturing and distribution companies seek-ing a total export manage-ment solution. The software maintains a comprehensive database and generates a full range of export doc-umentation, Commercial, Shipping,

Banking and Customs with additional functionality and ease of use proven since 1995 with our impressive customer base. ExportPro links with Tetra CS/3 (Sage Line 500), BAAN, MFG/Pro, BPCS, SAP and Robot Stores (www.resoco.co.uk) for small companies. TradingPro provides additional functionality in a multi supplier trading environment with automated Purchase Orders.

Formwise Export Limited

www.formwise.co.uk

Email: sales@formwise.co.uk

Since 1989 Formwise Export have produced a wide range of export documentation and management systems, for a variety of customers, from stand-alone users to multi-user systems, most having data transferred from business control software (currently approx 50 systems). The system includes a full range of United Nations and SITPRO documents, incorporating logos and signatures where requested, output can be by printer, fax or e-mail attachment files. A wide range of electronic data messages (eg NES) are included in the software.

i2i(Innovate to Integrate) Limited

www.i2i-solutions.net

Email: sales@i2i-solutions.net

i2i's 17 year commitment to making it easy to automate the production and distribution of export documentation, has resulted in both PC and browser based software solutions being developed, ensuring that the most appropriate technology is available.

GTA Net, is browser based so multiple sites can access the solution without the need to install on every user PC. The communication process is automated, from the easy interface with any business system, through to printing and distributing SITPRO documents and connecting to services such as e-Cert and NES. Global and multi-site organizations can share investment in a communication platform which handles today's document requirements, and the electronic communication requirements of the future.

Kenmare Systems Limited

www.kenmare.co.uk

Email: sales@kenmare.co.uk

Kenmare provides ManSys, a complete business support system for those dealing in physical goods such as chemicals, electricals, engineering parts, foodstuffs, military supplies, pharmaceuticals or tools. In some organisations it is a departmental system supporting the procurement team or the Export

Department. For other organisations ManSys, manages, tracks and reports on every aspect of the business from enquiry through order processing to shipment and documentation production. Functions include sourcing, quotations, sales orders, purchase orders, invoicing, stock control, shipping, product history, client history and reporting.

Precision Solutions Limited

www.precisionsoftware.com
Email: info@precisionsoftware.com
Established in 1984, Precision Software Ltd. has extensive experience in providing specialist export and import software solutions. This experience covers a wide array of industries including chemical, pharmaceutical, process, food & drink and the healthcare industry. Precision develops top quality, state-of-the-art software products specialising in the area of shipping, logistics, export, import, freight, transport and eCommerce.

TRA/X International Trade Logistics is Precision's fully integrated International Trade Logistics management system that ensures optimisation of all importing, exporting and transporting processes; Functionality includes Trade Compliance (Embargoed Countries, Denied Parties etc.), Shipping & Customs documentation, Hazardous Goods, Freight Management, Export Refunds, Duty and Landed Costs, Small Parcel, NES and NCTS Tracking & Tracing. TRA/X also supports standard interfaces with current versions of all major leading ERP suppliers in the marketplace.

9.2

Global trading trends

The IMF projections for the percentage growth of imports and exports of selected geographical groupings for the period from 2003 to 2007 are displayed in Table 9.3.1. In the bottom section of the table, the same data is shown for the World together with the US dollar values of global trade and it current account balance. Readers requiring absolute dollar values for the various groupings or similar data for individual countries should visit www.imf.org where this information and much more about the world's economies can be found.

Global trends

The IMF estimates that the value of global exports of good and services rose from $9,178 billion in 2003 to $12,684 billion in 2005 and projects further increases to $15,891 for 2007. The annual growth rate rose from sharply from 5.2% in 2003 to 10.3% in 2004 and is forecast to remain above 7% through 2007 with rather higher growth forecast for 2006. These are healthier growth rates than those recorded in the final decade of the last century except for year 2000 when world merchandise exports grew 11% before falling 1.5% in 2001.

Selected groupings trends

Advanced economies

As a whole, the projected growth rates in exports and imports are one to one and half percentage points below the world average. In 2006 and 2007, growth rates for goods are expected to be marginally higher than for goods and services combined. Over the five year period growth rates of imports and exports are roughly in balance.

Major advanced economies

Focusing on the G7 advanced economies, except for 2006, growth rates in both exports and imports are slightly lower than for the complete group of advanced economies.

Table 9.3.1 - Projections of Foreign Trade Growth for Selected Regions and Globally

	Groupings and Globally				
	2003	2004	2005 (e)	2006 (f)	2007 (f)
Advanced economies (%)					
Import volume of goods and services	4	9.1	6	7.5	6
Import volume of goods	4.9	9.4	6.3	8	6
Export volume of goods and services	3.3	8.8	5.5	8	6
Export volume of goods	3.8	8.7	5.3	8.6	6.1
Major Advanced Economies (G7) (%)					
Import volume of goods and services	3.5	8	5.9	7.6	5.7
Import volume of goods	4.3	8.2	6	8.4	5.7
Export volume of goods and services	1.6	7.8	5.4	8.7	5.7
Export volume of goods	1.4	7.2	4.9	9.4	5.8
Euro area (%)					
Import volume of goods and services	2.8	6.5	5.2	7.2	5.4
Import volume of goods	3.6	7.3	5.8	7.5	5.1
Export volume of goods and services	1.3	6.6	4.1	7.4	5.3
Export volume of goods	1	6.9	4.2	7.8	5.1
Central and Eastern Europe (%)					
Import volume of goods and services	10	15.9	8	9.2	8.8
Import volume of goods	12.4	18	8.6	11.2	9.4
Export volume of goods and services	10.5	15	9.4	10.4	9.7
Export volume of goods	12.2	16.9	9.9	11.7	10

Commonwealth of Independent States (CIS) and Mongolia

	(%)				
Import volume of goods and services	21.2	19.8	15.5	13.4	10
Import volume of goods	22.9	20.1	14.8	15.1	11.6
Export volume of goods and services	12.4	13.1	5.1	6.1	5.7
Export volume of goods	12.4	12.8	3.8	8.4	5.8

Middle East (%)

Import volume of goods and services	3.8	14.4	15	18.2	11.3
Import volume of goods	5.3	18.2	16.9	16	11.5
Export volume of goods and services	10.6	10.1	8	7.5	4.2
Export volume of goods	1.1	14.7	10.7	10.4	7.4

Africa (%)

Import volume of goods and services	5.9	8.9	12.3	10.9	13.8
Import volume of goods	7.2	9.2	10.7	10.5	13.1
Export volume of goods and services	5.2	7.1	6.2	4.9	11.8
Export volume of goods	6.6	7.2	5.2	4.3	12.2

Newly industrialized Asian Economies (%)

Import volume of goods and services	9.8	16.8	7.3	8	8.2
Import volume of goods	10.8	16.2	7.2	9.3	8.4
Export volume of goods nd services	13.6	17.8	9.3	8.9	7.9
Export volume of goods	17	18.5	10.3	9.9	8.1

The World

Import volume of goods and services (%)	5.5	10.9	7.6	9	7.8
Import volume of goods (%)	6.7	11.4	7.8	9.6	8
Export volume of goods and services (%)	5.2	10.3	7.3	8.8	7.5
Export volume of goods (%)	5.9	10.3	7.1	9.3	7.6

Table 9.3.1 (continued)

	Groupings and Globally				
	2003	2004	2005 (e)	2006 (f)	2007 (f)
Imports of goods and services (US dollars – billions)	9,178.10	11,123.5	12,585.90	14,284.90	15,707.50
Export of goods and services (US dollars – (billions)	9,242.60	11,208.30	12,684.30	14,464.20	15,890.80
Current Account balance (US dollars - billions)	-74.2	-55.3	-61.6	15.5	-16.3

Source: International Monetary Fund (IMF) database

Euro area

Growth rates of exports by the group of eurozone countries have been significantly lower by up to 2% than for the total grouping of advanced economies with 2004 a particularly poor year. However, the gap is forecast to narrow to less than one% in 2006 and 2007 and may reflect the mild recovery of some eurozone economies, notably Germany.

Central and Eastern Europe

Export growth of the CEE countries, which include the eight that are now EU members, has outstripped the world average and, in particular, those of the euro area. Growth rates of CEE exports are expected to remain 3% or 4% ahead of eurozone rates for 2006 and 2007. The differential for imports is rather less. Comparison with the eurozone is relevant to the decisions of the CEE8 whether and when to join the euro area.

CIS and Mongolia

Double digit growth in imports through to 2007 puts the CIS plus Mongolia well ahead of the world average and advanced economies as a target market for exporters. Surprisingly, in view of Russian exports of oil and gas the growth rates in exports are comparatively modest, lagging behind the world and advanced economies average and pointing to growing current account imbalances.

Middle East

Import growth rates are also in double digits from 2004 onwards and are forecast to exceed those of the CIS and Mongolia in 2006 and 2007. Export growth rates for goods are forecast to remain above the world average until 2007. There is an emerging current account issue for the region but not as acute as for the CIS.

Africa

Until 2007 when exports are expected to take off, growth rates of goods and services will remain 2 or 3% below the world average. However, growth rates in imports rose to double digits in 2005 and will continue to grow faster than exports through 2007. The endemic imbalances in the foreign trade of most African countries remain of grave concern to the G8 and all those seeking progress in the WTO Doha round of negotiations.

Newly industrialized Asian economies

Growth rates in the volume of exports, reflecting the performance of China's economic powerhouse and the growing but still nascent economy of India, will remain ahead of the world average. However, growth for the grouping has fallen back to single digits from the heady rates of 13.6% and 17.8% in 2003 and 2004. Reassuringly, the growth rates of imports are converging with those of exports, providing contrary evidence to the claim that China and other dynamic Asian economies are the major sources of global trade imbalance.

Appendices

Recommended Reading Lists for Advanced Certificate and Diploma in International Trade

Advanced Certificate

General

Schmittnoff: Export Trade, D'arcy, Murray & Cleave, Sweet & Maxwell
INCOTERMS, ICC United Kingdom

The business environment

The Business Environment, Institute of Export
Principles of Law Relating to Overseas Trade, Kouladis. N, Blackwells, 1st Edition
Charlesworth Business Law, Dobson P, Sweet & Maxwell 16th Edition
Business Law, Abbot KR & Pendlebury, Contavuum, 7th Edition

Finance and international trade

Finance and International Trade, Institute of Export, 2nd Edition 2001
Principles of International Trade and Payments, Briggs .P, Blackwells 1st Edition 1994
Finance of International Trade, Watson A.J.W, Bankers Books 5th Edition 1997
Uniform Customs and Practices for Documentary Credits (UCP 5000), ICC United Kingdom
Uniform Rules for Collections (URC 522)
Uniform Rules for Demand Guarantees
Guide to Documentary Credit Operations for UCP 500

Operating in the global economy

Operating in the Global Economy, Institute of Export 2nd Edition 1999
International Marketing, Bennett. R (Be), Kogan Page 2nd Edition 1998

International Marketing Strategy, Bradley F. (Br), Prentice Hall Europe 4th Edition 2002 *Marketing Research*, Kent R. (K), ITB Press 2nd Edition
International Marketing, Paliwoda S. (P), Butterworth & Heinemann
International Marketing, Walsh L. S. (W), Pearson Education 3rd Edition 1998
An Introduction to Modern Economics, Hardwick P. Langmead J. & Khan B. (HLK), Pearson Education 5th Edition 1999

International physical distribution

International Physical Distribution, Institute of Export 2nd Edition
Principles of International Physical Distribution, Sherlock J, Blackwells 1st Edition 1994
International Trade Procedures and Management, Walker A.G, Butterworth-Heinemann 4th Edition 1995
Understanding the Freight Business, Down D.E, Micor Freght UK Ltd 4th Edition 1992
The Merchant's Guide, Richardson J.W, P&O Nedlloyd millenlum Edition 1999

Diploma

General export management

Management, Bennett R (1997), 3rd Edition, Financial Times, Pitman Publishing, London
International Business, Bennett R (1999), 2nd Edition, Financial Times, Prentice Hall
Dictionary of International Business Terms, Capela J, Barron's Business Dictionaries

International logistics and purchasing

Handbook of Logistics and Distribution Management, Rushton A & Oxley J (1999), Kogan Page
International Logistics, Wood D et al. (1994), Chapman & Hall
The Importer's Handbook, Butler J (1994), Prentice Hall
International Purchasing Handbook, Ashley J (1998), Director Books

International marketing planning

Strategic Marketing Communications, Smith P, Berry C & Pulford A (1997), Kogan Page
Introduction to International Business, El-Kahal, S. (1994), McGraw-Hill

International Marketing Management, Jeannet, J.P. and Hennessey, H. (1992), Houghton Mifflin

Consumer Behavior and Marketing Action, Assael, H. (1992), PWS-Kent Publishing

International Marketing, Gilligan, C. and Hird, M. (1985), Routledge

International Marketing Strategy and Management, Gilligan, C. and Hird, M. (1986), Croom Helm

International Marketing, Terpstra V & Sarathy R (1997), Dryden Press

Marketing Management, Analysis, Planning, Implementation and Control, Kotler, P. (1988), Prentice Hall

Elements of Export Marketing and Management, Branch, A.E. (1990), Chapman and Hall

International Marketing, Cateora, P.R. (1993), Irwin.

Management of international trade

International Purchasing Handbook, Ashley J (1998), Director Books

International Business, Bennett R (1999), Pearson Education Ltd

Export Practice & Management, Branch A (2000), Thomson Learning

Trading in the Global Currency Market, Cheol S et al. (2000).

Index

Printed in the United Kingdom
by Lightning Source UK Ltd.
134139UK00001B/27-28/A